Power Corrupts

Power Corrupts

Cleaning Up America's Biggest Industry

Richard Munson

BLOOMSBURY ACADEMIC
NEW YORK • LONDON • OXFORD • NEW DELHI • SYDNEY

BLOOMSBURY ACADEMIC

Bloomsbury Publishing Inc, 1385 Broadway, New York, NY 10018, USA
Bloomsbury Publishing Plc, 50 Bedford Square, London, WC1B 3DP, UK
Bloomsbury Publishing Ireland, 29 Earlsfort Terrace, Dublin 2, D02 AY28, Ireland

BLOOMSBURY, BLOOMSBURY ACADEMIC and the Diana logo are trademarks of
Bloomsbury Publishing Plc

First published in the United States of America 2025

Copyright © Bloomsbury Publishing, 2025

Cover images © iStock.com/Harry Adam; iStock.com/ByM

All rights reserved. No part of this publication may be: i) reproduced or transmitted in any form, electronic or mechanical, including photocopying, recording or by means of any information storage or retrieval system without prior permission in writing from the publishers; or ii) used or reproduced in any way for the training, development or operation of artificial intelligence (AI) technologies, including generative AI technologies. The rights holders expressly reserve this publication from the text and data mining exception as per Article 4(3) of the Digital Single Market Directive (EU) 2019/790.

Bloomsbury Publishing Inc does not have any control over, or responsibility for, any third-party websites referred to or in this book. All internet addresses given in this book were correct at the time of going to press. The author and publisher regret any inconvenience caused if addresses have changed or sites have ceased to exist, but can accept no responsibility for any such changes.

Library of Congress Cataloging-in-Publication Data

Names: Munson, Richard, author.
Title: Power corrupts : cleaning up America's biggest industry / Richard Munson.
Description: Lanham : Rowman & Littlefield, [2025] | Includes bibliographical references and index. | Summary: "Power Corrupts explains the recent rise of racketeering and bribery by utilities seeking billion-dollar bailouts for dirty and uneconomic power plants. This corruption within America's utility industry has become the biggest barrier to tackling global warming and advancing greener solutions" — Provided by publisher.
Identifiers: LCCN 2024059255 (print) | LCCN 2024059256 (ebook) | ISBN 9781538199398 (cloth; alk. paper) | ISBN 9781538199404 (epub)
Subjects: LCSH: Electric utilities—Corrupt practices—United States. | Electric utilities—Government policy—United States.
Classification: LCC HD9685.U5 M86 2025 (print) | LCC HD9685.U5 (ebook) | DDC 333.793/20972—dc23/eng/20250307
LC record available at https://lccn.loc.gov/2024059255
LC ebook record available at https://lccn.loc.gov/2024059256

Typeset by Deanta Global Publishing Services, Chennai, India
Printed and bound in the United States of America

For product safety related questions contact productsafety@bloomsbury.com.

To find out more about our authors and books visit www.bloomsbury.com and sign up
for our newsletters.

Also by Richard Munson

Ingenious: A Biography of Benjamin Franklin, Scientist

Tesla: Inventor of the Modern

Tech to Table: 25 Innovators Reimagining Food

George Fabyan

From Edison to Enron: The Business of Power and What It Means for the Future of Electricity

The Cardinals of Capitol Hill: The Men and Women Who Control Government Spending

Cousteau: The Captain and His World

The Power Makers

To Kathryn

Power tends to corrupt. Absolute power corrupts absolutely.

—Lord Acton, April 5, 1887

There can be no crime more serious than bribery. Other offenses violate one law while corruption strikes at the foundation of all law.

—Theodore Roosevelt, December 7, 1903

Contents

I	The Stakes	1
II	Seeking Subsidies	7
III	Buying a Bailout	25
IV	Consequences and Entanglements	45
V	Securing Favors	73
VI	Swaying Elections	83
VII	Cut Corruption	99
Notes		111
Bibliography		151
Index		153
Acknowledgments		163
About the Author		167

Chapter I

The Stakes

We need electricity. In fact, we demand it, and that demand often outstrips our concern for how the power—for our homes, phones, computers, and even cars—is produced. Yet we should be concerned, very concerned, because as modern technologies challenge their outmoded generators, utility monopolies increasingly seek subsidies through political campaigns based on bribery and racketeering. Such growing corruption within one of the nation's biggest industries has become a drag on our economy, a threat to the rule of law, and a barrier to tackling climate change.

Charles ("Chuck") Jones epitomizes the bailout-buying utility executive. As CEO of utility giant FirstEnergy, he flew the future Speaker of Ohio's House of Representatives on the company's jet to Donald Trump's inauguration in 2017. Over posh dinners at The Palm and Charlie Palmer Steak, the executive and the politician plotted to have FirstEnergy secretly pay more than $60 million to the Speaker's allies in exchange for the House leader advancing a $1.3-billion bailout of the utility's uneconomic power plants.[1] On the day House Bill 6 (HB 6) passed, Chuck gloated about his team's victory: "Fuck anybody who ain't us."[2]

Chuck's is a tale about power—both electric and political. Imagine gambling sixty dollars and getting a $1,300 return. Now imagine adding six zeros to each number and you begin to appreciate the audacity, greed, and political might of these monopolies. In this case, Chuck wasn't banking on blind luck for his big win. To ensure a $1.3 billion payout, FirstEnergy's team bribed politicians, harassed bailout opponents, hired high-priced lobbyists, and blanketed the airways with xenophobic threats about China taking over Ohio's energy resources.[3]

It took three years for federal prosecutors—using home raids, wiretaps, and undercover agents—to expose this pay-to-play scheme. The consequences to date have been severe, and more indictments are expected. To avoid possible jail time, one FirstEnergy lobbyist committed suicide in the woods near his home.[4] Two others pleaded guilty. FirstEnergy fired Chuck, admitted to bribery, and paid a $230 million fine.[5] A federal judge in June 2023 sentenced the Republican Speaker to twenty years in prison. Almost a year later, Ohio's indicted utility regulator hanged himself, the second fatality traced to FirstEnergy's offenses.

Chuck Jones is hardly the only scandal-prone CEO. Anne Pramaggiore, Commonwealth Edison's leader, was found guilty in 2023 of distributing more than $1 million to allies of Illinois's Speaker in exchange for legislation worth more than $150 million to her power company. According to journalists, Arizona Public Service's chairman Don Brandt used dark-money political groups to install his allies as utility regulators.[6] Press reports also explained that Eric Silagy, Florida Power & Light's leader, paid for a ghost candidate to siphon votes away from a state senator who had proposed legislation that threatened the utility's revenue.[7]

Power corruption proliferates.

This book begins by highlighting FirstEnergy's scandals, but it reveals that fraud increasingly pervades utilities across the country. More than a collection of sordid tales, *Power Corrupts* explains why and how utilities mold regulations and legislation, and it suggests ways to increase the power industry's transparency and restrict its bribery and racketeering.

Shining a light on power corruption has broad implications. It exposes the influence of dark money, showing how one industry secretly spends millions to manipulate public policy to fund its ailing business practices. It reveals the deep pockets of corporate monopolies and the vulnerability of state legislators and regulators to having their pockets lined. It reflects how Supreme Court decisions favoring corporations make it harder for prosecutors to monitor and punish racketeering. Allowed to spread, deceitful and illegal practices by utilities are akin to a national brownout, dimming democracy and the public's faith in key institutions.

Power corruption also poses profound economy-wide impacts, since electricity generation and delivery constitute perhaps our nation's largest industry, with utility assets reaching approximately $2.3 trillion. Bailouts distort price signals, give preference to old and dirty generators, lead to waste and inefficiencies, and block energy innovation and clean power. Since utility monopolies also are our biggest polluters, their scandal-obtained subsidies result in massive amounts of unnecessary emissions that damage public health and the environment.

Electric utilities have faced a few scandals over the past century or so, but this book argues corruption is growing because the power industry's conventional business model is falling apart. Rapid technology advances—including sensors, smart meters, controls, smaller-scale generators, advanced turbines, microgrids, and battery storage—overwhelm their monopoly mindsets and outmoded generators. Threatened utilities, in turn, gun for taxpayer- and ratepayer-funded subsidies, which they increasingly seek through fraud-filled schemes.

Corruption, however, can be challenged, and this book offers options for increased transparency and ethics. We customers and citizens are paying not only for the electricity we use, but also for the taxes that pay to regulate, subsidize, and investigate utility companies. We should demand more power.

While their scope and scale have grown, utility scandals are not new. To grasp today's racketeering, let's consider a little history and discuss how electricity corporations became billion-dollar monopolies. Although utilities usually trace their roots to Thomas Edison and his founding of the Edison Illuminating Company in 1880, perhaps more responsible for the industry's basic structure is Samuel Insull, who arrived in New York City a year later at the age of twenty-one to be Edison's personal secretary.

Insull began his career by answering Edison's mail, organizing his office, and buying his clothes. In 1892, when bankers ousted Edison from his own company, Insull moved to Chicago and bought a power station there. Demonstrating what the inventor described as "a positive gift for borrowing money," Insull quickly moved to financing generators, bribing politicians, and buying up competitors. Within forty years, his empire spanned thirty-two states, and he became admired as a business tycoon. Thirteen years later, he would be arrested for racketeering. His legacies from that wild journey are monopolized utilities, manipulated regulators, and malfeasant executives.

Prospects for electricity's expansion did not appear bright at the dawn of the twentieth century. Only 8 percent of American homes had access. Manufacturers feared abandoning their steam-powered systems for unreliable generators. Homeowners tended to dismiss incandescent bulbs in favor of the less expensive and more pleasant glow of gas lamps.

Yet Insull took advantage of engineering improvements. When he became president of the Chicago Edison Company in 1892, it owned only one power plant and competed against more than forty other Windy City–based electricity suppliers. The biggest generators were streetcar companies that replaced horse-drawn public transportation. Industrialists and commercial building managers also tended to own their own electrical equipment.

Insull sensed that Chicago Edison would prosper only if it integrated these various power demands and built larger generators. So he began bribing the streetcar companies to purchase rather than produce power, thus obtaining a large load during morning and late-afternoon commutes. By offering special rates to large office buildings and manufacturers, he sold electricity throughout the day. Lavishing campaign contributions, he convinced Chicago aldermen to shut down their small street-lighting generators, thus acquiring a nighttime demand. The result was increased efficiency for Insull's growing number of bigger power plants, allowing him to cut costs, lower rates, and further increase sales.

The executive proved to be a master marketer. He created a twenty-five-person sales force and ordered them to offer service for less than the cost of gas. He even established an advertising department and widely circulated *Electric City* magazine.

It wasn't long before the expansionist bought other electricity companies. He initially targeted the much larger Chicago Arc Light and Power, inviting its president to lunch to announce his intention. That executive scoffed, and Insull admitted "relations at the end of the lunch were not quite as cordial as they were at the start."[8] Yet the aggressive financier issued more than $2 million in debt to buy all his competitor's stock.[9]

Insull then diversified, purchasing the coal mines and railroads that supplied fuel to his power plants. He also expanded beyond Chicago, first buying the Indiana-based Fort Wayne Electric Company and the power-and-light business in Rockford, Illinois. To finance additional acquisitions, he formed a holding company, Middle West Utilities, and convinced wealthy investors to purchase stock. Now called "the Chief," Insull grew his electric empire rapidly to serve four million customers across much of the heartland. The admired tycoon's face appeared on the cover of *Time* in November 1926 and again in November 1929.

No doubt other executives in the early twentieth century formed conglomerates, such as US Steel, American Tobacco, International Harvester, DuPont, and Anaconda Copper. Others also consolidated power firms, including J. P. Morgan, whose United Corporation managed numerous electricity companies in New England and the South. Ten holding companies by the late 1920s controlled more than three-quarters of the electricity industry.

As energy moguls bribed local politicians for permits needed to string wires across or under city streets, calls for reform grew. Unlike his power-company colleagues who abhorred government oversight, Insull joined Wisconsin governor Robert LaFollette and other progressives to criticize municipal corruption and advance "scientific" management. His goal was to strike a bargain that continues to dominate the industry: Power companies get to be monopolies in exchange for some state regulation. As the executive put it, "There is one great advantage that must follow regulation, and that advantage is protection."[10]

Wisconsin in 1907 became the first to pass legislation creating "an independent commission of experts" to approve rates for privately owned utilities.

New York and Massachusetts followed soon thereafter, and within nine years, thirty more states regulated power monopolies.

This arrangement convinced investors that utilities were safe bets. With assured returns on their every investment, utilities gained an incentive to build more and more generators and transmission lines, enabling Insull's expansionistic plans. Power company construction rose rapidly, from about $500 million in 1902, to more than $1 billion in 1907, and to almost $2 billion in 1912.[11]

Monopolization, however, shielded utility executives from the discipline of competition. They no longer worried whether another power company could build generators—and deliver electricity—cheaper. Managers, instead, focused on influencing or controlling state commissions, which periodically led to scandals. In 1925, for instance, when Frank Smith declared he would run against the incumbent Illinois senator—William McKinley, who had refused to sell to Insull his interurban electric railway and utility franchises in southern Illinois communities—the Middle West chief made political contributions totaling some $160,000, or almost $3 million in today's dollars. The problem was that Smith directed the Illinois Commerce Commission that was supposed to be an independent overseer of Insull's state-based companies.[12] A subsequent US Senate investigation found the power executive's self-serving payments to be "brazen" and "arrogant."[13]

The scandal grew as the Federal Trade Commission (FTC) criticized utilities for "buying" elections and spending enormous sums, surpassing $30 million annually ($538 million in inflation-adjusted dollars), on political advertising. Even more damning, the FTC concluded that 75 percent of power companies inflated their assets and that their holding companies regularly claimed fictitious income from their subsidiaries. New York governor Franklin Roosevelt in 1930 blasted Insull's network as "a kind of private empire within the nation" that represented a menace "of such a highly centralized industrial control that we may have to bring forth a new declaration of independence."[14] The future president expressed fear for our democracy in light of deceits by utility magnates.

The power industry, in fact, was a fragile house of cards. As the Great Depression accelerated and England abandoned the gold standard in 1931, investors panicked, and the value of Insull's securities fell $150 million in one week. A share of Middle West Utilities eventually plummeted from $570 to only $1.25.

The Securities and Exchange Commission charged utility holding companies with "stock watering and capital inflation, manipulation of subsidies, and improper accounting practices." The FTC's general counsel added that "words such as fraud, deceit, misrepresentation, dishonesty, breach of trust, and oppression are the only suitable terms to apply."[15]

Upon hearing he was about to be indicted, Insull fled to Greece under disguise, darkening his hair and mustache and abandoning his glasses "in such a manner as to avoid publicity." Inspired by a US-government bounty of $200,000—four times that offered for Al Capone—Turkish authorities boarded Insull's ship in international waters, arrested the disgraced tycoon, and extradited him back to the United States.[16]

A Chicago jury eventually sided with the elderly executive, who had taken the stand for three hours and woven a tale of being a public benefactor persecuted for the greed of an entire generation. While twelve of Insull's peers dismissed the charges, the scandal prompted more oversight of utilities. Congress approved the Public Utility Holding Company Act (PUHCA) of 1935, which broke up the parent companies and gave the federal government more oversight of the industry. Also in the 1930s, Washington financed massive public-power entities, including the Tennessee Valley Authority and the Bonneville Power Authority, which brought electricity to millions of rural residents that private utilities had ignored.

Such reforms tempered the most obvious corruption, but power scandals returned about eighty years later, in the early twenty-first century, after utility monopolies pushed aggressively to reduce government oversight. They convinced federal lawmakers in 2005 to reverse many provisions of PUHCA and to allow conglomerates to reconsolidate their markets and political power. Even more impactful, the Supreme Court in 2003—*McConnell v. FEC*—closed doors to prosecuting corruption and in 2010—*Citizens United v. FEC*—opened floodgates to corporate political spending.

This is where we are today, as federal prosecutors have been told to look the other way and the nation's highest court has given corporate sponsorship of political candidates its blessing. Yet utilities' moves to corruptly obtain subsidies for their old, dirty, and uneconomic facilities result as much from their own mismanagement—and misreading of economic trends.

Chapter II

Seeking Subsidies

A poster child for business mistakes and bailout scroungings is FirstEnergy, one of the largest private power conglomerates, with ten subsidiaries selling electricity to six million customers throughout the Midwest and mid-Atlantic regions. While that utility's former CEO, Chuck Jones, shares a name with the producer of classic animated cartoons—starring Bugs Bunny, Daffy Duck, Wile E. Coyote, and the Road Runner—there's nothing comical about his subsidy scandals.

Chuck is a native Ohioan, or "Buckeye," as he boasts. Born and raised in Akron, he briefly attended the US Naval Academy but returned home to graduate from the University of Akron with a degree in electrical engineering. In 1978, he joined Ohio Edison as a lowly substation engineer and methodically moved up the corporate ladder to become CEO in 2015.

Chuck supported numerous local causes, his favorite being the Akron-based All-American Soap Box Derby. The CEO, in fact, appeared all-American, despite his foul mouth and political cunning. Comedian John Oliver observed that the stocky Midwesterner "looks like he's left lengthy reviews for multiple gas grills on homedepot.com."[1]

Having spent his career within a monopoly protected from competitors, the new utility leader quickly misjudged economic signals, doubling down on coal just as fracking caused the cost of natural gas to plummet. That decision left his outdated facilities in dire straits and forced a FirstEnergy subsidiary into bankruptcy. It also moved the utility CEO to spend increasing amounts of time pushing others—state and federal legislators and regulators—to cover his billion-dollar losses.[2] By seeking such subsidies, he essentially converted FirstEnergy into a high-powered lobbying firm that happened to generate electricity.

The utility's bungling, admittedly, began before Chuck entered the executive suite. The company's very founding, in fact, resulted from a bad bet.

Ohio Edison acquired Centerior Energy in 1997 and changed its name to FirstEnergy, making it the country's eleventh-largest utility. Company executives should have known better than to spend $1.6 billion on Centerior, which had invested in three nuclear power plants after the Three Mile Island accident prompted more safety measures and drove up reactor costs. So high were the additional expenses that three years before the merger, Centerior canceled one of its nuclear units, slashed its dividend, and wrote off $349 million. Despite such warnings, Ohio Edison rolled the dice on a risky merger.

From the start, FirstEnergy's engineers suffered multiple safety citations from the Nuclear Regulatory Commission (NRC). In 2002, federal inspectors found a host of defective welds and borated water eating away a football-sized hole in the nuclear power station Davis-Besse's cover, threatening a massive radioactive leak.[3] Those government officials charged the utility with hiding the "serious" damage, what they described as the "most extensive" impairment ever seen at a US reactor.[4] They forced FirstEnergy to shut down the plant for two years of repairs and to pay $28 million in fines for what the NRC called "a series of problems that formed a long history of ineffective and inadequate attention and direction in the operation and maintenance of the Davis-Besse facility."[5]

The high costs for nuclear repairs led FirstEnergy to cut spending in other areas, like tree trimming. That decision came back to haunt the company in 2003, when unclipped branches swayed in the wind and knocked out a high-voltage transmission line near Lake Erie. Unprepared controllers then allowed the power surge to spread into a massive blackout that left fifty million people—across eight states and into Canada—without power for up to two days. The utility's colossal mistake caused eleven deaths and $6 billion in losses. FirstEnergy executives, trying to deflect blame, testified before Congress that the disaster was triggered by "the cumulative effect of occurrences in the region," but a subsequent US-Canadian investigation traced the culpability directly to the utility's ineptness.[6]

FirstEnergy also continued to bet heavily on coal even as clean-air regulations accelerated and cleanup costs increased. In 2011, it spent $4.7 billion to merge with Allegheny Energy of Pennsylvania, doubling the size of its coal fleet. The utility sealed the deal although it knew three of Allegheny's dirtiest coal plants were likely to close. Executives conducted business as if fixated on the black rock and loath to diversify, as evidenced by their selling in 2017 of five natural gas plants and one hydroelectric facility.[7]

FirstEnergy's treasurer admitted the company made strategic mistakes by devoting itself to coal and nuclear units as the fracking boom made natural gas–fired electricity much cheaper. "The coal assets weren't making money," he said. "Even the nuclear assets weren't making money. Energy prices were too low."[8]

FirstEnergy had committed to an antiquated utility business model that relied on outmoded generators. And despite its coal and nuclear units struggling to compete, the old-school monopoly increased its CEO's annual salary from $2 million in 2013 to a confounding $15 million in 2017.

Another colossal economic miscalculation occurred in 1999 when FirstEnergy pushed Ohio legislators to deregulate utilities, believing a subsidiary could earn more profits by competing in multistate, wholesale power markets than by relying on guaranteed profits by state-based regulators. Hoping, without much evidence, they could beat all contenders, the utility's executives happily established FirstEnergy Solutions, into which they spun off their biggest and oldest generation assets, mostly nuclear reactors and coal-fired units.

Dismissing Sam Insull's revelation that monopolization provides assured revenue and market protections, FirstEnergy's then-CEO declared competition "should remain a driving force for our business and industry in the years ahead."[9] Yet as a huge bonus, the utility convinced compliant regulators to charge Ohioans an extra $6.9 billion to cover what FirstEnergy claimed were assets at risk of being "stranded" in deregulated markets. Whereas regular companies and their shareholders absorb the costs of abandoning uneconomic facilities, the utility monopoly got paid for closing its units.[10] FirstEnergy's deregulation gamble turned south with the introduction of fracking, which, as noted above, reduced the cost and increased the output of natural-gas drilling. The power corporation failed to embrace that technological revolution, sticking instead with its uneconomic coal and nuclear generators, even as Ohio became awash in gas from the Marcellus Shale—which stretches from New York through Ohio and into West Virginia—and Utica Shale—located in eastern Ohio and considered to be one of the "biggest discoveries in US history." Suddenly, FirstEnergy Solutions was losing out to a new breed of independent power producers who entered competitive markets with now low-cost, natural gas–fired generators. That fuel's share of Ohio's energy supply jumped from around 2 percent in 2008 to 15 percent in 2013 and to 34 percent in 2018. Having failed to adjust, FirstEnergy Solutions admitted it was "just bleeding cash."[11]

The numbers looked bleak. The FirstEnergy's share price fell more than 30 percent between 2012 and 2014, even as the value of other energy companies soared. The struggling power corporation in January 2014 cut shareholder dividends by 35 percent, and its credit rating fell well below those of other utilities and competitive generators.[12]

Financial prospects were so bad for Chuck that when he became CEO in 2015, he launched a review of his options, including the sale of his coal and nuclear units. Yet according to a vice president, "You couldn't give the coal plants away," and the reactors were "just not marketable."[13]

Chuck decided to embrace "reregulation," hoping a return to monopolization would result in higher and steadier revenue. He also doubled down on bailouts. Even with the aforementioned $6.9 billion stranded-asset bonanza, he asked for an additional $4 billion to support his utility's two struggling reactors. Such subsidies, revealed a hopeful company treasurer, would "provide a fixed revenue stream" that would make the power plants alluring to investors and allow FirstEnergy to obtain a windfall profit from their sale.[14]

Chuck, however, faced two challenges. First, it proved hard to convince conservative Ohio legislators to fork over more government giveaways. Second, independent power producers, who enjoyed growing revenue and political clout, rather liked competitive markets and challenged FirstEnergy's reregulation. One of the most outspoken was Texas-based Dynegy, which owned eleven generators in Ohio. Its CEO said Chuck's appeal revealed FirstEnergy's real quest was for "big, fat margins so it can pay big dividends to shareholders," many of whom did not reside in the Buckeye State. He added, "Coal plants and nuclear plants in this market are losers. For some reason [FirstEnergy] wants to keep them. In order to keep them, they need them regulated because they can't compete." Going still further, the combative rival said FirstEnergy was "taking the weakest in the herd and putting it in the front to the benefit of [its] shareholders and the detriment of Ohio."[15]

Another competitive power producer, NRG, bluntly added, "FirstEnergy doesn't want to evolve. They'd rather go to the regulators and ask for a bailout."[16]

Indeed, Chuck was evolving, but into an aggressive subsidy seeker. In addition to his $4 billion entreaty, he sought a fifteen-year power purchase agreement that would guarantee revenue for his troubled nuclear reactors. With a good bit of irony noting his subsequent deceits, Chuck promised "transparent communications," saying, "I think one of the things that I have to start doing is saying what we are going to do and then doing what we say."[17]

You would think saying that your customers should subsidize your shareholders would be unpopular. You also might think seeking guaranteed profits would be rejected as "corporate welfare." Yet FirstEnergy proved it could spin rhetoric and tip political scales.

To appreciate how utility monopolies use their vast resources to obtain favorable regulations, let's examine Chuck Jones's response to his business mistakes. Rather than reduce executive salaries or cut shareholder dividends, court documents show he sought to have others—particularly captive customers and taxpayers—cover his losses through higher rates and government assistance.[18] In fact, well before the HB 6 scandal that sent the Ohio Speaker to jail, FirstEnergy, as will be explained below, became an insatiable bailout pleader.

Although the Akron-based corporation is among its most aggressive practitioners, subsidy seeking has become a national trend among power utilities. Such pleadings are striking because power monopolies already enjoy guaranteed profits and protection from competitors. Today's growing bailout appeals represent utilities' more desperate reactions to their poor business decisions and changing power-plant economics.

Subsidies are problems in part because they distort price signals in ways that discourage efficiency and innovation. Such business handouts also counter the basic tenets of free and fair markets, shielding inept managers from the consequences of their bad choices and placing those burdens instead on innocent, and sometimes impoverished, consumers. Frantic subsidy pursuits, moreover, often lead to bribery and other crimes that threaten the rule of law.

The thread of corruption from Insull to FirstEnergy highlights the need to reconsider our utility business model of monopolies manipulating regulators. At a minimum, we require true transparency of corporate lobbying and political payments, and we deserve independent oversight rather than rubber-stamping. Yet we also need to appreciate how competition advances modern technologies and how such innovations reveal the potential to move beyond monopolization.

Before exploring such solutions, let's trace the problem. Specifically, let's examine in some detail how one utility, FirstEnergy, exploited political systems to consistently seek subsidies. Let's assess how that monopoly deployed its substantial cash resources to sway regulators and legislators for ever larger bailouts. Let's trace the utility's troubling path from aggressive lobbying to illicit corruption.

As noted earlier, FirstEnergy was formed by expanding its coal commitments just as air pollution standards tightened and fracking made natural gas cheaper. It also embraced reactors after post–Three Mile Island safety requirements vastly increased nuclear power's costs. Such poor business decisions prompted Moody's to downgrade FirstEnergy Solutions and warn, "Both the probability of default and expected losses are high." Not so subtly declaring the company couldn't survive on its own, the ratings agency added, "There are no clear avenues for additional regulatory or political intervention aimed at providing any additional cash flows."[19]

FirstEnergy displayed an early proclivity toward bribery when, in 2003, it made improper gifts to the executive director of the Ohio Consumers' Counsel (OCC), pushing him to endorse an $8.7 billion rate increase and to hide his agency's own report showing that FirstEnergy should receive "only" $2 billion to $4 billion.[20] When news of the illicit payment surfaced, the OCC pressured its leader to quit, but FirstEnergy got little more than a slap on the hand. Unpunished, the utility grew unrepentant.[21]

Chuck became CEO in January 2015 and immediately accelerated the utility's lobbying. To bag a bailout, he cast his net widely—and repeatedly.

FirstEnergy's consistent calls for reactor subsidies need to be put in perspective. Recognize that by the HB 6 scandal of 2019, Ohioans already had paid three times over for the utility's two in-state nuclear power plants, one west of Toledo and the other east of Cleveland. Ratepayers first funded the units' construction in 1978 and 1987, as the utility monopoly received guaranteed returns on its expensive investments. They paid again in 1999, when Ohio restructured electricity markets and FirstEnergy obtained ten years of "transition charges" to make up for its assets alleged to be "stranded" by competition. And in 2008, Ohioans coughed up a third time when company-sympathetic regulators allowed utilities to collect higher rates under so-called electric security plans.[22]

Despite such multiple bounties, the utility's reactors continued to bleed money, so FirstEnergy tried a new approach, asking the Public Utilities Commission of Ohio (PUCO) to force consumers to underwrite power purchase agreements so the utility's unregulated generation affiliate could sell power at inflated rates to its regulated distribution subsidiary—with no competitive bidding, no price negotiation, and no consumer protections. FirstEnergy wanted to be paid to buy all the power its own subsidiary could generate for the next fifteen years, no matter how costly.

The utility had tried this trick before. When it was required to purchase a small amount of renewable energy in 2013, FirstEnergy avoided the market and bought clean power directly from its sister company, prompting Ohio regulators to calculate that the state's consumers overpaid by $43 million. John Finnigan, now a lawyer with the OCC, made the following comparison to these no-bid, self-dealing contracts: "Imagine if the owners of your company forced you and every employee to buy expensive health insurance from their cousin, even though you could easily get a better price if you shopped around."[23]

FirstEnergy also tried to block a new competitor—demand response, an innovative arrangement that paid consumers to conserve energy when the electric grid was stressed and generating expensive power. This low-cost, zero-carbon resource saved customers in the mid-Atlantic region $11.8 billion, but a threatened FirstEnergy argued electricity demand should be met only with more generators—its own generators. So the utility and its hired "experts" proposed that the regional grid operator kick demand response out of its market.[24]

FirstEnergy further attacked Ohio's clean energy initiatives, pushing state legislators and then-governor John Kasich for a two-year freeze on measures that helped consumers save electricity and money but cost FirstEnergy some sales.²⁵ Kasich, however, rejected FirstEnergy's plea, noting those existing provisions helped Ohio become the top state in wind-turbine manufacturing jobs; he also explained that the state's efficiency initiatives supported more than twenty-five thousand Ohio workers, reduced consumer electricity bills by more than $1 billion, and drastically slashed the state's toxic air pollutants.²⁶ Rob Kelter, with the Environmental Law & Policy Center, added that energy efficiency reduces energy bills, enhances system reliability, and lessens the need for expensive "peaking" power plants.²⁷ Rollbacks also were opposed by another Ohio-based utility, American Electric Power, as well as by the Ohio Manufacturers' Association, which declared "the program is working as intended and delivering substantial documented benefits for customers."²⁸

Less noticed but also challenging to clean energy, FirstEnergy and its allies advanced a provision within Ohio's budget bill that made it harder, if not impossible, to site wind farms. The existing zoning requirement called for a wind turbine to be at least 1.1 times the generator's height away from any property line, averaging 550 feet. The new, and quite arbitrary, provision nearly tripled that distance, meaning almost all existing wind projects could not have been built, and no new ones would be. Faced with such policy hurdles, wind energy developers moved to other states to invest in and construct turbines.²⁹

FirstEnergy, while blocking competitors, continued to plead for its own bailouts. Yet it faced substantial opposition. The grid manager testified that the utility's uneconomic power plants were not needed to keep the lights glowing.³⁰ Several alternative power-generating companies, such as Dynegy and NRG, offered to provide the same amount of electricity at significantly lower costs.³¹ Diverse groups, ranging from the Ohio Manufacturers' Association to the OCC, complained that FirstEnergy's subsidized power purchase agreements would unnecessarily burden the state's industries and homeowners.

Despite such criticism, the utility-supportive PUCO in December 2015 granted FirstEnergy a $4-billion bailout—spending less than six minutes to complete its formal consideration.³² Federal regulators, fortunately, gave the subsidy scheme a bit more scrutiny and called FirstEnergy's backroom bailout "abusive" for taking advantage of "captive" customers and distorting the multistate competitive power market. Mocking Ohio regulators, the Federal Energy Regulatory Commission (FERC) ruled the power purchase agreements to be misguided and illegal.³³

Not easily embarrassed, FirstEnergy responded with wordsmithing, renaming the subsidy a "surcharge" rather than a "power purchase agreement." The utility giant also said the bailout would go to its *distribution* affiliate (which the PUCO "regulates") rather than its *generation* affiliate (which the FERC oversees). Chuck assured his investors that such edits would obtain the original plan's result—a massive $4 billion bailout—but "without the need for FERC approval."[34,35]

Chuck's editing did not change the reality that Ohio consumers would be stuck with higher charges. As one analyst put it, "When all the jargon is stripped away, the [FirstEnergy scheme] requires regular people to pay an extra month's electric bill each year for eight years."[36] Another critic claimed the revised appeal was nothing more than a "rhetorical sleight of hand" that "would make Houdini blush."[37]

Without blushing, the grasping CEO tripled down. Adding to his "FERC-proof" stratagem, he asked for an additional $4 billion to reduce FirstEnergy's debt as well as another $4 billion to compensate FirstEnergy for keeping its corporate headquarters in Ohio. Yes, he sought a whopping $12 billion in subsidies.[38]

Even Ohio's rubber-stamp regulators flinched at that amount, yet they spent a fair amount of time lamenting how FirstEnergy's large debt led to credit downgrades, making utility borrowing more expensive. To avoid the appearance of bailing out reactors, commissioners in October 2016 advanced a new ploy: Just give FirstEnergy a lot of money, $625 million, so its credit rating would improve and allow it to borrow more money to theoretically modernize its grid with updated wires, meters, and transformers.[39]

To hide the appearance of an outright giveaway, the PUCO resorted to its own deceptive wordsmithing. One part of the regulators' order stated that the $625 million "should be conditioned upon the implementation of all grid modernization programs approved by the Commission." It even declared that regulators would annually review FirstEnergy's grid-modernization progress and adjust its receipts, "including any over- or under-recoveries."[40] Translated, that should mean that if FirstEnergy spent less on grid modernization than it earned from these new subsidies, it must make up the difference through credits to customers.

Yet hidden in the 192-page document were lines saying regulators "will not place restrictions on the use" of the funds and that FirstEnergy may deploy the resources "to indirectly support grid modernization investments." The operative word, of course, was "indirectly," and the PUCO added that such "investments" could "include outstanding pension obligations, reducing debt, or taking other steps to reduce the long-term costs of accessing capital." Translated, FirstEnergy enjoyed the flexibility to deploy the $625 million largesse to reduce its debt (making its bondholders happy), to increase its dividends (making its shareholders richer), or even to raise its salaries (making its executive ecstatic), without spending anything to actually modernize its grid. The only stand-up-to-the-utility provision within that regulatory ruling was a line saying FirstEnergy should maintain its headquarters in Akron.[41]

Even the utility-sympathetic PUCO chairman publicly admitted this approach was "undoubtedly unconventional."[42] That regulator, Asim Hague, secretly confessed to a FirstEnergy executive, "Knowing that [the no-strings-attached payment] would likely be found illegal and could not be refunded, I knew you would hold on to the funds."[43] As his term as commissioner was ending, Hague added, "Remember me fondly, my friend. I was the regulator that annoyed you the most, that simultaneously gave you the most. . . . I should have a small picture in memoriam in [FirstEnergy's] hallowed halls in Akron." When that exchange became public, Hague tried to claim his comments were "tongue-in-cheek."[44]

The Ohio Supreme Court found nothing humorous about the no-strings-attached payment. The justices ordered the illegal charge be removed, saying state regulators had failed to specify conditions for how FirstEnergy should spend the subsidy to modernize the grid. Yet, as Hague predicted, the court, because of legislation previously advanced by FirstEnergy, could not order those unlawful payments to be refunded to customers. As a result, FirstEnergy had collected—and got to keep—almost three-quarters of the $625 million that accumulated during the three years of legal appeals. In essence, the power company lost before both federal regulators and the state's highest court, but it still pocketed millions. A subsequent FERC audit found that FirstEnergy may have used some of these no-strings-attached payments to later push passage of HB 6, an even larger bailout scheme.[45]

Bob and Betty Buckeye probably viewed the $625 million subsidy as lavish, but it represented only about 5 percent of Chuck's requested $12 billion, prompting the utility executive to feel shortchanged, this time threatening to close his two uneconomic reactors and lay off hundreds of Ohio workers if he did not get more.[46] Chuck's threat sounded like a version of the old schoolyard taunt: *If I don't get my subsidies, I'm going to close my generators and go home.*

Noting its endless energy for seeking subsidies, FirstEnergy had become the Energizer bailout bunny. Despite millions already in hand, Chuck turned from regulators to legislators and demanded a bill that would provide an additional $6 billion. Unfortunately for the CEO, the Ohio House and Senate then were dominated by free-market conservatives who didn't take kindly to open checkbooks and corporate socialism.

As reported by Energy News Network, the CEO in early 2017 tried new rhetoric, this time saying his two nuclear generators deserved credit for not emitting greenhouse gases; he cutely labeled his requested payments "ZEN," for zero emission nuclear. Flabbergasted environmentalists pointed out that those reactors produced highly radioactive waste. With obvious irony, other Ohio utilities took up Chuck's expression and argued "clean-air subsidies" also should support their outmoded coal plants that spewed tons of soot, ash, and carbon dioxide.[47]

Chuck regularly threw out other rationales, but none stood up to scrutiny. He argued, for instance, that subsidies would be good for customers by providing certainty about future electricity rates, yet a bailout's only certainty was that consumers would pay more while corporate executives and shareholders enjoyed bonuses and dividends. The CEO further suggested bailouts would be good for Ohio's businesses, yet the state's leading industrialists, which consumed a lot of electricity, said the utility's income-guarantee plans "will make it more difficult for Ohio manufacturers to remain competitive in the global markets."[48] The subsidy-seeking executive then argued Ohioans should not rely upon out-of-state-power from FirstEnergy's competitors, forgetting electrons don't really care about state boundaries and ignoring the other Ohio-based generators willing to provide lower-cost electricity without subsidies.[49] Chuck also threatened lights would go dark without special support, but the electric grid's independent manager, PJM, again reported the system had plenty of reliable power even if FirstEnergy closed its old and uneconomic generators.[50]

When defending such roving claims, Chuck and his team occasionally shot themselves in the foot. To support one of his bailout requests before Ohio regulators, the CEO argued customers should pay the full costs of generating electricity from FirstEnergy's old and costly coal and nuclear facilities. If market prices turned out to be higher than those generating expenses, ratepayers would benefit, but if not, the utility won and ratepayers lost. Forecasts of future wholesale market prices, therefore, would be critical, so FirstEnergy hired a costly consultant willing to "predict" that such prices would rise rapidly, suggesting a short-term bailout would be a long-term bargain. Unfortunately for the power company, its witness's past predictions had not materialized, and during cross-examination he admitted wholesale electricity prices were about 10 percent lower and natural-gas prices 30 percent lower than he had forecast only a year before. The expert-for-hire also confessed to ignoring energy efficiency, which reduces electricity demand and, therefore, costs.[51]

Such embarrassments did not stop Chuck's plotting. In December 2016, to gain access to lower-cost money, he proposed substituting $700 million of FirstEnergy's secured credit for $1.5 billion of its unregulated affiliate's unsecured credit.[52] The CEO also tried to transfer a struggling coal plant from one of his unregulated affiliates to a regulated subsidiary in West Virginia. Such a move would have guaranteed profits for the company but cost customers a half billion dollars; federal regulators in January 2018 unanimously prevented the switch, which they labeled cross-subsidization.[53]

Frustrated with commissioners and legislators, Chuck turned his supplications toward the White House and secretly provided $5 million on May 1,

2017, to a Trump-aligned dark-money group, America First Policies.[54] (The bundler arranging that payment, a senior advisor at public affairs firm Akin, took the Fifth to avoid incriminating himself in a 2024 FirstEnergy bribery trial.[55]) The utility CEO, after becoming a Trump contributor, got the chance to plead his bailout case personally before the president, who, according to Chuck's notes, said, "We're doing it, period." To the chairman's delight, Trump added, "We are on the same team."[56]

To further secure the administration's support, Chuck engaged Corey Lewandowski, the president's tough-talking former campaign manager. Although denying he worked for the power corporation,[57] Lewandowski became part of FirstEnergy's "DOE Team" that pushed to have the US Department of Energy advance a federal bailout of uneconomic power plants. When Trump ordered DOE to "stop the loss" of coal and nuclear generators, Lewandowski boasted in an email to that team, "Boom!!!"[58]

Shortly thereafter, FirstEnergy's "friends" ponied up another $1.5 million at a Trump fundraiser in northeastern Ohio. One lobbyist noted that about a year later, a senior advisor to the president's campaign, Bob Paduchik, returned the favor and called Ohio House members to express support for HB 6.[59]

Amid this lobbying, Chuck got lucky in December 2017, when Trump's tax-cut legislation gave debt-heavy corporations, particularly electric utilities, a huge bonanza. Such good fortune helped FirstEnergy the next year obtain a $981 million net profit. Chuck expressed joy but gave no consideration to sharing the unexpected bonanza with his customers.[60]

The CEO obtained more benefits when private investors bet his battered company was undervalued and could earn substantial profits if it finally obtained a bailout and returned to the safety of being a regulated monopoly. FirstEnergy in January 2018, for instance, received $2.5 billion of financing from activist investor Elliott Management and private-equity firm Bluescape.[61]

Despite receiving massive dollar inflows, Chuck, in pursuit of federal assistance, hired other well-connected DC-based lobbyists, including one who had been senior advisor to Rick Perry, the new energy secretary. Those advocates argued the federal government should guarantee sales and profits for "traditional baseload resources such as coal-fired and nuclear" that tend to run constantly because they cannot scale up and down throughout the day and night in response to changing consumer demand. When he was governor of Texas, Perry advanced electricity markets that spurred huge investments in wind farms, but he reversed course as Trump's energy secretary and suggested awkwardly, "I don't think economics—I don't think that's the issue."[62] To lobby Perry and Trump, FirstEnergy executives flew the company's two aircraft on thirty-one trips to the District of Columbia, and in the same month, they spent almost $4 million at Akin, Washington's top-earning lobbying and law firm, where one of the partners charged as much as $1,475 an hour.[63]

Joining the advocacy push was Robert Murray, head honcho of Murray Energy, the giant coal-mining company that had long supplied fuel to FirstEnergy's plants. An outspoken climate-change denier and key Trump contributor, Murray met personally with the president and energy secretary to support a coal bailout, saying that "invoking this [bailout] provision would be an excellent action by the [Department of Energy]."[64] As another example of that coal company's political sway, Trump appointed a Murray Energy lobbyist to be administrator of the Environmental Protection Agency, where one of his first acts was to hand down a favorable ruling to the coal industry on its toxic coal ash.[65]

Also on the bailout team was Joseph Craft of Alliance Resource Partners, another major coal marketer, who donated a whopping $1.3 million to the president's inauguration. Despite Trump's promise to drain Washington's political swamp, it seems subsidy hunters continued to gain access by hiring expensive lobbyists and making huge contributions.[66]

Despite the political clout of bailout seekers, a significant number of Republican and Democrat legislators labeled the requested payouts "corporate welfare" and "just a tax on customers" designed to "do favors" for friends of the Trump administration. The FERC, though its new chairman had represented FirstEnergy when he worked at the law firm Jones Day, ignored FirstEnergy's political pressure and ruled that such special benefits would distort energy markets.[67]

Lewandowski expressed great displeasure with this decision by the five-member federal board, four of whom Trump had nominated. "The deep state is very real," he barked when attacking "government officials who don't support the Trump agenda."[68]

FirstEnergy and its consultants continued to grasp for some rationale—or any possible legislative vehicle—to bail out clunky, old, and uneconomic coal and nuclear power plants. Their next audacious plan was to invoke section 202(c) of the Federal Power Act—to guarantee profits so such generators could meet any "emergency" on the electric grid. Yet that proposal's cost estimates soared to a staggering $8 billion annually, sparking vocal protests from manufacturers, farmers, the AARP, and other consumers of electricity. Even a senior Republican on the House Energy and Commerce Committee had this to say about FirstEnergy's latest plea: "If you believe in free markets, it's difficult to stomach."[69]

Also mocking the notion of a national grid emergency, the electric system's operator confirmed that "nothing we have seen suggests there is any kind of emergency from these units retiring," calling the problem "fundamentally a corporate issue."[70] Other power generators joined in and argued that subsidizing hundreds of the oldest power plants would upend energy markets, undermine reliability, and undercut their investments in modern technologies.

Continuing to beg, Chuck tried another legal stretch—using a Korean War–era law designed to ensure a stable supply of resources needed to protect the nation *during a war*. The CEO argued the Defense Production Act of 1950 allowed for the diversion of federal resources to keep FirstEnergy's struggling units operating. Yet a Republican energy strategist admitted the law was "specifically premised on the idea that this stuff is essential to national security—that we're going to war. The problem in this instance is that some might think that an approach relying on the act trivializes national security."[71]

Blocked from multiple subsidy appeals, FirstEnergy Solutions in March 2018 filed for bankruptcy protection, although Chuck, probably a little embarrassed, waited until nearly midnight on the second night of Passover and the night before Easter to issue the blockbuster announcement. To critics, the bankruptcy proposal appeared to be just another attempt to protect the parent company, FirstEnergy, from the affiliate that owned the uneconomic power plants, FirstEnergy Solutions.[72] That subsidiary, not surprisingly, tried its own subsidy scheme before the bankruptcy court, proposing to pay $1 billion to its creditors in order to avoid $2.1 billion in claims, but—and it was a critical "but"—only if the corporation could skip out on all cleanup and decommissioning costs associated with closing its dirty coal and nuclear facilities. In essence, FirstEnergy Solutions hoped to walk away from steaming piles of hazardous waste in coal-ash ponds and landfills, transferring those cleanup expenses to consumers and taxpayers. The utility giant also wanted to ignore its multimillion-dollar shortfall in the trust fund for safeguarding the radioactive waste from its nuclear power plants; it hoped others would unknowingly pick up that tab too.[73]

When discussing this shift-the-liability ploy, Chuck had a hard time keeping his statements consistent. When trying to convince Wall Street analysts to invest in the corporation, he said that "there's just not that much risk" if FirstEnergy assumed the cleanup costs associated with toxic coal-ash pits and radioactive reactors. Yet when communicating with federal regulators at the Securities and Exchange Commission, he admitted such environmental liabilities "could have a material adverse effect on our results of operations and financial condition."[74]

Suspicions about FirstEnergy's statements grew when the power corporation's auditor asked the bankruptcy judge to terminate its accounting contract, claiming it had a "difference of position [with FirstEnergy Solutions] regarding the application of an accounting principle to a material transaction." That's a not-so-direct way of saying the auditor found the utility to be trying something fishy.[75]

The bankruptcy judge rejected the utility's pleas to avoid cleanup costs, calling them "patently unconfirmable."[76] Yet the amended deal did allow FirstEnergy Solutions (which became known as Energy Harbor after bankruptcy) to erase some $4 billion of debt from its books and become owned by its creditors, including major bondholders Avenue Capital Group, Nuveen Asset Management, and BlackRock.[77]

A key "activist investor" was John Kiani and his hedge fund, Texas-based Cove Key Management. He became Energy Harbor's executive chairman, referred to by a utility lobbyist as a demanding, hands-on boss with an "aggressive" temperament. As an example, Kiani obtained the Ohio Speaker's cell phone number and, according to the lobbyist, "overused" it.[78]

Kiani, after guiding the company through bankruptcy, claimed Energy Harbor was in an excellent position for a future based on zero-carbon-emitting reactors.[79] Yet the turnaround gambler still wanted subsidies to increase the value of the utility's generators and to allow existing hedge funds and bondholders to make massive profits spinning the units off to other investors.[80]

Court documents showed that these creditors agreed to "make political contributions, to have the Debtors use their efforts to get HB 6 passed, [and] to have the Debtors assist in the effort to defeat the referendum that followed the passage of HB 6."[81] The stakes were high, as Energy Harbor's board authorized up to $40 million for Generation Now, the dark-money group that was registered in Delaware and was at the center of this bribery scandal.[82] According to Kiani's aide, the financier stood to personally gain $100 million if the subsidy and reactor sale went through.[83]

Now with deep-pocketed gamblers in its corner, Chuck sought a grander bailout.

FirstEnergy's CEO may have had money for another subsidy campaign, but he most needed a political champion. A potential advocate landed in his lap when Larry Householder won reelection to the statehouse and reached out to FirstEnergy's chief lobbyist, Michael Dowling, for contributions to support his drive to again become Speaker of the Ohio House of Representatives. That connection nearly failed when Dowling "almost erased (Larry's email) and then saw his last name."[84]

Through an intermediary—Tony George, a Cleveland restaurateur who enjoyed financial contracts with FirstEnergy and political connections with Householder—in November 2016, Chuck detailed to the just-elected lawmaker the utility's urgent "need" for a government bailout. Without help, the CEO wrote, "It'll be too late. These plants will be shut, sold, or bankrupt." Sensing potential political contributions from the deep-pocketed utility, the wheeling-dealing Householder quickly replied that he wanted to talk.[85]

Realizing a bailout required Larry to become Speaker, Chuck arranged for the legislator and his son, as well as Tony George, to ride on FirstEnergy's private jet to Washington, DC, and attend Donald Trump's January 2017 inauguration celebrations. According to federal prosecutors, FirstEnergy consultants covered the Ohio politician's $1,557 hotel bill as well as expensive dinners for eight at the posh Charlie Palmer Steak and The Palm.[86] That trip cemented the relationship between Chuck and Larry that would lead to the concoction of a massive pay-to-play scandal. Describing this new alliance, the CEO announced, "We have to get Larry Householder over the line [to become Speaker] because I know he won't let anything bad happen to us."[87]

Upon returning from the Washington festivities, Larry had his top aide, Jeff Longstreth, set up a bank account for Generation Now, which would fuel his speakership campaign. The following day, the staffer emailed money-wiring instructions to Mike Dowling, clarifying that "this is the organization that Chuck and Larry discussed."[88] The day after that, Dan McCarthy—then a FirstEnergy lobbyist and later Governor Mike DeWine's legislative director—opened another secret funding mechanism, Partners for Progress.[89,90]

A bold Larry Householder made it clear he "expected" FirstEnergy Solutions to make "a multiple hundred-thousand-dollar contribution" to Generation Now. Juan Cespedes and another utility lobbyist "pushed back" by noting their client was in bankruptcy.[91] Yet sensing a promising path toward subsidies, senior utility executives soon got over their bankruptcy concerns and delivered one of their first payoffs at the State Street office in Columbus that Larry shared with the dark-money repository. In an almost-comical scene, the other lobbyist, Robert Klaffky, discussed bailout legislation while sliding across the table and under Larry's hand an envelope containing a check for $400,000. The corporation's consultant stated, "Our client cares very much about this issue." The politician tore back the sealed flap and replied: "Well, yes, they do."[92]

Utility executives had decided to initially give the legislator $500,000, but the lobbyists called that amount "far more than [Larry] expected." So the company split its early contribution, enabling FirstEnergy to later give a separate $100,000 "because we wanted another chance to get in front of him and show our support." Cespedes, who would be indicted for bribery, further explained the sordid pay-to-play deal: "We were trying to establish the fact that our support was specifically tied to [bailout] legislation."[93]

Larry, however, tied some of those and additional utility funds to himself. According to court documents, some $158,000 went to renovate and clean the pool at his Florida vacation home, $300,300 to settle a business lawsuit associated with his investment in an Alabama coal mine, and $19,800 to pay off his credit-card balances. An FBI agent would later assert that several

FirstEnergy lobbyists also profited handsomely, with one pocketing $2.53 million and another at least $650,000.[94]

During the final weeks of the 2018 political campaign, Larry traveled to Chuck's corporate office in Akron, where he pleaded for even more funding in a final push to elect allies who would make him Speaker and do the utility's bidding. FirstEnergy's CEO replied, "I'll help you with whatever you need."[95]

Chuck did not limit his political bets to the House leader. He also worked doggedly to ensure a utility champion became Ohio's chief regulator, a governor-nominated position that determined his utility's revenue and requirements.

On the evening of December 18, 2018, Chuck and Mike Dowling dined with the newly elected governor (Mike DeWine) and lieutenant-governor (Jon Husted) for ninety minutes at the private Athletic Club in downtown Columbus. They discussed a financial bailout for FirstEnergy and the appointment of Samuel Randazzo as chairman of the Public Utilities Commission of Ohio (PUCO).[96] Chuck commented, "When the governor elect asked me about [Sam's] attributes, I listed integrity."[97]

After that dinner, Chuck and Dowling drove about a mile to Sam's condo in the swanky German Village neighborhood. The threesome reviewed FirstEnergy's previous consulting contracts—totaling a whopping $22 million beginning in 2010—for which Randazzo secretly brokered rate deals between the utility and a few large Ohio industrialists. The high-priced lobbyist also had aggressively opposed competition from solar farms and wind turbines.[98]

Sam didn't mention that he made sure FirstEnergy contracts benefited his family. In an email to his wife, he explained, "In the agreements I set up monthly payments for a five-year term. In the event that I die or am disabled, the monthly payments (with a modest discount) still must be paid by FirstEnergy to Sustainability (a corporation that I own, and you will own in the event I die). This revenue stream . . . should go a long way towards helping you financially after I am not able to do so."[99]

With Sam wanting more, Chuck at the German Village meeting agreed to pay his voracious consultant an additional $4.3 million to help FirstEnergy with friendly administrative rulings if Randazzo became PUCO chairman.[100] The following morning, Chuck wrote to Sam that his extra money would arrive quickly, saying, "We're going to get this handled this year, paid in full, no discount."[101]

The utility's own attorneys argued against the payment, saying it would haunt FirstEnergy as a massive bribe that totaled two and a half times the average American's lifetime income.[102] Yet Chuck and Dowling overruled their staff and quickly forwarded to Sam a wire transfer "without ever having received an invoice for the payment and without any work or consulting services being performed."¹⁰³

FirstEnergy's CEO, virtually defining pay-to-play, wrote to Sam, "Don't forget about us or Hurricane Chuck may show up on your doorstep! Of course, no guarantee he won't show up sometime anyway." Chuck inserted an image of a venomous snake protruding from a hurricane, to which Sam replied, "Made me laugh.—You guys are welcome anytime and anywhere I can open the door."¹⁰⁴

Chuck's recommendation of Randazzo held a lot of sway with DeWine, in part because of the utility's numerous campaign contributions over the years. Evidence of the tight relationship was the Athletic Club dinner itself, when the new governor essentially asked FirstEnergy whom the company would find acceptable to be its regulator. The politician also felt pressure from a twelve-person nominating council, a supposedly independent body that just happened to be chaired by a former FirstEnergy lobbyist and on which Sam himself had long served.¹⁰⁵

The seasoned politician, however, received—and ignored—substantial warnings about Sam. A former DeWine staffer, J. B. Hadden, delivered a scathing 198-page dossier that revealed "Randazzo personally profits from a secret, for-profit entity funded by FirstEnergy Solutions. Randazzo is the entity's sole owner, and he utilizes it to purchase real estate (including eight properties in Ohio and Florida worth nearly $4.1 million) and other assets for his personal use and financial gain." The dossier, which DeWine's office obtained about a week before nominating Sam, further said the lawyer's "FirstEnergy relationship has always seemed sacrosanct" and that he long held "opaque and undisclosed" ties to the power corporation.¹⁰⁶

Hadden was a reputable messenger who understood state politics and energy issues. The Columbus lawyer for years had represented American Electric Power, the other giant Columbus-headquartered utility, and he served as DeWine's campaign treasurer from 2009 to 2015. "As a longtime supporter of Gov. DeWine," Hadden explained, "I've always been honest with him when I think he needs to know something to aid in a decision."¹⁰⁷

DeWine also ignored a separate letter from environmental organizations warning of Sam's "extreme bias" against renewable energy, noting, for instance, he had served as lobbyist for an anti-wind-power group that referred to climate change as a "hoax."¹⁰⁸ Good-government groups, moreover, expressed concerns that Sam ranked among the largest contributors to state legislative candidates, having given more than $282,000.¹⁰⁹

Randazzo's drive toward the PUCO chairmanship did hit a serious bump, at least from FirstEnergy's perspective, when an organization the lawyer controlled, Sustainability Funding Alliance of Ohio, showed up on FirstEnergy Solutions' bankruptcy filings as having received millions from that utility.

Reporters started inquiring, and Chuck started worrying he had no "backup plan" if Sam pulled out of the PUCO nominating process. Fearing his utility wouldn't have a sympathetic regulator, the CEO moaned, "This is awful."[110]

So Chuck and his lobbyists frantically placed calls to the governor and lieutenant governor. Utility officials initially wanted to avoid blame, with Dowling saying the DeWine administration is "going to be mad at Sam (and hopefully not us) for not disclosing the financial relationship; that's Sam's responsibility."[111] Yet within a day, the executives convinced the politicians that the financial connections between FirstEnergy and Randazzo—between a utility and a potential regulator—were not sufficiently embarrassing to block the nomination. "Forced DeWine/Husted to perform battlefield triage," Chuck boasted. "It's a rough game."[112] FirstEnergy's chief lobbyist added, "A bullet grazed the temple."[113]

DeWine nominated Sam as PUCO chairman on February 4, 2019. FirstEnergy's CEO immediately texted the nominee: "Congratulations!" Sam responded: "Thanks, Chuck—the last four days have been tuff. . . . Thanks goes to some great good friends."[114]

At his quick confirmation hearing in April before the Ohio Senate, Sam ignored his own significant self-promotion and claimed he had planned to retire before the DeWine administration asked him to take the job. Also overlooking his past work opposing wind and solar projects, he promised that as PUCO chairman, he would have no view for or against any specific technology. Sam, moreover, refused to comment on his past contracts with FirstEnergy or other utilities, claiming they were private affairs.[115]

With the Senate's approval, Sam became PUCO chairman.[116] Chuck had assembled his team.

Chapter III

Buying a Bailout

With a FirstEnergy consultant as the lead regulatory commissioner and an indebted Speaker overseeing Ohio's House of Representatives, FirstEnergy's CEO dreamed of a comprehensive subsidy package. The contours quickly grew into a utility wish list.

Chuck's initial ask was to "just" bail out two of the utility's reactors, which company executives called "unprofitable." Rather than "force creditors or any other parties to take on ownership and continued operation of units that are expected to lose money in the future," the executive decided Ohioans should become owners of these money losers and accept a surcharge on their electric bills.[1]

Other utilities wondered, *Why not provide similar subsidies to two dirty and uneconomic coal-fired generators?* American Electric Power (AEP) argued that to protect miners and coal barons, Ohio businesses and families wouldn't mind rate increases that supported both units—even though one was in Indiana.[2]

Feeling momentum, Chuck decided he really would appreciate guaranteed profits. With Sam Randazzo's help, he added a "decoupling" policy that separated the utility's revenues from its electricity sales, allowing the corporation to bill ratepayers for any shortfall compared to the $978 million it received in 2018—its best haul in a decade, thanks largely to high air-conditioning use during an unusually hot summer and to that year being the last that a giant General Motors factory operated and consumed a great deal of electricity in the state. Chuck boasted to his investors that this provision alone would provide $355 million of "unearned profit" over five years and make a good portion of the company "somewhat recession proof."[3]

While at it, Chuck essentially said, "Let's also get rid of the competition to our nuclear and coal units." Although wind, solar, and efficiency enjoyed broad support, the CEO added gutting the state's existing conservation and renewable-energy provisions that had been saving Ohioans money—but reducing the demand for electricity from FirstEnergy's generators.

Then to spread the pain, the power-corporation executive thought all Ohioans—not just those living in FirstEnergy's service territory—should shoulder these subsidies.

Thus, Buckeye State utilities assembled the framework for what would become House Bill 6.[4]

To obtain huge bailouts for reactors, Chuck threw out a lot of arguments, but most failed to stick or gain traction—at least until he bought political sway. The CEO claimed, for instance, that FirstEnergy needed subsidies because its reactors struggled economically, but the company refused to disclose its financial records, and several independent analysts found the plants to be quite profitable. According to the former chief economist at PJM Interconnection, the Davis-Besse and Perry nuclear units generated annual profits of $28 million and $44 million, respectively, and were "among the most profitable of their kinds in the nation."[5] The Ohio Consumers' Counsel found that FirstEnergy Solutions enjoyed a profit of $18.4 million in the single month of May 2019.[6]

Perhaps FirstEnergy's most stunning argument was that a massive bailout would benefit "Bob and Betty Buckeye," with a utility executive testifying that a $1.3 billion subsidy "saves Ohio consumers millions of dollars annually while also promoting clean energy."[7] An array of analysts found folly in this claim; one of the most direct rebuttals came from a state agency, the Ohio Consumers' Counsel: "The bill (HB 6) will transfer about a billion dollars in above-market charges from Ohio families and businesses to FirstEnergy Solutions' investors. That is bad. The bill similarly will allow the continued bailout of the two coal plants, at a total consumer cost of about $300 million. . . . That is also bad."[8]

The power corporation also tried this argument's inverse. Particularly in mass mailings to seniors, it threatened "skyrocketing" energy bills if the bailout legislation failed. That intimidation was even too much for one usually sympathetic regulator, who warned the utility to "stop trying to scare Ohioans."[9]

Chuck even claimed subsidies would improve the state's infrastructure: the set of roads, rails, generators, and water treatment plants that underpin the economy. Yet rather than modernize these substructures, HB 6 quite clearly would spend millions buttressing outmoded power plants.

The state-sanctioned monopoly also uttered obvious contradictions. While saying the government should not pick technology winners, it proposed showering benefits on nuclear reactors and coal burners. If the utility's bailout pleas for superseded technologies were reversed to one hundred years earlier, they would have subsidized buggy whips and attacked private investments in the emerging automotive industry.

FirstEnergy further asserted that it alone, if supported financially, could protect power-plant jobs. Yet various other companies, particularly Dynegy and NRG, were happy to employ Ohio workers and generate lower-cost power from their own nonsubsidized generators.[10]

When it came to counting jobs, FirstEnergy displayed a remarkable lack of mathematical prowess. The utility's executives claimed 4,300 jobs were at risk without the bailout, yet the firm's restructuring manager revealed that FirstEnergy Solutions' total employees numbered only 2,700 people, about half of whom were not working at the nuclear plants. Executives also must have forgotten that their own fact sheets showed Davis-Besse had 720 workers and Perry 760. To keep those 1,480 employees working, a $1.3 billion bailout would equal almost $880,000 of ratepayer-financed subsidies per job.[11]

Ohio enjoyed numerous, and better, employment options. Conservatives argued the money would be best utilized in the pockets of Betty and Bob Buckeye rather than in the coffers of FirstEnergy. Others suggested the funds could be more effectively deployed by JobsOhio, the nonprofit corporation that uses state liquor taxes to advance economic development projects; according to a McKinsey & Company analysis, JobsOhio paid out $1 billion in incentives that helped create or retain 154,000 jobs—for an average of only $6,500 per worker.[12]

FirstEnergy wasn't the only Ohio utility advancing questionable arguments. Since initial versions of the bailout bill focused on Chuck's reactors, AEP, as well as Duke Energy and Dayton Power and Light, felt left out and began demanding subsidies for the Ohio Valley Electric Corporation's (OVEC's) coal units, which were among the nation's dirtiest. It took AEP almost a month of pleading to get its provision included in a substitute bill. That utility's negotiating prospects probably improved when it formed a secret electioneering group that paid $900,000 to supplement Householder-managed dark-money groups.[13] Still, Nick Akins, AEP's CEO, had a difficult time justifying coal-plant subsidies within what Chuck billed as "clean air" legislation.[14] It was especially hard noting the particulars associated with these two dirty and outmoded units. Kyger Creek in Ohio and Clifty Creek in Indiana were built in the 1950s, during the Eisenhower administration, to power an Atomic Energy Commission facility that enriched uranium for use in nuclear bombs and the navy's shipboard reactors. A consortium of electricity companies formed OVEC to supply the needed electricity, yet as Cold War demands fell, military enrichment activities concluded in 2001, leaving the two coal-fired facilities to sell electricity to OVEC utilities or in regional markets.

By 2019, the aged coal plants still supplied a substantial 2,300 megawatts of electricity, but they could not compete against falling natural gas prices and rising environmental costs, such as the required installation of $1 billion scrubbers to limit dangerous emissions. One analyst calculated the coal plants would lose $5.3 billion if they continued to operate until their planned 2040 retirements.[15] An independent audit financed by the Public Utilities Commission of Ohio (PUCO) initially found that "keeping the plants running does not seem to be in the best interest of ratepayers," yet utility-supportive commissioners told the auditors to remove that line from the final report and to use a "milder tone and intensity of language."[16] The Ohio Consumers' Counsel subsequently subpoenaed PUCO staffers to testify about that "edit," but Sam Randazzo, then PUCO chair, barred them from doing so.[17]

Even though the enrichment plant had been closed for decades, utility pleaders tried to rationalize coal-plant subsidies by referencing national security. Yet if the Cold War could still be used to justify propping up outdated and dirty generators, I asked at the time, "What's next? Subsidizing a musket factory?" *Ohio Capital Journal* added pointedly that a coal bailout would force Ohioans "to pay to make themselves and their planet sicker."[18]

Perhaps recognizing the flimsiness of his arguments, Chuck turned to his newfound (and financed) political muscle.

Larry Householder, known as "Big Larry" for his size and brash political style, grew up raising corn and tomatoes on his modest family farm in Perry County, a region in southeast Ohio that ranked as one of the state's lowest-earning areas. He first won a tight election to the state's General Assembly in 1997 and worked his way by 2001 into the House leadership . . . where he enjoyed the political power. In that initial race for Speaker, Larry obtained support from the Republican Party's rural and socially conservative wings, and as Speaker he pushed through a concealed-carry law and a ban on same-sex civil unions. Perhaps a harbinger of future scandal, his four-year term became tainted by an anonymous memo in 2004 that claimed he laundered campaign contributions, deployed heavy-handed fundraising tactics, and overpaid some vendors in exchange for kickbacks.[19] Although the US Department of Justice decided against filing charges, the various controversies tarnished the politician's reputation and forced his return to selling insurance in southeast Ohio. He barely won election as Perry County auditor, where he faced more accusations, such as hiring supporters who did no work.[20]

Twelve years later, when a fellow Republican opted not to run for reelection to the Ohio House, Larry saw his chance for political redemption. Portraying himself as a gun-toting, camouflage-wearing "comeback kid," he won the general election in this conservative district by a large margin. Yet he wanted more, specifically to again be Speaker, a post made available in early

2019, when the then-current leader resigned while under FBI investigation for his lavish lifestyle.

To win back the gavel, Larry had to defeat Ryan Smith, who had the endorsement of the previous Speaker and the Republican establishment, as well as a pile of cash from scores of lobbyists.[21] Their appearances and styles differed greatly—with Smith being thin and soft-spoken and Larry seen as a burly, boisterous political hustler. The former insurance salesman also was known as the more persuasive promoter; one lobbyist described Larry as "a never-ending negotiator. Nonstop. He's going to fuck you till he wins."[22]

Householder viewed himself as a political outsider, distinct from Smith and other "country club Republicans" who then dominated the Ohio House of Representatives. Hailing from a rural county and often wearing a hunting cap, he presented himself as a simple country boy with a southern Ohio drawl. Yet that aw-shucks demeanor, as suggested above, disappeared when Larry wanted something. Smith, in contrast, was considered "a low-key, small-town financial advisor known for his sincerity, pragmatism, and fairness."[23]

Although both shared conservative values, a key policy difference was Smith's opposition to FirstEnergy's previous subsidy pleas, about which he argued corporations should not obtain taxpayer-funded bailouts. Larry, in contrast, conveyed a willingness to do the utility's bidding—and to accept its contributions. Also telling, Smith enjoyed affiliations with the natural gas industry, while Larry had built ties with coal companies prominent in his Appalachian region, which supplied fuel to FirstEnergy generators.

According to a utility lobbyist, "Householder had a close political relationship with the parent company" and was "very, very good on our issue. He was the preferred winner in this race [for Speaker], obviously, and someone whom we wanted to support."[24] As a result, FirstEnergy forwarded vast sums into dark-money groups—Generation Now and Partners for Progress—which the crafty politician used to elect Republican candidates who would support him becoming the House leader and the utility obtaining a giant subsidy.[25]

To promote one of his Republican contenders, Larry—despite his own previous arrests for alcohol-impaired driving[26]—used the utility's abundant cash to run deceptive ads painting the Democratic challenger as a drunk driver.[27] The charge was false, but the last-minute blitz allowed the Republican to win by 138 votes. That victor, like other winning candidates supported by Team Householder, would soon vote to make their benefactor the Speaker.[28]

Despite this core of support, Larry realized he and Ryan would split Republican votes, so he cleverly reached out to Democratic lawmakers and promised to reject "right-to-work" and other anti-union measures. It was a tough sell, because Larry was known for his conservative positions against abortion, gun controls, and same-sex marriage, yet Team Householder made it work. Even a critic admitted that the lawmaker "was a very sophisticated politician, a very good negotiator, knew how to count votes."[29]

FirstEnergy delivered both money and muscle. As the leadership vote approached, Larry frantically texted Chuck: "I literally need one more vote for speaker." The executive quickly responded: "I'm on it."[30]

The speakership scheme worked, but only by a very slim margin. All but one of the Team Householder candidates won their races, but Larry still lost the Republican vote by 26 to 34. Democrats made up the difference, with 26 splitting for Householder and only 11 for Smith, giving Larry in January 2019 a 52-to-45 victory.

The freshly elected Speaker immediately texted FirstEnergy's CEO: "Thank you for everything. It was historical."[31]

That same day, Cespedes wrote to Klaffky, "That 500K investment seems very wise right now . . . this is a good day." Klaffky responded, "High risk, high reward" and noted that with Larry in charge of the House, it became a "matter of when, not if," the bailout legislation would be introduced.[32]

The bureau chief for the (Cleveland) *Plain Dealer* offered at the time a clear forecast of what lay ahead, writing, "Larry Householder is driven by money and power. And he's a survivor. He took a beating in the past, and he's back and stronger and smarter." She added a prescient prediction: "Under a Speaker Householder look for deep-pocketed interests like utilities and payday lenders to get what they want. Look for consumers of all kinds to be hosed."[33]

Soon after being sworn in, "the comeback kid" kept his part of the bargain with Chuck and began working alongside utility lobbyists to assemble legislation—to be known as House Bill 6, or HB 6—that would have, as the CEO dreamed, Ohioans bail out FirstEnergy's two nuclear reactors, subsidize two outdated coal plants, guarantee the utility's profits, and overturn clean-energy measures that Chuck felt were a threat to FirstEnergy's sales.[34]

Further demonstrating a pay-to-play environment, one FirstEnergy lobbyist admitted the utility's checks to Householder-controlled accounts "constituted our expectation that we would receive this [subsidy] legislation in return." The new Speaker, he added, "gave us very strong verbals and nonverbals that he would introduce legislation."[35]

Larry continued being direct about his demands. Through his aide Longstreth, he instructed FirstEnergy to keep paying Generation Now "if it expected to . . . have continued support" of the legislation.[36] The company obliged, depositing $15 million from April 30 to July 5, 2019.[37]

The Speaker quickly assembled political support from diverse quarters. Labor unions that represented the 1,480 workers at FirstEnergy's two troubled reactors were willing to push their Democratic allies to embrace what they viewed as job-security subsidies. Other well-connected utilities, particularly

AEP, appreciated the amended bill's support for its old coal plants. Coal barons, including the well-endowed Koch brothers and Robert Murray, were pleased the proposal pushed power plants to keep burning their product. Also willing to weigh in were the deep-pocketed hedge funds and private-equity firms that placed bets on a bailout-fueled FirstEnergy turnaround.[38]

That said, Larry had to overcome numerous opponents. Environmentalists abhorred subsidizing coal plants that spewed pollution. Consumer and manufacturing advocates objected to higher rates. Well-endowed natural gas companies opposed bailouts for competing coal and nuclear generators. The grid operator responsible for reliability complained that subsidies distorted markets. Conservative think tanks detested corporate welfare; one called HB 6 "a disastrous bill" and "a publicly funded money grab" that would provide FirstEnergy's investors a return of more than 3,000 percent; another right-wing group labeled the bill "cronyism on full display; in other words, a bailout" that might initially enrich FirstEnergy's hedge-fund vultures but be "a long-term financial loss for Ohioans."[39] Some Republican legislators simply objected to Larry's haranguing and bare-knuckle tactics.

The Speaker ignored such critics and demanded loyalty from his supporters, saying he wanted "casket carriers" who would be with him until the very end. "I can protect you when you're in the fort," Larry told his collaborators. "Don't leave the fort and get shot at." Noting the Speaker's doggedness, one legislator fearfully said, "He knows all. He sees all. He hears all."[40]

Larry regularly threatened those outside the fort. When a Republican lawmaker announced his intent to vote against the bailout, the Speaker promised retribution: "If you're going to fuck with me, I'm going to fuck with your kids."[41]

When Rep. Dave Greenspan expressed his opposition, Larry texted him, "I just want you to remember when I needed you, you weren't there. Twice." He ominously added, "Nobody comes after the [Householder] team without consequences." A FirstEnergy lobbyist piled on, telling the Republican legislator to expect repercussions since the Speaker managed which bills moved for a House vote and would block Greenspan's favorite measures "because the sponsor pissed off the speaker." Larry also controlled the Republican caucus's finances, allowing him to withhold campaign support from Greenspan and other politicians who crossed him.[42]

Yet in this case, the powerful Speaker's heavy-handedness backfired by pushing the Republican renegade to contact the FBI, which began an investigation. While Greenspan met with a federal agent at a Columbus Bob Evans restaurant in late May 2019, the day before the House passed its initial version of HB 6, the maverick legislator received a text from Larry again pressing for his vote and demanding that he delete all messages associated with the legislation.[43]

One lobbyist observed that Larry "went to war for [FirstEnergy]." The Speaker pressured Ohio House leaders to move the complex legislation with almost-lightning speed, even demanding hearings during the Assembly's spring break. He harangued lawmakers, to the point that one conservative member complained, "This is some next-level pressuring. . . . After every conversation I had with someone on [this bill], I felt like I needed a shower."[44] Another Republican representative objected, "I have never experienced such pressure for any other bill."[45]

The HB 6 enterprise required money, lots of it, and one lobbyist admitted, "We call FirstEnergy 'The Bank.'"[46] Another described the utility's waterfall of pay-to-play funds as "Monopoly money . . . you know, it's like not real."[47]

FirstEnergy and FirstEnergy Solutions spent lavishly to obtain and protect the HB 6 bailout. In a wiretapped conversation, Neil Clark, one of the indicted consultants, boasted of FirstEnergy's "unlimited money," and he cautioned that "they've got too much money, too much power." The tough-talking Clark added, "I spent close to $20 million in the last eight weeks, $20 million. FirstEnergy got $1.3 billion in subsidies, free payments. So, what do they care about putting in $20 million a year for this thing? They don't give a shit."[48]

That money flow was made possible by the Supreme Court's *Citizens United* ruling, allowing corporations to secretly fund dark-money groups—technically known as 501(c)(4) nonprofits that can spend unlimited amounts to influence elections without revealing the sources of those funds. A federal prosecutor described such an organization as "a perfect entity to receive a secret bribe."[49]

Even noting dark money's inherent secrecy, FirstEnergy went out of its way to camouflage its remittances. One $400,000 disbursement passed anonymously through two groups—One Ohio United and Citizens for a Working America—before being sent to Hardworking America, another secret funding vessel controlled by the Speaker.[50]

With such large war chests, Chuck supported his allies as well as attacked his critics. Consider the fate of Republican state representative Christina Hagan, who rebuffed the bailout as corporate welfare, saying, "I didn't budge when [FirstEnergy] came into my office to lobby me." When Hagan decided to run for Congress, she claims she "became the target of the company." A subsequent investigation by the Center for Public Integrity found that a slew of negative television ads was paid for by the Conservative Leadership Alliance, whose treasurer had been a longtime FirstEnergy lobbyist. According to Hagan, "I'm sure [FirstEnergy] just wanted to make an example of me in my race for higher office that if you don't play well, this is what will happen to you."[51] Although an avowed supporter of then-president Donald Trump, Hagan lost her Republican primary.

To bolster its Statehouse-based lobbying, the FirstEnergy "bank" also provided campaign contributions to local officials in areas where the utility operated. The power company and its consultants, in turn, pressured those mayors, county commissioners, and school superintendents to submit testimony and letters of support for HB 6. FirstEnergy, moreover, created a foundation that annually granted some $8 million to the favorite charities of key politicians or to money-hungry nonprofits that would endorse utility-crafted proposals.[52]

FirstEnergy and FirstEnergy Solutions also hired some twenty lobbyists to push the bailout bill through the legislature. They even peeled consultants away from bailout opponents, offering substantially higher pay. For example, they lured Josh Rubin, who had been DeWine's 2018 campaign advisor, from the Environmental Defense Fund, where I and others had been actively opposing utility bailouts. In addition to providing the FirstEnergy enterprise with insights on the resources and tactics of subsidy critics, that consultant-for-hire lobbied DeWine staffers, his former colleagues, to promote and quickly sign HB 6. Rubin also spent considerable time advancing Sam Randazzo's PUCO appointment; he briefed, and joined, Chuck Jones and Mike Dowling for their dinner meeting with DeWine and Husted at the Athletic Club; and to ensure DeWine's deniability, he advised the executives not to tell the politicians of their later-that-evening session with Sam.[53]

According to one consultant, the FirstEnergy/Householder enterprise represented an "unholy alliance" that brought together opposing political forces. Neil Clark and Matt Borges, for instance, hated each other from past lobbying conflicts, but the utility and the Speaker recognized the need for a diverse lobbying team. Executives also saw benefits from Borges, who supported former governor John Kasich for president, cooperating with Larry Householder, a MAGA Trump advocate.

With so much utility money on the table, those lobbyists sniped at each other regularly, each jockeying for a larger share. Juan Cespedes disparaged Neil Clark as "a psychopath" and said, "I don't trust him to do it right." He and Borges kept dropping hints to FirstEnergy executives that Clark and other lobbyists should "stay out of our lane."[54] The tough-talking Clark, of course, countered with his own blunt allegations. Still, utility executives controlled the purse strings and demanded cooperation.

The power corporation and the Speaker directed a good portion of their lobbying and largesse toward wavering lawmakers, making the Statehouse something of a policy bazaar. One politician, whose district included the massive but economically troubled Sammis coal-fired power plant, complained that initial versions of HB 6 would benefit only nuclear reactors in other parts of the state. The power corporation quickly arranged a community meeting in the senator's district, at which an executive announced that the amended legislation "would make our company economically healthy enough that we would be able to look at other investments, like investing in the Sammis Plant." Hearing that the utility would use $40 million to $50 million of its bailout slush fund to keep Sammis open and its workers employed, the senator changed his position on the subsidy bill.[55]

Like others, however, that politician had been duped. About three years later, the out-of-bankruptcy utility, then named Energy Harbor, acknowledged Sammis's continued financial frailty, closed the power plant, and laid off 140 employees. The utility's public-relations specialists offered a pablum-filled justification, saying, "It has been made abundantly clear to us that our customers, communities, and capital markets partners recognize the value of partnering with Energy Harbor as we help transform clean energy supply."[56]

The utility monopoly tried to pull lots of different strings to obtain Chuck's wish list. When Larry informed Chuck that HB 6 was a few votes short and three supportive lawmakers were attending a conference in Chicago, FirstEnergy executives asked DeWine to send a state-owned plane to fly the politicians home. Laurel Dawson, the governor's chief of staff, signed off, even though the special flight would cost Ohio taxpayers nearly $5,700. FirstEnergy's Mike Dowling gloated about the utility's political power, since Dawson was married to a company lobbyist; referring to Laurel, he boasted, "Mike Dawson's wife. Boom."[57] Yet after a newspaper revealed the extravagant scheme, the governor's office ditched that plan, forcing a few lawmakers to take commercial flights or drive 350 miles.[58]

FirstEnergy also spent heavily on advertising, including some $16 million for mailers and television ads urging Ohioans to encourage their legislators to support HB 6. The airwaves seemed blanketed with pleas from utility workers worried they would become unemployed without government action. Even hard-nosed Larry complained about repeatedly watching "that poor sumbitch drive that pickup truck down the road and cry about losing his job."[59]

Even years since these bailout efforts, journalists and investigators keep finding more covert utility payments that advanced HB 6 in the Ohio legislature. In April 2024, for instance, the *Cleveland Plain Dealer* reported that Senator Matt Huffman received, between 2019 and 2020, five checks worth $300,000 from Liberty Ohio, a FirstEnergy front group that one lobbyist referred to as "the Huffman C4."[60] Mike Dowling had texted Chuck Jones that Huffman "wants us to give him A LOT." Another utility lobbyist observed the politician to be "transactional and can get shit done,"[61] while yet another noted that the then–junior senator "is much stronger on our issue than I expected, . . . [and] he could be our champion in leadership."[62] Huffman, in fact, became Senate president and in January 2025, having moved over to the House due to term limits, and became Speaker.

Such ongoing revelations expose the extent of FirstEnergy's secret spending and suggest that even more disclosures are pending.[63]

Meanwhile, at the PUCO, Sam Randazzo, known for "his aggressive, litigious tactics,"⁶⁴ was answering FirstEnergy's pleas. Referencing the need for a "rescue project," Chuck wrote, "Stock is going to get hit.... Need Sam to get rid of the 'Ohio 2024' hole," referring to a requirement that the utility file a "rate case" in 2024 that would have commissioners extensively review the utility's finances and likely reduce customer charges and, therefore, power-company income.⁶⁵ Morgan Stanley already had downgraded FirstEnergy's credit rating due to fear of such rate reductions. With support from sympathetic legislators and regulators, the utility had escaped audits since 2007, regularly raising its rates with "riders," supplemental charges that the PUCO embraced with little review. Dowling met with Sam "to solve the 2024 issue" and subsequently noted that "no one internal [within PUCO] knows we met with him."⁶⁶ Not long thereafter, Sam ignored his staff and issued an order saying FirstEnergy's rate case was "no longer necessary or appropriate."⁶⁷ Chuck quickly texted Sam—"Thank You ... It wouldn't happen without you"—and he brashly attached an image of his company's stock price rising.⁶⁸

As PUCO chair, Sam also directed the Ohio Power Siting Board, which had authority over the location of electricity generators. Before making the appointment, as noted above, Governor DeWine ignored complaints from renewable-energy advocates about the lawyer's previous work with groups trying to block wind turbines. In his new position, Sam expanded such efforts to obstruct competitors to FirstEnergy's coal and nuclear plants. In one instance, he ruled that a proposed wind project on Lake Erie, which could have provided clean power for approximately seven thousand homes, must turn off its blades every night for eight months per year. Sam claimed to be protecting bats, but wind-energy supporters called his decision a poison pill. Chuck again texted his appreciation.⁶⁹

Yet even the CEO acknowledged that the regulator's continued favors for FirstEnergy were raising eyebrows. He noted there was "a lot of talk going on in the halls of PUCO about does [Sam] work there or for us."⁷⁰

Perhaps Sam's greatest payback to the utility that showered him with consulting contracts came in his behind-the-scenes drafting of, and lobbying for, sections of HB 6. As noted above, Randazzo crafted the "decoupling" provision that virtually guaranteed future utility profits by separating its revenues from its sales.⁷¹

Sam increased his legislative clout by arranging for one of his staffers, Pat Tully, to become HB 6's chief crafter as the senior policy expert for the House Republican caucus, which the Speaker controlled. Rather than have Tully approach Larry Householder directly, Sam sent his aide's résumé to a FirstEnergy lobbyist, and only after receiving the utility's blessing did the lobbyist forward that vita to the Speaker.

In his new position, the well-placed staffer consulted almost daily with utility representatives, but according to a company lobbyist, "Tully did not want to have emails or an electronic trace of us sending information back and forth." That FirstEnergy consultant, who later pleaded guilty to bribery, added, "I found it to be extremely odd behavior, but I understood why" he wanted to escape detection.[72] To avoid a message trail or running afoul of open-records laws, Tully printed hard copies for utility executives and Sam, who returned memos with detailed amendments as well as political strategies for dealing with the bill's supporters and opponents. Adding to the subterfuge, when Sam did transmit emails about HB 6, he used his private, rather than his PUCO, account.[73,74]

Chuck and Sam conspired many times, and in many places, to craft and advance HB 6. For example, in early February 2017, a prime time to leave wintery Columbus, three senior legislators joined them for a two-day retreat in Naples, Florida. They held their 5:15 p.m. cocktail reception at "Sam's house," a $3.9 million rambler.[75]

Sam's engagement, when it became public, raised alarms. "It is clear from these emails that Sam Randazzo, while employed as the top energy regulator in the state of Ohio, assisted in writing components of House Bill 6, and specifically pieces of legislation that would impede development of wind energy and damage the renewable portfolio standards," complained Miranda Leppla, then with the Ohio Environmental Council. "It is absolutely inappropriate for someone charged with being an independent arbiter of energy policy for the state of Ohio to be involved in drafting legislation that picks winners and losers in the types of generation operating in our state. His job as chair of the PUCO was to implement the law—not create it."[76]

FirstEnergy's payments and subterfuge paid off—but barely. The House count of 51 to 38 was just one vote more than the fifty required for HB 6's passage; fifteen Republican lawmakers opposed the measure, while Democrats cast nine of the pro-bailout votes. The Senate tab of 19 to 12 was only two more than the minimum, with Democrats providing three. Thus Larry did heavy lifting with Republicans, but HB 6 would have failed without support from minority-party members, who felt last-minute pressure from labor unions representing workers at the troubled power plants.[77]

Governor Mike DeWine signed House Bill 6 into law on July 23, 2019, only a few hours after the measure's passage. One journalist described the unusually quick action as "a resounding stamp of personal approval [by the governor] that almost never happens."[78]

The reason for rapidity soon became clear, proving duplicity would not stop with the bill's adoption. The day after the governor ratified that massive subsidy, FirstEnergy Solutions argued before the bankruptcy court that it could no longer honor existing union contracts, including those associated with retirement and salary benefits. This revelation contradicted FirstEnergy's previous promises that had prompted the International Brotherhood of Electrical Workers and other unions to persuade Democratic lawmakers to supply the critical votes for the "job-saving" bailout. One Democratic politician accused FirstEnergy Solutions of "spitting in the face of every Ohio taxpayer," and he added that the utility was "clearly more concerned about taking care of Wall Street than they are of taking care of workers at their plant. I think this is such a damaging piece of information that if this had been known before the vote, I don't know [if the bill] would have passed."[79]

Another strategist bluntly added, "The unions got duped." Others suggested Householder (and DeWine) cleverly rushed the vote (and signature) because they knew the pension-gutting announcement would have cut support in the General Assembly.[80]

With HB 6's passage, FirstEnergy lobbyists, in the bro-vernacular of Ohio's Capitol Square, gloated, "Bang Bitches!"[81] As noted in chapter I, Chuck expressed his glee in a similarly raunchy note within which he Photoshopped a picture of Mount Rushmore that supplanted the four presidents with faces of Sam Randazzo, Mike Dowling, a longtime FirstEnergy lobbyist (Ty Pine), and a coal company executive (Matt Evans of Boich Companies).[82] Pine was so happy with the legislative victory that he broke out a bottle of Pappy Van Winkle whiskey, a twenty-three-year-old rare bourbon worth some $7,000.[83]

Chuck further boasted to one of his colleagues, "We made a bbiiiiiig bet and it paid off." That other executive responded immodestly (and greedily): "Huge bet and we played it all right on the budget and HB 6—so we can go back for more!"[84]

Mike Dawson, the governor's legislative director who used to lobby for FirstEnergy, added to the fraternity-like swagger by retweeting a newspaper's depiction of the Ohio Statehouse renamed "FirstEnergy Stadium" and Larry dressed as a football star. Demonstrating the close link between the governor and First Energy, Dawson made sure DeWine's pen used to sign the legislation went to Mike Dowling at the utility.[85]

The raucous celebrations continued for months. Sam distributed an image of himself—wearing a mask and cape that featured a large "R" surrounded by a lightning bolt. Taking some credit for the legislative victory, the regulator added a variety of names for himself, including "Randazzler," "captain," "hunter," "King," and "Poppa Dazzo."[86]

An FBI agent described the coconspirators' bravado as "jaw-dropping."[87]

As expected, bailing out FirstEnergy's outdated coal and nuclear plants caused investors in modern technologies to walk away from Ohio. Just over a month after HB 6's passage, LS Power abandoned its $500 million advanced natural gas unit that would have created hundreds of construction jobs in Troy. Then, Clean Energy Future terminated plans to build a $1.1 billion next-generation gas plant in Lordstown; the company's president blamed HB 6, saying, "Political tampering with Ohio's free electricity generation markets has very real impacts and results."[88]

Much happier, of course, were Energy Harbor's investors. Wall Street gamblers who recently bought utility debt or shares enjoyed a windfall, and they quickly pushed the company to repurchase $800 million of its own stock, a move that increased equity values by reducing the number of shares available on the market. As a result, Energy Harbor's stock price more than doubled in the month after the renamed company emerged from bankruptcy.[89]

Ned Hill, an economic development professor at Ohio State University, called the legislation "an act of socialism, where you socialize the risk and privatize the benefits."[90] Clean Energy Future's president labeled HB 6 a "classic case of 'Ohio Main Street bailing out Wall Street.'"[91] A Republican state senator further complained, "The Ohio taxpayer should not be paying to prop up a private company just so New York investors can make more money than they are making now."[92]

If they cared enough to listen, Ohio legislators would have heard the swooshing sound of their bailout monies leaving the state.

FirstEnergy, cocky after its HB 6 win, expanded its use of secret money payments. As an example, it gave more than $550,000 to a front group, Consumers Against Deceptive Fees, that smeared Cleveland Public Power, a not-for-profit utility that competes for customers with Cleveland Electric Illuminating Company, a FirstEnergy subsidiary.[93] That deceptive political organization drafted legislation threatening Cleveland Public Power's revenue, and it funded widespread advertisements undermining the public utility, with the goal of expanding FirstEnergy's monopoly control throughout the city. To present at least the appearance of support in minority communities, the group paid $6,000 to two pastors associated with the Cleveland Clergy Council; yet one had been convicted of bribery and served six months in prison, while the other had recently pleaded guilty to a separate felony charge. When FirstEnergy's actions came to light, Cleveland's city council blocked the private utility's power grab and pushed to have FirstEnergy's name removed from the town's National Football League field; despite seven years remaining on the $107 million naming-rights deal, the facility reverted to its former name, Cleveland Browns Stadium, in April 2023.[94]

Revealing similar greed, Larry's initial lesson from the FirstEnergy bailout was that other businesses might be willing to engage in similar pay-to-play schemes. In a wiretapped conversation, the Speaker said he "expected big things in [dark] money from payday lenders," the scandal-prone industry that spends large sums to avoid regulations against its high-interest loans that burden the poor.[95]

Soon after Governor DeWine rushed to sign HB 6, a coalition of bailout opponents launched a campaign to have Ohioans overturn the law with a referendum. The state's constitution allows voters to reject provisions passed by the General Assembly if they first collect enough signatures—at the time, from at least 265,774 registered Ohio voters—within ninety days of a bill's passage.[96]

The threat to their bailout sent Chuck and Larry into frenzied overdrive. Their polling starkly showed that only a third of the public supported the billion-dollar bailout of a giant corporation. According to one FirstEnergy lobbyist, "If it makes the ballot, we're dead."[97] A Householder advisor admitted, "Polling shows the more we explain it, the worse it gets."[98] Utility executives also appreciated that the collection of enough signatures would pause HB 6's implementation; even if voters eventually upheld the legislation, the delay until Election Day would reduce FirstEnergy's benefits by approximately $150 million.[99]

For Larry, the referendum represented a personal affront, and he declared that protecting House Bill 6 was about preserving the legislature's power to determine state policy. During a $2,720 dinner meeting at the exclusive Aubergine Private Dining Club in Ohio's capital, the inebriated Speaker further asserted, "It is so important that [HB 6 opponents] are not successful because when the legislature votes on something, it needs to stay law."[100]

Larry sought to defend bailout-supporting legislators taking heat from oil and gas companies. A staffer alerted the Speaker, "It's the beginning of your speakership. [A rejection] sets a bad precedent for the next six years. What we need to make them realize is that you [Householder] can't be fucked with."[101] Larry understood that threat and announced, "Nobody screws with my members,"[102] and he ordered attack ads against his natural gas–company critics that exposed fracking's environmental damage. The Speaker turned again for money to Energy Harbor, which responded, "We will gladly pay for as many anti-fracking ads as [Larry] wants."[103]

Dollars became key, particularly since deep-pocketed natural-gas firms and the American Petroleum Institute (API) were spending some $4.9 million to block subsidies for their nuclear and coal competitors. A FirstEnergy lobbyist warned, "Oil and gas groups mobilizing to oppose nuke bailout. Aren't interested in any deals on carbon. Just want to drive nuclear out of the market."[104] Yet the API amount, while substantial, would pale in comparison to the utility's ultimate financial commitment; and, in comparison to Energy Harbor's laser focus, one anti-subsidy insider admitted, "The natural gas companies had other political priorities and were not full in on overturning HB 6; they were happy to have others, such as environmental and consumer groups, pick up more of the tab."[105]

Energy Harbor, although just emerging from bankruptcy, managed to dole out some $38 million to Generation Now, which funneled funds to Ohioans for Energy Security, the front group fighting against the referendum and for the bailout. "We have more money than they think," crowed one of the corporation's lobbyists. "Who would ever assume a bankrupt company is willing to spend [millions of dollars]. What a joke? lol."[106]

Noting the bailout's unpopularity, Chuck and Larry realized they needed a heavy-handed, multipronged drive to "make sure the thing never makes the ballot."[107] To block the collection of sufficient signatures, utility executives "imposed a timeline" and demanded the hiring of private detectives and bullies to harass the petition circulators with "goon-squad tactics."[108] According to one politico, "I've done campaigns in several states but have never seen such a brutal effort based on violence, xenophobia, and outright lying."[109]

Subsidy supporters paid "blockers" to surround and scream at signature collectors, preventing them from approaching voters. A referendum organizer observed: "It (became) like a war zone out there. . . . Our employees were stalked. They were harassed. They were intimidated. Some of them were assaulted. It was quite something."[110]

Bailout defenders also paid private investigators more than $100,000 to track petition gatherers, sometimes by secretly attaching GPS devices to their vehicles. A few of the key referendum coordinators confronted multiple violence-threatening notes on their car windshields. Allegations of assaults eventually prompted the state's Republican attorney general, David Yost, to issue a rather mild warning to individuals or groups disrupting the state's referendum process: "Knock it off."[111]

The utility's harassment squads, instead, accelerated their efforts. They bought, and then destroyed, completed signature forms. They bribed referendum organizers with retainers and plane tickets to leave the state or with $2,500 in cash to switch sides and work for Ohioans for Energy Security. They spent $450,000 in a single month to pay "signature collections people to not work."[112] One referendum opponent admitted, "We have to go out on the corners and buy out their people every day. . . . If we knock off 25 people collecting signatures, it virtually wipes them out in the next 20 days; this ends the whole fucking thing."[113]

To further limit the bailout-opponents' options, the FirstEnergy-Householder enterprise paid twenty-five signature-gathering firms an average of $65,000 to avoid Ohio and do nothing to support the referendum. Put another way, subsidy supporters signed contracts with virtually every national signature-gathering company, paying them not to work for HB 6's overthrow. A FirstEnergy lobbyist texted, "I was hoping that we could take out all the big players and limit their chances. It's impossible to referendum proof imo. We can make it tougher."[114]

Although swamped by the utility's dark-money payments, referendum organizers, known as Ohioans Against Corporate Bailouts, caused some of their own problems. Since gatherers usually need to obtain at least two signatures to get one valid one, they had to collect some 554,000, meaning about 10,000 each day, seven days a week. Yet anti-bailout campaigners decided not to work on Sundays, and they often sent out far too few crews. After three weeks of effort, they accumulated only 80,750 signatures.[115]

FirstEnergy's hired guns, in addition to being thuggish, could be clever, as when they split up a possible progressive coalition between labor and environmentalists by underwriting unions to highlight and protect HB 6's job-saving subsidies.[116] They also pushed some conservation groups opposed to fossil-fuel burning to avoid cooperating with natural gas companies.[117]

Funders of environmental organizations—including the George Gund Foundation and the Energy Foundation—became alarmed by the utility's pressure tactics, and they encouraged their grantees to shift energies from the HB 6 referendum to less-confrontational issues, such as asking city councils throughout Ohio to adopt pro-solar resolutions. Said one insider, "Environmental groups backed away at the first sign of threats, in part out of sheer fear and in part because some of their leaders had political aspirations and didn't want to get on the wrong side of unions."[118]

To further hinder the referendum effort, FirstEnergy and the Speaker crafted their own initiative, which they admitted "was largely symbolic," that asked Ohio legislators to prevent foreign investments in the state's energy grid. When it became clear this second petition was not needed, Neil Clark and Jeff Longstreth directed a staffer to delete related files on her computer. They "told me kind of more privately after the fact that they were afraid maybe at some point the anti–House Bill 6 people would use us," she testified. "So just go ahead and remove everything."[119]

Top Ohio politicians seem to have aided the anti-referendum effort. According to Chuck Jones, secretary of state Frank LaRose and Speaker Larry Householder provided "private" filings and information on the initiative, intelligence that would have helped the bailout enterprise learn the repeal effort's strategies and prospects.[120]

A more blatant spying effort was conducted by Matt Borges, Ohio's former Republican Party chair and then–Energy Harbor lobbyist. He offered to pay a referendum coordinator, Tyler Fehrman, $15,000 for information on the number of collected signatures and the planned locations for petition gatherers. "I promise this will be worth your while," asserted Borges.[121]

Privately, Borges didn't fully trust Fehrman, whom he once considered a friend. Speaking with another FirstEnergy lobbyist, the gun-for-hire joked,

"If we gave him too much money, would he spend it irresponsibly [in ways] that would embarrass us, buy a luxury car, or, who knows, whatever it might be." He feared Fehrman doing "something that would raise eyebrows."[122]

Fehrman, in turn, grew to distrust Borges. Saying, "There is zero doubt in my mind that Matt from the very beginning was offering me a bribe," Fehrman approached the FBI and agreed to wear wires, which agents tucked into the brim of his dark blue Under Armour baseball cap and into a fob attached to a set of keys he would place on a restaurant table. "I'll be really honest, it was probably the most difficult thing I've ever done," the campaign organizer reflected. "It's not just awkward. It's terrifying."[123]

In one recording, Borges said, "We can take care of all those things [Fehrman's car debt and child support payments], I just need you to provide me with inside information about what's going on." On another tape, the utility lobbyist added, "Dude, I don't have a mortgage anymore. Like, I'm so taken care of. And we could do the same for you."[124] Borges further admitted money was no object, describing FirstEnergy's payments into Generation Now as "fucking Monopoly money."[125]

During a late-in-the-campaign meeting, at a Columbus-area Starbucks, a more aggressive Borges declared to Fehrman, "No matter what—don't ever tell anyone about our conversation." He added, threateningly, "It would be bad for both of us if the story came out. But it would be worse for you." Then, after saying, "You better not be screwing me," Borges warned, "If you're messing with us, we'll blow up your house." Fehrman, who once considered Borges to be a "mentor," told federal prosecutors, "I don't think it was a joke at all. . . . In politics, there's a lot of dark humor, but we were past that point."[126]

To get a sense of this scandal's bizarreness, consider that outside this over-coffee meeting were FBI agents listening to their wire as well as private investigators hired by Borges to track Fehrman. Later, according to a federal official, "We kind of joked that it made for a congested parking lot of interested parties."[127]

To further dissuade Ohioans from signing the anti–HB 6 petition, Chuck and Larry blanketed Ohio's TVs and radios with xenophobic assertions that China bankrolled the effort to repeal Ohio's nuclear subsidies. That sixty-second ad claimed Beijing was trying to take over the state's energy grid and disrupt its elections. The "decline-to-sign" clip began with an image of Chinese president Xi Jinping raising his fist, and it ended with a baleful narrator telling viewers and listeners to "say no" when asked to sign the HB 6 petition. A separate mailer warned Ohioans that if they signed the petition, they'd be giving their "personal information to the Chinese government." The *Plain Dealer* called these claims "the sleaziest scare ad in recent memory."[128] Not surprisingly, Chuck's team did not reveal that FirstEnergy itself had received a $111 million investment from a Chinese state–owned bank.[129]

Perhaps the most bizarre advertisement featured flames leaping from the Ohio Statehouse. Subsidy proponents might have been suggesting, *Give us a bailout or we'll burn down your government*. Lobbyist Neil Clark called that ad "hilarious" and "fucking cold-blooded."[130]

Larry and Chuck also launched a legal campaign to postpone the signature gathering. The Speaker personally called the attorney general, Dave Yost, to discuss a delay, and Larry later scrubbed the two fifteen-minute conversations from his phone.[131] Chuck also asked Matt Borges, who had coordinated Yost's previous political campaigns, to convince the Republican attorney general to deny "the language of the people seeking the ballot referendum."[132] Borges pushed the AG to define the HB 6 subsidy as a tax, which would have made it ineligible for a referendum challenge.[133] In a note to a colleague, the lobbyist boasted he "had dinner with Yost and put the [repeal] referendum issue on his radar." According to Borges, "If there's any way that the law will allow him to reject the language, he will do it."[134]

Yost—in a six-page, 1,535-word document released in August 2019—dismissed the tax argument and decided to delay rather than outright reject the summary. The AG suggested twenty-one minor language changes, thereby forcing initiative organizers to rewrite the document and lose valuable time, leaving them with only fifty-four of the original ninety days to obtain about a half million signatures.[135] Said an anti-bailout organizer, "It was a significant impediment."[136]

Two months later, in October 2019, using money FirstEnergy had funneled to Generation Now, Borges donated $10,000 to Yost's campaign.[137] At the lobbyist's criminal trial, federal prosecutors appeared to link that contribution to Borges's claims of assistance from the AG.[138]

Subsidy critics asked a judge for additional days, but FirstEnergy's lawyers objected. Time simply ran out on the referendum.[139]

FirstEnergy's money and hardball tactics prevailed, with one referendum organizer complaining, "We were up against a tsunami of money and corruption."[140] Another observed of the FirstEnergy-Householder juggernaut, "Whenever you're corrupt, you're willing to do whatever, especially if you have an unlimited bank account."[141] According to an assistant US attorney, the utility's various schemes "prevented Ohio voters from exercising their right to reject this corruption. Ohioans never had the opportunity to vote up or down on this legislation."[142]

A boastful Larry wrote to Chuck, "We win again."[143] Yet neither of these arrogant men recognized the looming challenges to their corrupt enterprise.

Chapter IV

Consequences and Entanglements

The bribes-for-bailouts scheme became a full-fledged scandal at six o'clock in the morning on July 21, 2020, when FBI agents arrived with search and arrest warrants at Larry Householder's farm in Appalachia's Perry County. Wearing a gray Carhartt T-shirt, baggy jeans, and an N95 face mask, the politician refused to make any comments, but his wife, Taundra, "barricaded" the house. According to a federal law-enforcement official, "It turned into quite a scene with her at the door and refusing to let agents in and some of the comments that she made."[1]

Later that day, a federal grand jury released an eighty-two-page criminal complaint outlining how Larry, then sixty-one years old, received some $64 million from dark-money groups to help him obtain political clout, which he used to push for FirstEnergy's $1.3 billion bailout.[2] Also arrested were three utility lobbyists—Matt Borges (forty-eight years old), Neil Clark (sixty-seven), and Juan Cespedes (forty)—and a Householder aide, Jeff Longstreth (forty-four)—all of whom federal prosecutors accused of bribery, specifically of creating and using a "slush fund" to steer a utility and subsidy bill through the Ohio legislature.

Prosecutors further charged Larry and the others with conspiring to violate the Racketeer Influenced and Corrupt Organization Act (RICO) that was approved in 1970 to convict Mafia dons who had insulated themselves from the crimes of their made men. They chose RICO because it defines guilt in broad terms and remains one of the few anti-corruption laws the Supreme Court has not scaled back. Federal officials called Team Householder a criminal enterprise masquerading as a political operation.

The defendants made brief appearances at a federal court in Columbus, where a magistrate judge released them on their own recognizance but imposed travel restrictions and ordered the surrender of their passports and weapons. When Larry walked out of the courthouse, a crowd of noisy protestors surrounded his car and chanted for his resignation. Police intervened and arrested one activist.[3]

With more than a touch of irony, just a few months before these grand-jury indictments, the Edison Electric Institute, the national trade association for private power corporations, gave FirstEnergy its annual lamp-shaped advocacy award. Referencing HB 6, the trade group praised FirstEnergy's "efforts to ensure Ohio customers would continue to have access to clean, reliable, and affordable 24/7 power sources for years to come."[4]

The US attorney found nothing to praise, and he blamed FirstEnergy's corruption on dark-money organizations that Chuck and Larry used to launder millions of dollars to bribe politicians and orchestrate sleazy campaigns. "I don't see how [the conspiracy] could possibly have happened" if not for the misuse of these [dark-money] groups that are supposed to advance "social welfare," the federal prosecutor observed. "Not one dime went to any social program."[5]

Less than an hour after Larry's arrest, FirstEnergy's stock price plummeted 20 percent, forcing trading to be automatically stopped. Shares dropped another 18 percent the following day.

The federal grand jury's charges were only the beginning of FirstEnergy's legal woes. Ohio's attorney general, David Yost, introduced in September 2020 the state's own civil lawsuit against the power corporation and the Speaker. The utility initially countered, "The Attorney General's lawsuit unjustly targets the company for lawfully engaging in the political process."[6] The AG responded in August 2021 by adding Jones, Dowling, and Randazzo to his targets, saying, "This is the justice system working, holding bad actors accountable. To restore public trust, everyone involved in this sordid matter needs to pay a price."[7] The attorney general in February 2024 announced additional corruption charges against the former FirstEnergy executives and Public Utilities Commission of Ohio (PUCO) chairman.[8]

In late July 2021, the power corporation flew a white flag and signed a deferred prosecution agreement with federal attorneys, admitted to one count of wire fraud, paid a $230 million fine, and hoped the settlement would shield it from further legal jeopardy.[9] In that agreement, FirstEnergy confessed to bribing the likely-to-be PUCO chairman and to creating a dark-money group that secretly advanced a pay-to-play scheme that led to Larry Householder's election as Speaker and a massive public bailout for the utility. FirstEnergy also admitted, "Although Partners for Progress appeared to be an independent 501(c)(4) on paper, in reality, it was controlled in part by certain former FirstEnergy Corp. executives, who funded it and directed its payments to entities associated with public officials."[10] Also acknowledging wrongdoing was Generation Now, another FirstEnergy-funded nonprofit that coordinated the growing scandal's flow of money; it forfeited $1.5 million to federal authorities.[11]

In February 2022, FirstEnergy agreed to pay an additional $180 million to settle derivative lawsuits from shareholders claiming to have lost money from the HB 6 scandal and the utility's failure to forthrightly report its questionable lobbying and electioneering efforts. That payment represented one of the largest such settlements ever, although most of the amount was covered by FirstEnergy's insurance for its directors and officers.[12] (The utility subsequently tried to charge its customers for the resulting higher insurance rates.)

In April 2024, FirstEnergy hinted it might spend even more money to avoid additional scrutiny. After being reminded by the Ohio attorney general that the power corporation had previously admitted bribing Sam Randazzo to obtain special regulatory benefits, FirstEnergy's new CEO suggested the utility may—as it did in July 2021 with its deferred prosecution agreement—again try to buy its way out of criminal charges. Brian Tierney bluntly said the company "may have to put a little bit of money on the table" to move past state criminal investigations and a civil suit.[13] In August 2024, in fact, FirstEnergy quietly signed a $20 million settlement with Ohio attorney general Dave Yost to avoid prosecution. According to one Ohio newspaper, "The settlement amounts only to less than a third of the bribes Akron-based FirstEnergy paid, and it is dwarfed by the benefits Ohio utilities have received from ratepayers as a consequence of the corrupt legislation those bribes paid for."[14] The journal further noted that FirstEnergy consultants previously estimated the fine would reach $3.8 billion.[15]

One month later, FirstEnergy agreed to pay a $100 million penalty to the Securities and Exchange Commission (SEC). The federal agency had said FirstEnergy made misrepresentations to investors and the SEC about its role in the bribery-for-subsidies enterprise.[16]

Other consequences of FirstEnergy's corruption fell on an array of politicians, lobbyists, regulators, and executives.

Despite facing felony charges, the folksy but shrewd Big Larry won reelection in a November 2020 landslide. Exposing his ongoing gall, the politician used dark money to blast his opponent for accepting "dirty" dark money. Yet Larry's legislative colleagues, embarrassed by his indictment, unanimously stripped him of the speakership. In June 2021, almost a full year after his arrest, they booted him totally from the Ohio House, the first such expulsion in 164 years.[17]

The federal trial of Larry Householder and Matt Borges began in Cincinnati in January 2023. The former Speaker, appearing relaxed and confident when he took the stand in his own defense, regaled the jury with textbook stories about how bills become laws. He cockily denied attending swanky

Washington dinners, talking regularly with FirstEnergy executives, soliciting utility suggestions for House Bill 6, or planning attacks against bailout opponents.

Yet government lawyers and FBI agents revealed an array of surveillance photographs and wiretapped conversations that unraveled Larry's claims. Having obtained the Speaker's cell phone, for instance, they showed that during bailout debates, the House leader talked eighty-four times with Chuck Jones and held more than two hundred conversations with other senior FirstEnergy officials.

The US attorney enjoyed cross-examining the politician, calling it a "Matlock moment" to use her extensive evidence to expose the former Speaker's lies. That lead prosecutor concluded Larry "ripped off the people he was elected to serve and made backroom deals to exchange his power for money."[18]

Householder tried to argue he could not be charged for Generation Now's actions since his name was not on the group's initial paperwork. But when asked how the dark-money organization was used, he boasted, incriminatingly, "It was used to educate the public on issues that were important to me."[19]

Jeff Longstreth, Householder's long-term aide who had cut a deal with federal prosecutors, testified that Larry failed to repay him for covering the Speaker's settlement associated with a defaulted Alabama coal company, his credit card debt, as well as repairs to his Florida home damaged by a hurricane. When asked why he stiffed his assistant, Larry lamely claimed, "Well, by this time, Mr. Longstreth was a witness in this case for the government, and my concern was that if I gave him money, I'd be in trouble with the Court."[20]

The trial turned testy. The judge scolded Larry's lawyers for unprofessional and "bush league" behavior after they made faces and clicked pens during the government's opening statement. One of those defense lawyers even questioned the jurist's fitness, saying he got bad "vibes" from US District Court Judge Timothy Black and wondered if he might hold "personal animosity" toward the former Speaker because Larry had donated money to a dark-money group that opposed Black's run for the Ohio Supreme Court. "The answer to your question is no," the judge responded sharply.[21]

The most detailed, and damaging, testimony came over several days from an FBI agent who described the evidence obtained from roughly 250 subpoenas. He carefully charted the flow of money from FirstEnergy to its dark-money affiliates and then to "Team Householder."

Defense lawyers tried to argue FirstEnergy's payments were nothing more than "politics as usual." The jury foreperson, however, would later say that justification "left a sour taste in my mouth."[22]

The twelve-member jury, on March 9, 2023—after a twenty-six-day trial and almost ten hours of deliberations—found Larry Householder and Matt Borges guilty of racketeering and bribery.[23] The politician's attorneys pleaded for leniency, arguing that he "is a broken man. He has been humiliated and disgraced." Government lawyers called for a sixteen- to twenty-year prison sentence and declared, "Householder once occupied one of the three most powerful offices in the state of Ohio. He now faces a substantial prison sentence for causing immeasurable damage to the institution of democracy in Ohio, through his direction of a criminal enterprise." Prosecutors concluded that Larry "illegally sold the statehouse."[24]

At his actual sentencing hearing in late June 2023, the former Speaker expressed no remorse and called for mercy on behalf of his family and in recognition of his "good deeds in the community." The judge, imposing a twenty-year sentence, labeled Larry a "bully with a lust for power" and a "puppet master" who had "conned the people of Ohio and then tried to con the jury, too." The judge further asserted the politician lied on the witness stand about his plotting with FirstEnergy executives during Trump's inauguration, his regular interactions with utility leaders, and his control over substantial dark-money spending. Judge Black added, "How many lives could you have improved, but you took that away from the people of Ohio and you handed it over to a bunch of suits with private jets." For a stinging conclusion, the judge declared, "Beyond financial greed, I think you just liked power. You weren't serving the people. You were serving yourself."[25]

Larry asked to remain free while he appealed the verdict, baldly arguing bribery fell within his First Amendment rights, but Black responded bluntly, "The court and the community's patience with Larry Householder has expired." After the former Speaker emptied his pockets, US marshals cuffed his hands behind his back and whisked him into custody. Looking disoriented and reddened, Larry glanced back at his wife, Taundra, who was sitting in the first row and holding his trademark Perry County Ducks Unlimited hunting cap. Larry's mug shot from the Butler County jail revealed him to have gray hair and blue eyes, standing at six feet and three inches, and weighing three hundred pounds. One pundit quipped that the former Speaker was moving from the Ohio House to the Big House.[26]

Larry, not surprisingly, appealed the federal conviction, arguing prosecutors had made him a "scapegoat," but government attorneys responded, "Householder could not have lawfully received millions of undisclosed dollars from FirstEnergy for campaign or election purposes."[27] Perhaps hoping to take advantage of his and FirstEnergy's past engagements with Donald Trump, Larry's lawyers in November 2024 also announced they'd ask the incoming president for clemency or a pardon.[28] The jury foreman expressed fury, arguing that such actions would be the same kind of corruption for which Householder had been convicted.[29]

Several months earlier, in March 2024, Householder confronted ten new state felony charges, including the alleged theft of $1.2 million from his campaign fund to pay for his criminal defense against federal indictments.[30] According to Ohio's attorney general, the former Speaker also failed to report on his ethics forms gifts from FirstEnergy officials as well as loans and legal fees associated with his failed coal mine. The AG observed, "The sheer breadth and continuity of these omissions shows a concerted effort by Mr. Householder to hide his obligations, to hide his personal finances and his business connections." A conviction in state court would bar Larry permanently from serving again in public office in Ohio, ensuring he would never again be a comeback kid.[31]

One FirstEnergy lobbyist—Juan Cespedes—and the Speaker's chief staffer—Jeff Longstreth—pleaded guilty in October 2020 to participating in the pay-to-play conspiracy, and they agreed to testify against other defendants and the corporation. Cespedes, who had received a monthly lobbying retainer of $10,000, admitted, "I did many things as part of a conspiracy that were illegal."[32] Cespedes, in fact, had a long history in shady politics, having been kicked out of Ohio State University's undergraduate student government because of misappropriating funds.[33] Longstreth, whose firm received $10.5 million in "consulting" payments, placed some $1 million into his personal brokerage account.[34] To a federal grand jury, the Speaker's strategist admitted, "I handled the money. By doing that, I facilitated everything else that happened because of that."[35] As of early 2025, sentencing for Cespedes and Longstreth had not been scheduled.

A second indicted lobbyist, Matt Borges, had peddled influence in Ohio for decades. An Ohio State graduate, he ran Joe Deters's 1998 campaign for state treasurer, but then was convicted of steering state contracts to his boss's political donors. Borges paid a $1,000 fine, avoided a six-month jail sentence, and later expunged his record.[36] (Deters was not charged and now sits on the Ohio Supreme Court, having been appointed by Governor Mike DeWine.) Beginning in 2005, Borges also was embroiled in a decade-long dispute over unpaid taxes and liens.[37]

Despite such controversies, the political operative became a rising star in the GOP and managed several more campaigns, including Dave Yost's 2014 reelection as state auditor. With backing from then-governor John Kasich, he became chairman of the Ohio Republican Party, yet President Donald Trump had Borges removed, finding him not sufficiently loyal. The political campaigner turned to lobbying for state-based companies, including FirstEnergy Solutions. When an FBI informant, wearing a wire, asked him why he allowed the "unholy alliance" between his advocacy firm, the utility, and the Speaker, Borges replied bluntly, "People are going to get fat off this. . . . So why the fuck not us?"[38]

At the federal trial, Borges opted against testifying, leaving it to his lawyers to distance himself from Larry; in the courtroom, the lobbyist was overheard saying he didn't even like the politician. Yet the jury found both Borges and Householder guilty. At the sentencing hearing, the lobbyist admitted, "I'm here today for one reason and one reason only. My behavior, my decisions, my poor judgment. I should have known better."[39]

Judge Black agreed and observed that Borges worked alongside FirstEnergy and the Speaker with "eyes wide open," and that he diverted about $366,000 of dark money for his own personal benefit. The court sentenced him to five years in federal prison.

Rather than allow Borges to turn himself in, as occurs with many white-collar criminals, the judge had the lobbyist remove his wedding ring and tie and ordered marshals to cuff his hands and take him to the jailhouse. On his way out of the courtroom, Borges mouthed, "Bye, babe," to his wife, Kate, who blew him a kiss. It was the second time in two decades the influence peddler had been convicted of a corruption-related crime.

The third indicted lobbyist, Neil Clark, committed suicide at a wooded area near his Florida home in March 2021.[40] A bicyclist found his body near a small pond, with a handgun and his 2019 Lincoln nearby. Perhaps signaling his frustration with being indicted while the governor had largely avoided scrutiny, Clark, when he shot himself, wore a blue "DeWine for Governor" T-shirt.[41]

Clark's wife claimed his suicide resulted from the financial stress of having lost all his nearly three dozen clients after being indicted and having accumulated more than $2.2 million in federal tax liens.[42] Clark's attorney summed up his client's fall: "He went from being a major powerbroker in the Ohio Statehouse to being a pariah. No one wanted to touch him."[43]

The lobbyist's self-published memoir ends with a discussion about death, declaring, "If you know me, you know my end. Respect it."[44] That autobiography, completed not long before his suicide, reveals Clark's tough upbringing, during which his father, a mafia foot soldier, often was in prison, and young Neil faced beatings on the football field and mockery from teachers. The book explains how Clark became a ruthless lobbyist, doing whatever it took to triumph, and he swore never to face incarceration like his dad. He, therefore, rejected the prosecutor's proposed cooperation in exchange for a short jail sentence.

Clark—described often as a superlobbyist and sometimes as "prince of darkness"—had helped Larry become Speaker in 2001, but the politician felt the lobbyist grabbed too much credit; at a press conference, the House leader asserted that Clark was "an illusion, he doesn't exist." In response, Clark claimed he "went to mother-fucking war" and, as suggested above, anonymously pushed a string of allegations against the Speaker, bragging, "The whole gambit of shit, that was me."[45] Referencing Larry, Clark even told a *Cleveland Plain Dealer* reporter in late 2004, "I've never seen anybody abuse that position as much as he has."[46] The two men did not speak for fifteen years.

Yet with the urging, and largesse, of FirstEnergy, the politicos buried their hatchets, with Larry saying to Clark, "You and I have been at war for two decades, and at my age and at your age, we need to make friends, not enemies."[47]

The lobbyist attracted diverse clients, even helping the Natural Resources Defense Council (NRDC) oppose FirstEnergy's early subsidy seeking. That experience gave Clark insights into the anti-bailout coalition's assets and tactics, which proved to be valuable to FirstEnergy and the Speaker when they launched HB 6 and reconnected with the lobbyist.[48]

The advocate-for-hire enjoyed displaying his success, securing a regular table at the Hyde Park Prime Steakhouse in downtown Columbus, but he seemed to flirt regularly with scandal. He participated in a "pancaking" scheme during the 1990s that gave lawmakers multiple $500 checks, each just at the allowed limit, for speaking at events,[49] and he represented a slew of controversial clients, including the beleaguered Electronic Classroom of Tomorrow's online charter school.[50] Suspicious of the lobbyist's aggressive tactics, the FBI had tapped Clark's phone and recorded his meetings with undercover agents pretending to want help obtaining a real estate license for a sports-betting operation in Cincinnati.

Clark initially expressed caution about the undercover agents, telling his driver, "Good meeting, but they acted the way I thought FBI agents would. I wondered what they were investigating."[51] The lobbyist found it odd that men posing as sports-betting developers would pay for dinners and drinks with cash, and he couldn't find any online information about the "entrepreneurs," who claimed to be Rob Miller and Brian Bennett. Still, Clark let his guard down, accepted them as clients, and talked freely—over expensive meals, one of which featured a $400 bottle of cabernet—about political slush funds.

The lobbyist also expressed trepidation about working with FirstEnergy, whose executives he found to be demanding, reckless, and lacking political sophistication. Clark became startled during a Sunday morning conference call, on August 4, 2019, when John Kiani and other utility officials spoke in "borderline-panicked tones" about the anti-bailout referendum, prompting the lobbyist to observe that FirstEnergy "didn't know a lot about campaigning, they knew a lot about bullying."[52] Clark later identified the utility giant as the state's most corrupt corporation, beating out nursing homes and gambling racetracks; he added, "No company, no group, no individual has ever owned as many politicians as FirstEnergy."[53]

To get Larry elected and FirstEnergy subsidized, Clark claimed to have become the Speaker's "proxy" and "hitman" who would do the "dirty shit." He explained that "every politician has got to have somebody that's the hit man," and he boasted that his job was "to beat [his political opponents] and beat them soundly."[54]

The former Speaker publicly offered no reaction to his proxy's suicide.

Ohio's chief regulator first felt the scandal's consequences when a team of federal agents—dressed in navy-blue jackets with "FBI" emblazoned in yellow—searched his German Village condo on an early Monday morning in November 2020 and took away computers and files. Pressures increased dramatically when both federal and state prosecutors indicted the lawyer. Presumably wanting to avoid trial and jail, like Neil Clark, Sam Randazzo in April 2024, then seventy-four years old, committed suicide, hanging himself with a blue nylon rope strung from the metal rafters of a Columbus warehouse his shell company controlled. A brief handwritten note found on a nearby table did not mention the corruption charges, but instead lamented his death's effects on his wife, family, and friends.[55]

Not long after the FBI's initial raid, Sam emailed a friend: "Pretty stressful few days which started Monday at 6:00 when 10-12 FBI agents with their guns drawn announced their arrival at our home."[56] Repeated newspaper images of federal agents carting off scores of boxes added to Sam's anxiety. He quit his PUCO post a few days later.

The then-former regulator, despite appearing glum, strongly maintained his innocence. His two-page resignation letter to Governor DeWine focused on his triumphs rather than his scandals. He boasted, "Since being appointed by you, much has been accomplished inside the PUCO," and he bragged that he "put the PUCO on a better foundation to serve the public interest."[57]

Sam regularly tried to justify FirstEnergy's $4.3 million as the final payment of a long-standing consulting agreement, but blamelessness and triumphs were a little hard to swallow after FirstEnergy, in its deferred prosecution agreement, admitted forwarding the funds "with the intent and for the purpose that, in return, [Randazzo] would perform official action in his capacity as PUCO Chairman to further FirstEnergy Corp.'s interests relating to passage of nuclear legislation and other specific FirstEnergy Corp. legislative and regulatory priorities, as requested and as opportunities arose."[58]

The power company's 2020 annual report to the SEC added "that payments under the [Randazzo] consulting agreement may have been for purposes other than those represented within the consulting agreement."[59]

Sam, moreover, made sure FirstEnergy's payola would benefit his family. Upon obtaining the $4.3 million payment, he gleefully emailed his wife: "I hit the $4 mm jackpot with FirstEnergy." He also happily reached out to Chuck Jones: "I'm enjoying my new beach home. Thanks$$." Court filings later revealed that Sam spent much of this largesse on himself—paying $1.5 million to cover overdue federal taxes, $1.4 million for mortgage payments on a Florida house, and $100,000 to wipe out a loan to his daughter's Columbus-based restaurant, Ambrose & Eve, which closed in late 2020.[60]

Sam also sought to protect his funds from government prosecutors. He outright gave his son a $500,000 home, and, to avoid having land absconded, he sold $5 million of properties in Florida, Columbus, and Akron and moved the funds to a new brokerage account jointly controlled with his wife.[61] Trying to get beyond Ohio's reach, he allegedly placed some $3 million with out-of-state law firms.[62]

Sensing Sam's obfuscation, Ohio's attorney general convinced a county judge to block him from transferring or hiding further properties or assets, such as his pink Porsche convertible. Although that decision was overturned on appeal, the state supreme court in January 2024 ruled unanimously that Sam's assets could be frozen, allowing the state to claw back some of FirstEnergy's $4.3 million bribe.[63] That decision prompted the AG to declare, "We are pleased that the court recognized that Mr. Randazzo cannot spend down his bribe proceeds and render himself judgment-proof."[64]

Other incriminating fingers pointed toward Sam. FirstEnergy's assistant controller, for example, when asked under oath "with whom did FirstEnergy conspire to commit honest services wire fraud," responded bluntly, "Sam Randazzo and Larry Householder."[65]

Sam, it seems, had a history of negotiating secret deals for his clients and then skimming funds for himself. One such Randazzo arrangement had Duke Energy pay "unlawful and substantial rebates" to sixteen large industrial energy users, including General Motors and Marathon Ashland, allowing the utility, according to court documents, "to benefit from an allegedly illegal, secret side deal." That filing said Sam became "deeply intertwined" in the Duke effort, which, according to Ohio's attorney general, taught him "lessons" needed to negotiate—and keep secret—larger side deals with FirstEnergy, in which the lawyer's coalition of well-endowed industrialists received substantial payments to endorse rate increases that would fall on common consumers.[66]

When asked at his confirmation hearing before the General Assembly if he "or the companies [he owns or controls] ever had contracts or done business with FirstEnergy or FirstEnergy Solutions," Sam responded, "I have never represented as a lawyer or as a lobbyist any electric utility regulated by the Public Utilities Commission of Ohio."[67] That proved not to be true.

FirstEnergy, just between 2016 and 2019, had paid $13.2 million to Industrial Energy Users of Ohio, a nonprofit trade group which Randazzo controlled, in order to obtain support for FirstEnergy's rate increases. Sam covertly gave only $7.7 million of that amount to his industrial clients and transferred $5.5 million to his personal accounts.[68]

The power corporation sought secrecy in its dealings with Sam. Michael Dowling, for instance, failed to list him as a paid lobbyist within the utility's required notifications to the Joint Legislative Ethics Committee.[69] Company executives also asserted in legal filings that those side "deals" resulted from "serious bargaining among knowledgeable, capable parties"—meaning real, and thereby legal, negotiations between FirstEnergy and its industrial customers. Yet the utility did not disclose that Sam had been on its payroll, making the negotiating quite one-sided, unserious, and fraudulent.[70]

When prosecutors revealed Sam's machinations, Fitch downgraded FirstEnergy's credit score. The rating agency stated, "Disclosure of the payment [to Randazzo] will significantly and adversely affect [FirstEnergy's] regulatory standing in Ohio and could affect rate regulation in the utility holding company's other jurisdictions."[71]

After months of expectation, a federal grand jury in late November 2023 indicted the former PUCO chair on eleven counts of bribery and racketeering. The government charged Sam with using FirstEnergy's $4.3 million bribe "for his own personal benefit" and devoting his "official actions [to] the benefit of" FirstEnergy.[72]

That federal charges focused (1) on Sam taking FirstEnergy's pay-to-play payments to shape HB 6, and (2) on embezzling from his own association of large industrial corporations. To hide such misappropriations, even from his financially sophisticated clients, the lawyer allegedly moved $1.1 million regularly between bank accounts under his control.[73]

After surrendering to federal officials, Sam, wearing a black Columbia parka and appearing somber, pleaded not guilty and was released with conditions, such as not traveling outside Ohio without permission. He faced twenty years in prison if convicted as charged.

The judge ordered the former regulator to wear an ankle monitor, which Sam's lawyer called "downright mean." That attorney subsequently asked that the tracker be removed, disclosing that "a mental health professional has opined that the GPS monitor that Sam is required to wear as a condition of his bond has negative health consequences." The judge had not ruled on that request before Randazzo took his life.[74]

More legal consequences arrived in February 2024, when Ohio's attorney general added Sam, Chuck, and Dowling as defendants to his civil lawsuit against FirstEnergy. Those charged, according to the AG, "were literally as thick as thieves. Together, they would steal money from FirstEnergy, write legislative provisions worth unearned millions of dollars to FirstEnergy, guarantee continued FirstEnergy profitability, and take over the state government in ways that allowed FirstEnergy to regulate itself."[75]

It should be noted that AG Yost came late to subsidy bashing. When Matt Borges, the indicted lobbyist who had run some of his election campaigns, asked the attorney general to reject the proposed anti–HB 6 referendum language, Yost told him, "I would be out front [in opposition to the anti-bailout initiative] if not for FE support and your [Borges'] involvement."[76] In fact, Yost had received $24,000 in political contributions from FirstEnergy, as well as a subsequent $10,000 of utility funds funneled through Borges. As noted before, the AG effectively killed the anti-subsidy referendum by asking for amendments to that initiative's summary, thereby costing the signature gatherers thirty-six of their ninety days.[77]

Whatever the arc, Yost did turn aggressive, at least temporarily, against the FirstEnergy-Householder corruption enterprise. "Shout it from the public square to the boardroom, from Wall Street to Broad and High. Those who perversely seek to turn the government to their private ends will face the destruction of everything they were working for," declared the AG.[78] He slung his harshest criticism toward Sam, alleging the $4.3 million payment "was not a gift," that Randazzo "would work hard for FirstEnergy from inside the government," and that he was "skimming money from his client, the Industrial Energy Users-Ohio." The state's indictment liberally portrayed the former regulator's efforts with words like "stole" and "embezzled."[79]

Yost highlighted the covert side deals discussed above, particularly Sam's "well-lawyered theft in 2010" when FirstEnergy made cash payments—and the promise of favorable pricing—to Sam's coalition of industrial energy users in exchange for them withdrawing their opposition to FirstEnergy's electric security plan, thereby transferring higher electricity costs from manufacturers to homeowners.[80] The sense of sleaze heightened when Sam, then a FirstEnergy consultant, ran this settlement and others through his own shell companies, and skimmed off substantial fees. The AG's indictment further asserted that Sam and FirstEnergy's Mike Dowling hid the side deals from the PUCO and Ohio consumers.[81]

Yost's charges of February 2024 also revealed that Sam, while still PUCO chairman, worked diligently, but quietly, to advance HB 6 and block its repeal. The regulator, the AG added, regularly urged Governor DeWine's staff and key legislators to "manage the political chaos" and to remain "consistent" with HB 6's principles of subsidizing coal and nuclear plants while gutting efficiency and renewable provisions.[82]

After Larry's arrest, Chuck vehemently defended his company, saying, "I believe that FirstEnergy acted properly in this matter." Despite allegations of extensive corruption, the CEO, managing a straight face, added, "Ethical behavior and upholding the highest standards of conduct are foundation values for the entire FirstEnergy family and me personally. . . . We strive to apply these standards in all business dealings, including our participation in the political process."[83] The SEC had a different perspective, labeling comments by Chuck and his utility as "misrepresentations to investors about FirstEnergy's role in the political corruption scheme."[84]

Yet consequences caught up with Chuck in October 2020, when "his" power corporation abruptly fired him, purportedly for not informing the corporation's directors about the $4.3 million bribe to Sam Randazzo. (Jones, in a subsequent court filing, asserted he had disclosed that payment to FirstEnergy's Executive Council on December 19, 2018, one day after his German Village meeting.[85]) Claiming a few executives "violated certain FirstEnergy policies and its code of conduct," the utility board also ousted Michael Dowling, the senior vice president of external affairs who coordinated the utility's HB 6 lobbying, as well as Dennis Chack, the senior vice president for product development and marketing.[86]

Trying to sound diligent, the board's compensation committee made a "recoupment demand" for $56 million, equaling Chuck's salary over roughly the three years before HB 6 became a scandal. Yet hidden within its complaint, the panel admitted, "There can be no assurance that the efforts to seek recoupment from Mr. Jones will be successful and the approximately $56 million recoupment demand has not been recognized in FirstEnergy's financial statements."[87] Noting Chuck's contract allowed the utility to claw back his salary, the board's refusal to do so reveals the lack of consequences for an executive whose company admitted to a multiyear political corruption scheme.[88]

The utility's board replaced Chuck with Steven Strah, who had been FirstEnergy Service Company's chief financial officer. Strah promised to foster "a strong culture of compliance and ethics," and he signed the $230 million deferred prosecution agreement that admitted FirstEnergy conspired criminally.[89] Yet according to subsequent court filings, Strah was culpable for having "reviewed and determined the company's accounting for its payments and political contributions," including the illicit bribe to Sam Randazzo.[90] Text messages further revealed that Strah had been involved in FirstEnergy's "under the radar" strategies to craft portions of HB 6,[91] and a shareholder lawsuit argued the executive made false or misleading statements on an investor call. Strah resigned unexpectedly after a bit less than two years as CEO and just after the FirstEnergy board completed a still-secret review of its management team.

As noted above, the state of Ohio in February 2024 indicted Chuck and Dowling on multiple counts of bribery, theft, money laundering, record tampering, and a pattern of corrupt activity.[92] The court released both on their own recognizance but limited their outside-the-state travel.[93]

Chuck and other senior executives also confronted a shareholder lawsuit for allegedly being "engaged in insider trades, which rendered them unable to exercise the independent judgment required of them to investigate the allegations relating to FirstEnergy's participation in the illegal scheme involving passage of Ohio's House Bill 6."[94] Attorneys for investors claimed that between 2017 and 2020, the then-CEO "sold or otherwise disposed of over 788,000 shares" of FirstEnergy stock, worth $31 million. Just three months before the governor signed HB 6, Chuck cashed in another 148,302 shares, making a tidy profit of $6 million, allowing him to purchase the expensive condo in Naples, Florida.[95]

The former CEO, as well as Michael Dowling, in September 2024 also were indicted by the SEC on an additional conspiracy charge for their alleged roles in the bribery enterprise. In a separate lawsuit, the SEC charged Jones with misleading investors about FirstEnergy's payments to Larry Householder.[96]

Chuck did himself no legal favors by trying to delete thousands of scandal-relevant text messages from his phone shortly after being fired.[97] When Ohio's attorney general indicted the former CEO, the Department of Justice's prosecutor hinted Chuck also might face federal charges, saying investigators "are only coming to the end of Act 1." A lot of additional indictments, in fact, are likely.[98]

Those hints became real in January 2025 when a grand jury indicted Chuck and Dowling on racketeering conspiracy charges associated with their bribery of Larry Householder and Sam Randazzo. In their 42-page charge, prosecutors asserted that the two executives participated in "a pattern of racketeering activity—including bribery, money laundering, and obstruction—to increase the company's stock price and enrich themselves." The government attorneys added that Chuck told a FirstEnergy executive to lie to investigators about consulting contracts.[99]

Corruption tends to permeate institutions and make reform difficult. After Larry Householder's arrest in July 2020, for example, several Ohio lawmakers introduced legislation to repeal HB 6, but Republican leaders, despite promising a "fresh start," blocked such efforts and instead advanced provisions that further benefited power corporations.[100] Even as the scandal spread, Ohio politicians waited a full eight months before overturning a portion of the bailout bill, specifically the subsidies for FirstEnergy's failing nuclear plants. Yet even that move wasn't particularly noteworthy since the Federal Energy Regulatory Commission (FERC) already had adopted rules that penalized utility companies receiving state benefits; Energy Harbor, in fact, had asked Ohio legislators for permission to ignore the HB-6 subsidies so its two reactors could sell power in regional markets.[101] Governor DeWine in late March

2021 signed the weak measure with little fanfare, making no statement and taking no questions.

Remaining in effect are HB 6's bailouts for two dirty, Eisenhower-era coal plants that provide American Electric Power (AEP) and other Ohio utilities approximately a half million dollars in subsidies every single day. Other ongoing beneficiaries are the companies that supplied coal to the Ohio Valley Electric Corporation's (OVEC's) generators; HB 6, for example, allegedly allowed Resource Fuels—owned by Boich Companies, whose president Chuck Jones Photoshopped onto Mount Rushmore—to overcharge OVEC for its coal by some $12.6 million.[102]

Protecting OVEC's benefits was a new Speaker—Jason Stephens, who had been a Team Householder member and voted against expelling that indicted politician. More telling, Stephens's district includes one of the subsidized coal-fired units.[103] The House leader blocked hearings and ignored a discharge petition that would have moved repeal legislation directly to a full House vote. A Republican bailout critic complained that Speaker Stephens "made a procedural move to stop OVEC repeal so corporate welfare can continue on the backs of Ohioans."[104] The Ohio Consumers' Counsel added, "That [coal] subsidy is preventing the competitive market from benefiting Ohioans with lower electric bills and a cleaner planet."[105]

State legislators also failed to investigate corruption or advance ethics reforms. Rather than provide more transparency and accountability, in fact, several political "leaders" in 2024 advanced a measure that, according to the Ohio Manufacturers' Association, will "stack the deck in the utilities' favor." Many of Ohio's biggest companies asserted the bill would "limit customers' rights and further increase customers' costs."[106] Noting the proposal would mean some stakeholders "will no longer have a seat at the table," one legislator moaned, "It's just another example of the legislature doing the bidding of their Big Energy overlords."[107]

Ohio regulators, meanwhile, have hidden behind protective orders and confidentiality claims to avoid disclosure of their role in the bailout scheme. The PUCO, despite stakeholder protests, also approved more than $100 million in consumer charges for OVEC's aging coal-fired power plants, but it has not authorized an independent management audit nor reexamined case decisions made when Sam Randazzo was in charge.[108] According to Maureen Willis of the Ohio Consumers' Counsel, "The agency itself has not had to answer to the public."[109]

Alleged conflicts of interest—and charges of regulators being captured by the regulated—run deep at the PUCO. One striking example was a hearing examiner, a supposedly independent arbiter of complex utility cases. Behind the scenes, he helped craft and advance HB 6, and, after the bill passed, he took on judge-like roles that blocked inquiries into FirstEnergy's schemes and he "limit(ed) access to documents and information sought by the Office of the

Ohio Consumers' Counsel." Only after news coverage grew about his dual roles as advocate and arbitrator did the hearing examiner recuse himself from FirstEnergy cases.[110] Such slow and half-hearted "scrutiny" prompted Dave Anderson of the Energy and Policy Institute to observe that "FirstEnergy [is still] driving the bus on the investigation and accountability."[111]

Sam's influence, and perspective, remains at the commission, in part because his top assistant, Scott Elisar, became the commission's chief of staff. Elisar had worked with Sam at the law firm of McNees Wallace & Nurick and then went with him to the PUCO, where he began as the legislative and policy director and became a key proponent of HB 6.[112] Repeated comments among advocates appearing before the commission are that Elisar "is close to the utilities" and "wields enormous power and influence."[113]

FirstEnergy has tried diligently to distance itself from the ongoing controversy. To avoid being criminally prosecuted on multiple charges, as noted above, the power corporation in July 2021 entered into a deferred prosecution agreement with the US Department of Justice and paid a $230 million fine, reached a $180 million agreement in early 2022 with shareholders, and in August 2024 it settled charges from the Ohio attorney general for $20 million.[114]

Those penalties, while substantial, pale against the utility's $1.1 billion earnings in 2020 or the $1.3 billion of subsidies associated with HB 6. Attempting to justify the federal fine's amount, the acting US attorney observed, "The principle here is trying to come up with a number that stings but doesn't annihilate."[115] Yet that final figure held little bite, as evidenced by investors increasing FirstEnergy's stock price a substantial 4.4 percent after the federal agreement's announcement.[116]

A judge questioned how attorneys reached the $180 million derivatives deal with shareholders without an adequate period "to review and analyze the documents that were provided." He further asked why the insurance-covered settlement was derived without any testimony under oath from any of the utility's officers or directors.[117] The judge concluded, "Here, no one's had to pay, essentially. No one has had to suffer the consequences here." He added that former and current FirstEnergy executives will "just ride off into the sunset."[118] He became visibly angry when FirstEnergy's lawyers would not answer his basic question: "Who paid the bribes?" After several minutes of sparring, with utility attorneys claiming confidentiality over their mediation process, the judge barked, "I'm wasting my time. You're not here to answer any questions. You're here to duck and evade." He then stormed from the bench, leaving thirty shocked lawyers sitting silently in his courtroom.[119]

Even Larry Householder complained that FirstEnergy got off easy and "bought its way out of criminal prosecution."[120]

Most of the key people pushing HB 6, in fact, kept their jobs. FirstEnergy replaced only a few executives and directors. Largely because past gerrymandering eliminated most competitive legislative races, all forty-five lawmakers who backed the bailout bill and were up for election in 2020 won their races.[121]

Hoping attention and accusations would go away, FirstEnergy claimed to have "accepted full responsibility for its actions related to House Bill 6" and to have "taken significant steps to put past issues behind us."[122] While admitting to one count of bribery to commit wire fraud, the utility claimed its "core values and behaviors include integrity, openness, and trust."[123]

FirstEnergy, however, continues to block disclosures. It fought aggressively in several states, especially Ohio, against the release of internal investigations into its actions associated with House Bill 6. The utility even appealed an order from a special master of a US District Court demanding the release of two audits by supposedly independent law firms—one by Squire Patton Boggs and another by Jones Day.[124] A US district judge in May 2024—and an appeals court in July 2024—upheld the special master's ruling and ordered FirstEnergy to make public its internal investigation results.[125] Utility lawyers, however, continued to hide those possibly incriminating documents.[126]

Rather than embrace transparency, as its press releases suggested, the utility monopoly objected when the Ohio Consumers' Counsel tried to question its former ethics and compliance officer.[127] FirstEnergy, moreover, has yet to disclose its dark-money payments for the years 2018 through 2020, and it tried to suggest the $4.3 million bribe to Sam Randazzo was simply an "improperly classified" expense.[128] When asked for openness, a FirstEnergy spokeswoman cannily claimed, "We're committed to sharing all the information we can when we are able to share it. However, because of the ongoing investigations, that's not information we're able to provide at this time."[129]

The supposedly reformed utility even backed off its pledge, made during the scandal's height, to cut greenhouse-gas emissions 30 percent by 2030. That commitment lasted just three years, evidence of the power monopoly again doubling down on coal-fired power plants, particularly two aging and uneconomic units in West Virginia that executives want to be paid to operate. Sounding a lot like Chuck, FirstEnergy's latest CEO, Brian Tierney, declared in July 2024, "We don't see a pathway" to a coal phaseout.[130]

FirstEnergy continues to sway regulators. Its top executive in August 2023 cavalierly asserted that commissioners in Ohio, New Jersey, and West Virginia "want FirstEnergy to keep up with the normal day-to-day business of investing in our utilities" by increasing charges to consumers and earnings for shareholders. Ignoring the ongoing scandal, Tierney, who took home $26.4 million in 2023, added: "I have detected no regulatory overhang associated with the past."[131]

FirstEnergy's new executive team has tried to pin blame solely on Chuck Jones, the utility's now-former CEO, and Michael Dowling, who led the company's lobbying efforts, saying those two "devised and orchestrated FirstEnergy's payments to public officials in exchange for favorable legislation and regulatory action."[132] Yet investors suing the utility complained, "FirstEnergy has drawn from its internal investigation to partially inculpate Jones and Dowling while attempting to partially exculpate itself and others by asserting the purported absence of any evidence against others at the company."[133] These attorneys representing allegedly stiffed investors further asserted that FirstEnergy selectively released portions of its findings to throw the two fired executives under the bus while protecting the company, board members, and remaining senior executives.[134]

Other charges came from FERC, which, in an eighty-four-page audit, reported that the utility's rate officials tried to camouflage hundreds of thousands of dollars sent to Generation Now, the dark-money conduit, as charges for poles, wires, and transformers.[135] In one instance, company executives mischaracterized the utility's political payments as vegetation management expenses, otherwise known as tree trimming.[136] In January 2023, FirstEnergy agreed to pay a relatively small civil penalty of $3.9 million for such misstatements.[137]

The utility giant, despite such fines and allegations, hasn't scaled back its politicking. It continues pushing regulators for higher rates, claiming increased customer charges are part of the "normal course of business trying to update the rate base and costs." In Pennsylvania, it sought an additional $500 million, which prompted the Commonwealth's Public Utilities Commission to vote unanimously to suspend and investigate that proposed hike.[138] In Ohio, it pursued an extra $4 billion over the next eight years for grid modernization,[139] and it asked the PUCO to double its proposed rate increase to $190.3 million per year, far higher than the $94 million requested just two months earlier.[140] (Recall that FERC and the Ohio Supreme Court rejected FirstEnergy's last such subsidy plea, yet the company still collected hundreds of millions of dollars without modernizing its grid.) The Ohio Manufacturers' Association labeled these new pleas "anticompetitive, unreasonable, imprudent, and not in the best interests of consumers."[141] The state's consumer watchdog, moreover, called out FirstEnergy's $1.4 billion rate increase in 2023 as unnecessary since regulators already allowed higher-than-normal profits.[142]

The power corporation, moreover, persists in pushing for—and often obtaining—additional subsidies. In December 2023, Ohio's Tax Department unexpectedly—and without explanation—reduced the assessed value of the Davis-Besse nuclear plant by $54 million, thus cutting Energy Harbor's taxes as well as reducing funds for the local county's schools and libraries.[143]

Scandals usually are complex and hard to unravel and overcome. They often involve a myriad of individuals and interest groups. To acknowledge the entanglements associated with utility controversies, let's examine the involvement of a few other FirstEnergy executives and Ohio politicians.

Accusations abound within the monopoly's executive ranks. According to an internal audit, Dennis Chack, a fired senior vice president, "may have had an immediate family member who worked at a vendor company that resulted in a conflict of interest."[144] The utility's director of state and regulatory affairs, wanting to avoid self-incrimination, refused to answer some three hundred questions during a deposition about his role in the bribery scandal.[145] FirstEnergy's chief ethics officer allegedly signed misleading statements to investors about FirstEnergy's misconduct and helped process the $4.3 million payment to Randazzo that the company later admitted was a bribe.[146] The utility also fired its chief legal officer amid the federal corruption probe.[147]

One key, although often overlooked, corporate player is John Kiani, the hedge-fund investor who guided FirstEnergy Solutions through bankruptcy, to subsidies, and into a lucrative sale. This executive chairman got his professional start at Enron, the energy giant that collapsed in 2001 because of financial scandals. Even the convicted Matt Borges, who worked closely with Kiani, described this previous connection to corruption as "shocking."[148]

Kiani and his investment fund took a minority stake in FirstEnergy Solutions to redirect its activities and gamble that aggressive political actions—from dark money to signature blockers—would allow him to sell subsidized assets and obtain a bailout bonanza. According to a FirstEnergy lobbyist, Kiani "was more than willing, as he had done before, to spend money in exchange for legislation."[149]

The financier proved to be a hands-on commander of the pro–HB 6 and anti-referendum campaigns, which he dubbed "black op" operations. He talked and met regularly with the Speaker, often over lunch at Plank's Café & Pizzeria in Columbus. He coordinated with GOP public-relations consultants to create xenophobic TV ads, and he pushed his team to defeat the repeal effort with "whatever it takes," which ended up including a $15,000 bribe that sent Borges to prison for five years.[150]

Kiani saw Householder as his ticket to riches. "Larry has been very generous in telling me not to worry," texted the utility's executive chairman. The Speaker, in fact, assured Kiani that "he would do everything in his power to help defeat the referendum," that the company was "in good hands with Generation Now."[151] Even if voters or a judge blocked HB 6, the executive felt assured Larry would introduce an alternative bill to bail out his nuclear reactors.[152] Noting such promises, Kiani and Chuck forwarded another $38 million to Generation Now between August and October 2019.[153]

While the investor craved government subsidies, he opposed government oversight. Kiani pushed hard for language in HB 6 that would limit "the state's ability to audit how FirstEnergy Solutions used nuclear bailout money that the legislation produced." He found an ally in Sam Randazzo, who asserted, "I am engaged and hope I can help." To which Kiani approvingly commented to a colleague, "Randazzo is a bad ass."[154]

Kiani's bailout justification had long been suspect, particularly since FirstEnergy Solutions (and later Energy Harbor) released no financial data to support his claim that the two Ohio-based reactors were so economically challenged that they would close—and jobs would be lost—without government welfare. Proof of that falsehood came in March 2023, about two years after the scandal-shocked Ohio legislature repealed HB 6's nuclear subsidies, when a Texas-based company saw enough value in the supposedly uneconomic—and now unsubsidized—power plants to buy them for $6.3 billion. Energy Harbor's very happy shareholders received $3 billion in cash and a 15 percent stake in the newly formed Vistra Vision.[155] Shares of Vistra gained more than 5 percent in premarket trading that day, but Kiani would not say whether he collected his expected $100 million. The executive chairman, however, did gloat that he had achieved "the successful operational and financial turnaround of Energy Harbor into a leading, carbon free power infrastructure and energy supply company."[156]

Vistra in March 2024 announced that the merged company would be headquartered in Irving, Texas, causing an economic blow to Chuck's beloved Akron. With the addition of Energy Harbor, Vistra became the nation's largest competitive power generator, with most of its forty-one thousand megawatts of capacity coming from what it called the "greener energy sources" of nuclear reactors.[157]

AEP's executives, including its former chairman, Nick Akins, also touched on the scandal in several ways. As noted above, this Columbus-based utility paid $900,000 to Empowering Ohio's Economy, a dark-money group that supported Team Householder's candidates.[158] Akins and other executives also regularly discussed strategy with legislative leaders, pressed aggressively for HB 6 to include OVEC subsidies,[159] and long lobbied for OVEC utilities to continue collecting some $500,000 each day.[160] AEP in January 2025 agreed to pay $19 million to settle the SEC's investigation of its dark-money engagements with the HB 6 scandal.[161] While Akins consistently hailed the legislation's provisions, even he lamented the blemish resulting from subsequent investigations, stating, "It certainly was a tainted process. It made the whole state look bad. And it made all the utilities look bad. And we suffered from that."[162]

The most prominent political player is Mike DeWine, who appointed a FirstEnergy consultant to be the state's chief regulator, pushed HB 6 aggressively, and rushed to sign the legislation. The Ohio governor's ties to FirstEnergy were substantial and complex. There's certainly nothing illegal about DeWine's campaign having received $50,000 from the utility's political action committee, executives, and lobbyists. There's also nothing criminal about the candidate traveling with FirstEnergy executives to highlight one of their nuclear plants. And to lobby for a piece of legislation, the governor had every right to use his official residence for an "energy discussion" with Larry Householder and Sam Randazzo two days before HB 6 was introduced and an additional "Nuclear Bailout Bill Discussion" on the day the legislation faced blistering criticism at a statehouse hearing.

Yet one of the indicted lobbyists asserted that "DeWine agreed to accept a $5 million contribution from FirstEnergy/FirstEnergy Solutions [funneled through a dark-money group] in exchange for his support of a planned bailout." Neil Clark gave numerous details, saying the offer was made on October 10, 2018, at the Columbus Club.[163]

In response to such serious charges, the governor's press secretary simply stated, "We are not commenting on this."[164]

Bolstering the lobbyist's account, government prosecutors in their Householder sentencing memo mentioned "troubling" evidence FirstEnergy paid multiple millions of dollars to dark-money groups supporting Governor DeWine and Lieutenant Governor Jon Husted.[165] Other court documents revealed an array of secret FirstEnergy payments, including at least $2.5 million through State Solutions (affiliated with the Republican Governors Association [RGA]), another $500,000 directly to the RGA, $1 million through Freedom Frontier (which initially supported Husted before he joined DeWine's team), and $300,000 through Securing Ohio's Future. Journalists also reported the utility quietly transmitted $200,000 to the Citizens Policy Institute, coordinated by restaurateur Tony George, to blast DeWine's Democratic opponent.[166]

DeWine proved to be an active fundraiser, allegedly soliciting election contributions from FirstEnergy for both his campaign and supportive dark-money groups. Less than a month before his first gubernatorial election, for example, DeWine texted Chuck, "Can you call me?" and he added that "OEA [Ohio Education Association, a liberal-leaning teachers union] put in a million yesterday for Cordray (DeWine's Democratic opponent)."[167] Although Chuck and Dowling grumbled that their company had done "more than anyone" for DeWine, FirstEnergy's chief lobbyist shortly thereafter texted the CEO, "Go ahead and call Mike DeWine on the $500k. It's going to RGA's C (4) called state solutions. All set."[168]

Despite the clarity of such text messages, DeWine's press secretary denied the candidate solicited a contribution to a dark-money organization, which may have been illegal. He called it "sick and disgusting" and "highly offensive and irresponsible" to suggest otherwise.[169]

DeWine himself admitted FirstEnergy's overall dark-money payments supporting his election reached some $4 million in 2018, but he claimed to have not known anything about the contributions at that time.[170] Yet a University of Cincinnati political scientist observed, "The notion that [DeWine] was just this fumbling, naïve grandpa who has no idea about seven-figure flows [supporting] his campaign is perhaps the single most far-fetched thing he's even said."[171] A journalist added, "There's also the fact that it's questionable for a company to make such a huge expenditure and not make sure the public official benefiting from it knew about it."[172]

There's no doubt FirstEnergy, often quite publicly, supported Mike DeWine. In addition to the $50,000 from the utility's political action committee, Chuck hosted a fundraiser for the candidate at his home, and he promoted a Dallas event sponsored by Texas governor Greg Abbott. In his invitations to the latter fundraiser, Chuck stated, "This fall's governor race is very important to FirstEnergy from both a legislative and regulatory perspective and getting Mike across the finish line is critical."[173] At his house, the CEO added, "[DeWine and Husted's] vision, experience, and strong leadership will be great for our state, our communities, our company, and our shareholders."[174] After the event, Chuck wrote the candidate, "We are glad to be able to help out. Ohio needs you." DeWine responded, "Many many thanks."[175]

Signs of close cooperation continued even to Election Day, when the executive texted both DeWine and Husted, "Good luck today. We will be pulling for and praying for you." Although swamped with get-out-the-vote efforts, Husted found the time to respond: "Thanks for all you've done to help." DeWine added, "Chuck, we are very grateful for all your help."[176]

In fact, the governor and the utility enjoyed tight relations for more than three decades. An article on cleveland.com, which shares ownership with the *Plain Dealer*, observed, "DeWine has also long been a reliable instrument for FirstEnergy's sordid ways," which include "lavish statehouse spending on consultants, lobbyists, and in-house 'government-affairs' types." That cozy relationship, according to the veteran journalist, began early in DeWine's career when he befriended Alex Arshinkoff, who was both Summit County's powerful Republican Party boss and a FirstEnergy agent.[177]

The politician and the power monopoly maintained numerous other ties. Michael Dawson—husband to Laurel Pressler Dawson, DeWine's longtime chief of staff—had for many years been a FirstEnergy lobbyist.[178] He received a $10,000 loan from Randazzo in 2016, a couple of years before his wife recruited Sam to be the state's top utility regulator; neither party reported the loan nor explained its purpose.[179] Media reports also asserted Michael Dawson secretly participated in early 2020 ex parte (and likely improper) communications with the regulator and FirstEnergy's Dowling about rate cases and decoupling, important matters then before the PUCO.[180]

Laurel Dawson, whom DeWine called "my most trusted adviser for over two decades,"[181] testified that she did not inform the governor of FirstEnergy's $4.3 million payment before he nominated Sam; without explaining the delay, she admitted revealing the apparent bribe to the governor only after FBI agents raided Sam's German Village condominium in November 2020.[182] The chief of staff, according to court documents, also did not forward to the governor revealing dossiers and letters from Sam's critics, nor did she explain how she could fairly vet the lawyer to be PUCO chairman when he had given her family a $10,000 loan.[183] As reporters made such information public, Dawson quietly moved to another state job, which pays more than $185,000 and where she continues to advise the governor.[184]

Dan McCarthy represents another link between the utility and the governor. DeWine's now-former legislative director—responsible for pushing the politician's priorities (including HB 6) in the General Assembly—had been a FirstEnergy lobbyist for more than a decade, and he launched and led one of the utility's dark-money groups that secretly funneled millions to politicians and organizations supporting Larry's election and the company's bailout. The utility monopoly's deferred prosecution agreement disclosed that McCarthy, while employed by DeWine, was "fighting" to extend the subsidy's terms from eight years to ten years and to concoct language that would make the controversial bailout harder to challenge in a popular referendum.[185] Even after the scandal broke, the governor continued to support McCarthy for another year, and in May 2023, DeWine appointed him to the Ohio State Racing Commission.[186]

FirstEnergy tried to hide the link between McCarthy and DeWine. When Partners for Progress needed to file its regular update to the Internal Revenue Service, a utility executive, probably thinking it would not look good to have the governor's aide publicly associated with the company's dark-money group, texted, "Please make sure Dan McCarthy's name is not on the filing." When told IRS rules required identifying the nonprofit's former president, he responded, "There must be a creative way to handle this. It's important that [McCarthy's] name not be listed."[187]

Journalists showed more evidence of this cozy relationship, reporting that DeWine asked the utility giant to provide $75,000 to advance the unsuccessful bid of his daughter, Alice DeWine, to become Greene County's prosecutor, a job that had launched his own political career some five decades before.[188] The governor also appointed key FirstEnergy people to plum positions, including Michael Dowling to the University of Akron's board of directors and, even after revelations of Josh Rubin's role in the Athletic Club dinner, DeWine selected the FirstEnergy lobbyist to be chairman of the JobsOhio board of directors, a move the *Toledo Blade* editorialized as "appalling."[189]

In addition to supplying money, FirstEnergy and its allies worked diligently to ensure the governor's active engagement. The utility, as an example, responded quickly when DeWine, using his personal email, asked Randazzo, "Sam, what do we know about whether nuclear plants need this boost? One editorial suggested testimony was not conclusive."[190] The very next day, FirstEnergy's chief lobbyist visited the governor's residence, and the day after that Sam delivered a lengthy memo trying to debunk the studies described in the referenced editorial.[191]

No doubt DeWine pushed the bailout. Chuck informed one of his lobbyists, "DeWine's on board. I talked with him on Wednesday." After his own conversations with the governor, Dowling wrote to Chuck, "We know that DeWine called Senate President to express support for HB 6."[192]

Despite clear warnings to his office, the governor never seemed to investigate Sam's finances, and he later justified his nomination by saying "everybody knew" about the lawyer's connections to FirstEnergy. Countered one journalist, "Maybe in their good-old-boys club everybody knew, but I assure you, the public did not. The public did not widely know their governor appointed an electricity corporation stooge as the state's head watchdog over electricity corporations."[193]

Noting the governor knew of Sam's dealings with FirstEnergy, the *Toledo Blade* opined, "Advocacy for a Randazzo appointment by the utility he was opposing [when he represented Ohio's largest manufacturers] should have been highly suspicious to the long-experienced governor." The newspaper's editorial board added, "Anyone smart enough to be governor should realize if Mr. Randazzo was serving his [manufacturing] clients well, he would have been the last man FirstEnergy wanted as PUCO chairman."[194]

Even as the scandal intensified, DeWine continued to support his PUCO pick. Just after the FBI raided Randazzo's house, the governor suggested there was "no indication" Sam was the target of an investigation. A few days later, when accepting the regulator's resignation, DeWine added, "He has done very, very good work as chair."[195]

Only after state authorities indicted Sam on twenty-two counts did the governor begin to change his tune, suggesting his appointment might have been an error: "We all make mistakes, every call I make as governor is not right." Yet DeWine still added that Sam had been the best person for the job and he hadn't been aware the regulator was FirstEnergy's hand-picked regulator.[196] The slight tone change resulted, in part, from rising public criticism, with the *Toledo Blade* editorializing, "If Mr. DeWine did know of the connection between FirstEnergy and Mr. Randazzo, the governor deserves to be impeached and will end his career in scandal."[197]

In a February 2024 press conference, DeWine stated, "I wish we hadn't appointed him." He justified that more-significant switch in position by claiming, "We did not know all of those facts." Then, perhaps remembering that his chief of staff had been aware of FirstEnergy's $4.3 million bribe, he slightly amended his statement to, "I did not know all those facts at that time."[198]

The governor seems to have not known, or to have forgotten, a lot. When asked about meeting with FirstEnergy executives at an RGA fundraiser, he said, "I don't remember that. I'm not disputing it. I just don't remember. I don't remember the meeting."[199] About the ninety-minute gathering at the Athletic Club, where Chuck sang Sam's praises, DeWine claimed to not recall if Randazzo's name came up, and he again declared, "I don't really have any great specific recollection of what was talked about."[200] When asked about FirstEnergy's dark-money payments supporting his election, he asserted he didn't know about them.[201] When pressed about soliciting Chuck near Election Day for an extra $500,000 to a dark-money group, he professed not to remember those conversations: "I'm making a lot of calls to a lot of people asking for money. And if that call was made, I have no doubt it was made."[202]

To check the credibility of such statements, journalist Morgan Trau asked "a dozen public officials across the political spectrum with different positions if they would forget a $500,000 donation. All said no." One state representative added, "You're aware of everything going on, especially in the home stretch. You remember—unless you try not to—or conveniently can't."[203]

Despite the growing scandal, DeWine continued to embrace House Bill 6, calling it good policy.[204] Only after the US attorney referred to the matter as "the largest bribery scheme ever perpetrated against the people of the state of Ohio"[205] did the governor begin to waver, saying, "No matter how good this policy is, the process by which this bill was passed is simply not acceptable. That process, I believe, has forever tainted the bill and now the law itself."[206] To distance himself from FirstEnergy's growing political taint, DeWine made a monetary donation to the Ohio Association of Foodbanks, but only in the amount fired executives and indicted lobbyists directly contributed to his campaign committee, leaving in place the far larger amounts that FirstEnergy funneled through dark-money groups.[207]

The DeWine administration faces other pressures at the time of this writing. Large investors bringing a civil suit against FirstEnergy, for instance, subpoenaed testimony and documents from the governor and lieutenant governor.[208] Michael Dowling, moreover, said he plans to call both officials as witnesses in his criminal trial.[209]

DeWine's Democratic opponent in his 2022 reelection campaign focused on the FirstEnergy scandal, saying, "This corruption case reaches the highest levels of government in Ohio." She added, "Enough is enough. It's time for Governor DeWine to come clean about his knowledge and involvement in this scandal."[210] Despite such hard-hitting charges, the governor won a second term in a landslide, 62.4 percent to 37.4 percent.

While DeWine's engagement with FirstEnergy was substantial, Jon Husted enjoyed even tighter connections. Michael Dowling, the utility's vice president, praised the lieutenant governor for being "highly engaged" and "fighting to the end . . . to make sure FirstEnergy got the beefiest bailout possible."[211] He added that Husted performed "battlefield triage" to save Sam Randazzo's nomination.[212] At the 2018 political fundraiser at his home, moreover, Chuck remarked about Husted, "Jon has always been very accessible and great to work with, and I can say without question, he is a good friend of FirstEnergy."[213]

Husted was particularly close to Dowling. On the day the politician pulled out of the governor's race to join DeWine's team, Dowling said he was proud of him, to which Husted responded: "Your support means a lot to me. I admire you and value your friendship. I hope I didn't disappoint you, but it is the right decision for all concerned."[214]

During the HB 6 legislative debates, Dowling told his colleagues, "The admin is engaged—especially John (*sic*) Husted, which is who we want engaged."[215] Backing up that statement, Husted's personal cell phone number came up at least thirty times in call logs with Dowling and Chuck.[216] On the day the bill was signed, FirstEnergy's CEO thanked Husted for his "leadership on a very challenging issue."[217] And after being indicted, Chuck and Dowling, in a shareholder lawsuit, asserted that Husted played a significant role in the bailout and was "likely to have discoverable information."[218]

Yet when subpoenaed in that civil case against FirstEnergy, Husted repeatedly claimed to have no memory of meetings or conversations associated with FirstEnergy's bribery enterprise. When asked at a press conference about texts suggesting such a scheme, the lieutenant governor barked, "I don't know what you're talking about. We weren't involved."[219] When specifically asked to explain his role pushing HB 6, he asserted flatly, "None."[220]

Husted long has been a friend of utility monopolies, with one lobbyist referring to him as FirstEnergy's "Golden Boy."[221] When serving as Speaker of the Ohio House of Representatives in 2008, he pushed for the passage of Senate Bill 221, which allowed electricity corporations to avoid scrutiny and obtain higher profits by filing "electric security plans" instead of full rate cases. That legislation also enabled cross-subsidies and added numerous charges to customers' bills. According to a former PUCO commissioner, "It was a humongous gift for the utilities."[222]

A utility lobbyist boasted that "Husted's history with FirstEnergy goes back decades."[223] The politician also had a long relationship with Sam Randazzo, having appointed him in 2007 to the PUCO Nominating Council.[224]

FirstEnergy's political action committee donated some $50,000 to Husted's early campaigns, but the utility's secret payments seem to have soared after the Supreme Court's *Citizens United* ruling. When Husted was Ohio's secretary of state and running for higher office, FirstEnergy paid $1 million to another dark-money group, Freedom Frontier, designating those funds to the "Husted campaign."[225]

Husted's campaign claimed it "never received this [$1 million] donation and is not affiliated with any of these groups."[226] His spokesperson ignored the fact that Freedom Frontier received such secret payments, which it used to support Husted.[227]

Husted also had staff ties to FirstEnergy. Dan McCarthy—who had been a utility lobbyist, the administration's legislative director, and coordinator of the dark-money Partners for Progress—was considered the lieutenant governor's right-hand man.²²⁸

DeWine in January 2025 promoted his lieutenant governor to take over J.D. Vance's US Senate seat, ironically on the very day federal prosecutors charged FirstEnergy executives with bribery associated with the subsidy legislation advanced by DeWine and Husted. When asked about the connection, the governor simply said, "No comment."²²⁹

Another prominent politician engaged in the FirstEnergy drama is Ohio secretary of state Frank LaRose. After Householder was sentenced, LaRose claimed that everybody knew Larry was "a crook,"²³⁰ yet he had failed to speak up as the racketeering enterprise schemed. Federal prosecutors criticized such actions, saying, "It's interesting that some people are piling on [Householder] after the fact. So many knew what was happening in real time and did nothing about it. Not only did they do nothing about it, they helped facilitate it."²³¹

LaRose, in fact, had many connections to the scandal. A consultant with his Super PAC worked with Larry's campaign committee.²³² LaRose himself received more than $25,000 from FirstEnergy for his 2018 campaign to be secretary of state.²³³ According to FirstEnergy's CEO, the politician also passed along "privileged" information about signature gatherers associated with the HB 6 referendum.²³⁴

Two of FirstEnergy's indicted lobbyists, moreover, plotted about how to protect the secretary of state if he were pressured to recuse himself as chair of the Ohio Ballot Board, which reviews referendum language headed for a ballot. "He's going to be a friend in this process," texted Borges, "so let's be prepared to speak up for him." Cespedes responded, "We will support him more than anyone."²³⁵

LaRose expressed interest in building even tighter relations with the power corporation making large political contributions. The secretary of state, for instance, sent messages saying he "wants to get to know" Kiani, then–executive chairman of FirstEnergy Solutions.²³⁶

Although once considered the frontrunner in Ohio's Republican primary to become a US senator, in March 2024, LaRose suffered a distant, third-place finish.

Scandal's web ran deep in Ohio. The corruption—and the failure to confront it—cost ratepayers millions and tarnished trust in the state's business and government institutions. Unfortunately, utility fraud has escalated well beyond the Buckeye State.

Chapter V

Securing Favors

Utility misconduct in the Land of Lincoln demonstrates that fraud can span political affiliations. A jury in May 2023 found Commonwealth Edison's CEO, and three of her lobbyists, guilty of conspiring to bribe the Democratic Speaker. Those executives paid $1.3 million in jobs and consulting contracts to associates of the House leader in exchange for favorable legislation worth more than $150 million to ComEd.[1] While these utility officials await sentencing, the nation's longest-serving legislative leader faces twenty-two counts of official misconduct.

For years, Michael Madigan had been no friend of ComEd and its parent company, Exelon. Steeped in utility regulation as a young lawyer, he was widely known to be skeptical of power monopolies and particularly annoyed at ComEd for its high rates and poor customer service, especially after a summer 2011 storm left 850,000 customers without power, some for several days.[2] The angry politico from Chicago's Southwest Side "torpedoed a rate hike"[3] and helped freeze the utility's charges for eight years, causing a ComEd executive to say the giant corporation was in "dire" straits and on the verge of bankruptcy.[4] To further express his ire, Madigan ignored meeting requests and forced Exelon's former chief executive officer to sit alone for hours in the Speaker's antechamber.

Anne Pramaggiore, a rising star within the company, became ComEd's CEO in 2012 and quickly realized two facts. First, the utility, considered one of the nation's worst performing, needed to update its infrastructure and customer service. Second, its political relations also needed repair, particularly with the House Speaker, who managed the legislative agenda and controlled energy policy. While these utility officials await sentencing, the nation's longest serving legislative director was found guilty of conspiracy, bribery, and wire fraud. The measure also offered ComEd a controversial "formula rate" that enabled it to increase revenues but bypass regulatory reviews. In return, the Speaker demanded stiff penalties associated with poor customer satisfaction as well as strict limits on ComEd's profitability.

Pramaggiore initially found Madigan to be a "classic Democrat, very pro-consumer," and she acknowledged the influence of the Speaker's daughter, attorney general Lisa Madigan, who, according to the ComEd executive, "was always in opposition to us." To make progress, the company's new leadership team realized they needed "to play nice."[5]

Illinois political observers referred to the Speaker as the "Velvet Hammer" for his smooth but vigorous use of political power. Madigan had served in the Illinois House since 1971 and been its leader for all but two years between 1983 and 2020. One of his colleagues observed that he ruled the legislature through "fear and intimidation."[6]

Madigan had been a protégé of the late Chicago mayor Richard J. Daley, considered "the last of the big city bosses." He learned to cover his tracks, rarely using cell phones or emails that could be traced or recovered. He also mastered reading people's motivations, and he quickly realized ComEd's new CEO needed his help if she was to save her company.

The Speaker's initial requests seemed insignificant. He asked, for instance, that students from his suburban Chicago district jump to the front of the line for ComEd's paid and coveted summer internships. Playing nice, utility lobbyists made sure his constituents didn't have to compete against the larger pool of applicants, and they waived grade-point-average requirements for applicants from the Speaker's power base in Chicago's Thirteenth Ward.[7]

Yet Madigan quickly began to think bigger and "suggested" in October 2011 that ComEd's general counsel sign a generous contract with a law firm headed by Victor Reyes, one of the Speaker's top fundraisers.[8] When ComEd's in-house counsel later tried to reduce the consultant's contracted 850 hours of attorney work per year, one of the utility's lobbyists, Michael McClain, declared that "our Friend," his code word for Madigan, was unhappy, and he complained to Pramaggiore, "I know the drill, and so do you. If you do not get involved and resolve this issue of 850 hours for his law firm per year, then [Reyes] will go to our Friend" and Madigan "will call me, and then I will call you. Is this a drill we must go through?"[9] John Hooker, another ComEd lobbyist, shared his own tough-guy take on what the Speaker would say if ComEd cut back on the lawyering contract: "You're not gonna do it? You're not going to do something for me. I don't have to do anything for you."[10] Wanting support from the legislature, Pramaggiore renewed Reyes's contract.

Madigan next "hinted" that a few of his closest associates—including a pair of former Southwest Side aldermen and two of the Thirteenth Ward's top precinct captains—would appreciate consulting work. The Speaker had advanced the idea at least once with the previous ComEd CEO, Frank Clark, who rejected it before he retired in September 2011. When Pramaggiore initially heard of the proposal, she, too, expressed dread, saying, "Oh my God."[11] Yet in January 2014, she directed money to one of ComEd's subcontractors so Madigan's allies could receive monthly retainers of $4,000 to $5,000. According to a ComEd lobbyist, "We had to hire these guys because [Madigan] came to us. It's just that simple."[12]

On an FBI recording, which federal prosecutors would later replay several times in court, another utility lobbyist admitted the Speaker's associates did "not much" in exchange for their pay. One of the recipients, who collected monthly checks of $4,500 for six years, added that his only activities were door-to-door canvassing for the Speaker's Democratic allies and that he did nothing for the utility.[13]

Madigan would defend his job-placement scheme as "routine constituent service."[14] Yet in a separate wiretap, he admitted to McClain, "Some of these guys have made out like bandits, Mike." To which the lobbyist responded, "Oh my God, for little work too. Very little work."[15]

In hindsight, the selection of a few of the do-nothing consultants seemed strategic . . . or sordid. A Chicago alderman, for instance, received $5,000 a month after he agreed to resign with one year of his term remaining, allowing a Madigan loyalist to be appointed to replace him and run more effectively for a full four-year term as an incumbent. The retiring city council member's daughter-in-law, moreover, got appointed, at Madigan's recommendation, to be chair of the Illinois Commerce Commission, which regulates ComEd and other state-based utilities.[16]

The Speaker continued to want more, expressing interest in returning a political favor by having Juan Ochoa be appointed to ComEd's board of directors, a $78,000-per-year part-time position. Ochoa, the good friend of a Madigan ally, had directed the Metropolitan Pier and Exposition Authority, known as McPier, a municipal corporation that owns Navy Pier and McCormick Place and attracts trade shows, conventions, and public events to those Chicago venues. After some ComEd officials pushed back on this board appointment, expressing concerns about the nominee's past financial problems, including foreclosure on a property in suburban Chicago, Pramaggiore asked if the Speaker would be okay with Ochoa being given a different job but with the same amount of money. Madigan "suggested" the CEO "keep pressing," and he testily told the lobbyist McClain, "I would suggest that we continue to support Ochoa." In a subsequent internal memo, Pramaggiore acknowledged that "our friend" had taken "good care of me" and "I will do the best that I can to, to take care of you."[17] The utility's general counsel expressed additional "concerns about [the appearance of] someone from the Speaker's office serving on the board," but he would later testify that Pramaggiore "wanted to go forward. She thought it was important."[18]

The key lobbyist coordinating these sleazy deals, as suggested above, was Mike McClain, who served in the Illinois House of Representatives in the 1970s and early 1980s and was a close confidant of Madigan. Although long a consultant for ComEd, the lobbyist referred to the Speaker as his "real client." Other ComEd executives half-jokingly called McClain a "double agent" because of his close ties to the legislative leader.[19]

To get a sense of McClain's power, when an elected representative expressed reservations about a last-minute legislative change, the lobbyist approached and said simply, "It was fine, and to adopt the amendment." Although that politician admitted knowing little about energy or ComEd, the Speaker had appointed him to sponsor electricity-related bills and to follow McClain's lead.[20]

The well-connected lobbyist claimed to have retired in December 2016, but ComEd continued to pay him $361,000 for "legal services" in the two subsequent years. Breaking his usual reticence toward public comments, Madigan on McClain's supposed retirement praised the lobbyist, who would be indicted and found guilty on multiple charges, for his "complete honesty and integrity."[21]

Prosecutors alleged that McClain used "threats, intimidation, and extortion" to realize the Speaker's desires. In one recorded discussion, the hard-charging lobbyist referred to ComEd executives complaining about the no-work hires as "dumb fucks."[22]

Behind the scenes, federal agents confronted another utility official, Fidel Marquez—arriving at six o'clock in the morning at his mother's home and laying out their vast amount of incriminating evidence against him. To avoid a harsh sentence, that ComEd senior vice president, who began working at the utility thirty-seven years before as an intern, agreed to cooperate with the government, wear a wire, and provide testimony against his colleagues during an upcoming trial.

In one such recording at a restaurant in Springfield, the state capital, Marquez got McClain to explain how the Speaker's allies obtained no-work consulting assignments without making it appear ComEd paid them. McClain claimed the arrangement—through Jay D. Doherty & Associates—protected the utility, saying, "Doherty's the one that has to prove that if the IRS ever comes in and says, 'Who are these guys, what do they do?' . . . Doherty's gotta prove it."[23] In addition to being a longtime ComEd consultant, Doherty was well connected, having led the City Club of Chicago, a respected century-old civic group that organized popular speaking events with leading politicians, executives, and authors.

Marquez, on a separate occasion, asked Doherty, "As far as I know, and maybe you can tell me different, all these guys do is, they're a sub under you and you cut them a check. Do they do anything? What do they do? What do you have them doing?" Doherty replied, "Well, not much, to answer the question." He added that these "workers" would "keep their mouths shut," and that their subcontracts were designed "to keep Madigan happy. I think it's worth it because you'd hear otherwise." Doherty continued, "ComEd should not tamper with the arrangement because your money comes from Springfield."[24] To advance the power corporation's interests in the state capital, those no-work payments between 2011 and 2018 totaled $3.1 million.

In another discussion taped by Marquez, this one from a dimly lit table inside Saputo's, a popular Italian restaurant in Springfield, McClain described how ComEd's relationship with Madigan had evolved over the past few years from "play nice" to "how can we help you?"[25] In another recorded phone conversation, Pramaggiore argued against changing the no-work jobs, saying, "We do not want to get caught up in a, you know, disruptive battle where, you know, somebody gets their nose out of joint . . . because we're in the middle of needing to get something done in Springfield." That "somebody," of course, was the Speaker.[26]

Building on Marquez's recordings, prosecutors at trial would assert that "Pramaggiore viewed Madigan as immensely powerful in the General Assembly and wanted him to be favorably disposed toward ComEd, and it was not uncommon for her to ask what Madigan's position was on an issue."[27]

By 2014, before ComEd's various payments became a scandal, the utility's parent company, Exelon, turned from requesting higher rates for infrastructure investments to seeking bailouts for struggling nuclear reactors. Over the next few years, the corporation negotiated with environmental and consumer groups to obtain a compromise bill—the Future Energy Jobs Act—that provided some nuclear subsidies but also expanded energy efficiency programs, fixed the state's renewable energy laws (thereby sparking billions of new investments in Illinois-based wind and solar projects), and cut incentives for dirty coal plants. Negotiations continued to the last day of the legislature's fall veto session in December 2016, with ComEd's forty contract lobbyists making sure no legislators left Springfield before the vote; quipped one utility lobbyist, "Guarding elevators was a job task."[28]

Clean-energy advocates hailed the legislation as "a big win,"[29] and Exelon executives in spring 2018 were pleased enough with the negotiated results to promote Pramaggiore to oversee all the company's power-distribution utilities, including those in New Jersey, Pennsylvania, Maryland, Delaware, and Washington, DC. Her first call, tellingly, was to inform Madigan of her new job, and then she wrote to one of her lobbyists that her advancement "never would've happened without you . . . and the Speaker." She then gushed, "And you guys have been my spirit guides."[30]

Replacing Pramaggiore at ComEd was Joe Dominguez, an Exelon veteran whom Mike McClain did not trust to please the Speaker. Revealing his aggressive approach, the lobbyist described how he would convince the new CEO to continue the no-work contracts. "Now look it, asshole," McClain would bark at Dominguez, "if you want to pass this bill, this is what it requires." Speaking of the need to accommodate Madigan's requests, he added, "So, either you're gonna play in the tier-one game here or you're gonna keep playing in your tier-two game. . . . And if you wanna fire me today that's fine but, uh this is like serious business, it's millions of dollars. So either you wanna look like you're the leader, and be the leader, but that means you've gotta authorize your people to do things."[31]

The federal investigation became public in May 2019, when FBI agents, armed with search warrants, raided McClain's home in downstate Quincy, as well as the house of a Madigan operative who had been a Chicago alderman. Two months later, ComEd and Exelon received grand jury subpoenas for information about their lobbying activities. Three months after that, Anne Pramaggiore, the promoted CEO, resigned.[32]

To avoid more severe charges and to shift the public spotlight away from the utility, ComEd in July 2020 entered into a deferred prosecution agreement, described its misconduct, pleaded guilty to one count of bribery, and agreed to pay a $200 million fine. In the legalese-laced settlement, the utility "admitted it arranged jobs, vendor subcontracts, and monetary payments associated with those jobs and subcontracts, for various associates of a high-level elected official for the state of Illinois, to influence and reward the official's efforts to assist ComEd with respect to legislation concerning ComEd and its businesses."[33] Stated more succinctly, the utility confessed it spent eight years paying the Speaker's associates in order to obtain legislative benefits worth millions of dollars.[34]

Federal prosecutors, while cutting a deal with the company, remained free to pursue ComEd executives and contractors, and in November 2020, a grand jury handed down criminal charges against the "ComEd Four": former CEO Anne Pramaggiore and three utility lobbyists, Michael McClain (Madigan's friend and confidant), John Hooker (longtime utility executive), and Jay Doherty (consultant and onetime City Club president).[35]

With the scandal diminishing ComEd's and Exelon's political clout, environmental and consumer advocates pushed for an even more aggressive clean energy bill, referred to as the Climate and Equitable Jobs Act (CEJA).

That legislation called for Illinois to transition by 2045 away from carbon-emitting coal and natural gas plants, to obtain 100 percent renewable energy by 2050, to electrify the transportation sector, and to adopt stronger energy efficiency standards. While CEJA provided $694 million for two of Exelon's money-losing but carbon-free nuclear reactors, the legislation focused on clean energy and related job-training programs, particularly in underserved and low-income communities. Noting the swirling charges of utility fraud, the bill also ordered increased accountability and transparency by the state's power corporations.

Exelon and ComEd, despite the charges against them, were not powerless in Springfield, and the well-financed corporations had environmentalists over something of a policy barrel. Conservationists wanted non–carbon-emitting electricity, and since nuclear reactors generated more than half of Illinois's total electricity, an odd coalition formed between Exelon advancing the carbon-free benefits of nuclear energy and environmentalists highlighting the climate advantages of wind and solar. Jack Darin of the Sierra Club observed that if reactors retired quickly, "renewables wouldn't be ready in time to take their place." While his environmental group didn't support nuclear power as a long-term solution, it disliked the alternative of building new natural-gas facilities that likely would spew pollution for decades.[36]

Exelon also enjoyed labor-union allies, which wanted to maintain high-paying jobs at the reactors, and it had additional support from public officials near the troubled generators who depended upon the plants' property taxes to fund schools and public safety. Governor J. B. Pritzker signed CEJA in September 2021. The Citizens Utility Board said the nine-hundred-page legislation "could be a national model on how states can fight the most devastating and expensive consequences of climate change while controlling costs for energy consumers."[37]

Several months after CEJA's passage, in May 2022, a grand jury filed a 106-page, twenty-two-count indictment against the Illinois House Speaker, charging him with running a "Madigan Enterprise" that criminally enriched himself and those loyal to him. The charges related mostly to ComEd, but also accused Madigan of illegally steering legal work to his property-tax law firm. The indictment accused the Speaker "of leading for nearly a decade a criminal scheme whose purpose was to enhance Madigan's political power and financial well-being while also generating income for his political allies and associates."[38]

Recognizing he no longer had enough support from scandal-shocked legislators, Madigan gave up the Speaker's gavel and then resigned from the House seat he'd held for fifty years. In an awkwardly worded statement, Madigan's aides denied wrongdoing: "The speaker has never helped someone find a job with the expectation that the person would not be asked to perform work by their employer, nor did he ever expect to provide anything to a prospective employer if it should choose to hire a person he recommended. He has never made a legislative decision with improper motives and has engaged in no wrongdoing here."[39] Madigan's racketeering trial began in October 2024 with federal prosecutors saying the case was "about corruption at the highest levels of state government."[40] After ten days of deliberations, the jury in February 2025 convicted him on ten counts.

The ComEd Four, at their own court case, which started in March 2023, argued they offered only "classic, honest, legal lobbying." They labeled the government's accusations a "dark theory" and denied that the utility's legislative strategy relied on hiring people recommended by Madigan. Declaring that "lobbying and politics are not illegal," they asserted the CEO and her consultants simply negotiated with a wide assortment of consumer, environmental, and labor groups to craft compromise legislation that garnered enough Democratic and Republican support.[41]

Yet in a seventeenth-floor courtroom at Chicago's Dirksen Federal Courthouse, government prosecutors presented substantial evidence that the four defendants worked together to provide "a continuous stream of benefits" to corruptly influence the Speaker in exchange for his support of ComEd's legislative agenda.[42] The trial lasted six weeks, during which time the jury heard from fifty witnesses, listened to over one hundred wiretapped conversations, watched dozens of secretly recorded videos, and read hundreds of text messages and emails.

The prosecuting US attorney observed, "This [utility scheme] was not the $10,000 in a grocery bag in the back room; it was much more complex. And the dollar amounts involved, and the gain involved was much more significant as well. So, it was a different type of [bribery] case."[43]

Federal prosecutors painstakingly explained to the jury that the fortunes of ComEd and Exelon depend on the actions of legislators and regulators who set electricity policy and rates. They highlighted how the companies benefited from laws approved during the bribery years, particularly formula rates and reactor subsidies. Prosecutors further showed that these payments buoyed the utility's stock price, to the benefit of both executives and investors. Using McClain's own words about playing in the tier-one game, the assistant US attorney concluded, "[The four] spent years playing this 'tier-one' game to get legislation that ComEd needed. This was not lobbying, this was not building goodwill, this was not politics, this was not normal business operations. These were crimes."[44] In her closing arguments, the prosecutor repeated the criminal mantra: "Madigan wanted, ComEd gave, and ComEd got."[45]

Government attorneys labeled the four "the grandmasters of corruption,"[46] but a jury member said her colleagues grew to like the defendants over the course of the trial, suggesting, "All in all, they're good people that made bad decisions."[47] Yet she added that Pramaggiore's decision to give nine hours of testimony did her little good, particularly since government attorneys repeatedly highlighted her acting studies in college, leading the jury member to believe the former CEO was simply performing on the stand.[48]

As with the FirstEnergy scandal described in earlier chapters, the Illinois-based jury grappled with the question of when lobbying becomes bribery. After the trial, the foreperson observed that the defense argument—that ComEd's various payments were part of the normal course of business—"did not sit well with us."[49] Another juror stated, "All of us agree lobbying is necessary for our legislators to be educated. This is not lobbying."[50]

The twelve jurors—seven women and five men—deliberated for some twenty-seven hours over five days, returning guilty verdicts for each of the defendants on all counts. The ComEd Four face up to five years in prison for conspiracy, ten years on each bribery charge, and as many as twenty years for each count of falsifying records.

The four defendants remained stoic as the US district judge read the verdicts at around 5:00 p.m. on Tuesday, May 2, 2023. In addition to a few sobs from family members and friends, the only other voice heard was McClain's wife saying softly, "Oh dear God."[51]

The federal judge set sentencing hearings for January 2024 but postponed those dates until the US Supreme Court reviewed a separate case that could further restrict the definition of *racketeering*.[52] After the justices again narrowed federal bribery laws in their Snyder decision—ruling that bribes are criminal only if received in exchange for official acts—the ComEd Four in August 2024 asked a new judge to acquit them of all charges.[53] Government prosecutors countered that no relief should be granted since the "continuous stream of high-value benefits over a long period of time provided powerful evidence of an intent to influence Madigan."[54] As of this writing, in January 2025, that judge had issued no decision.

Investors, meanwhile, reached a $173 million settlement with Exelon and its ComEd subsidiary. Their class-action lawsuit had alleged that revelation of the bribery scandals caused the utility's stock price to drop and stockholders and bondholders to suffer substantial losses.[55]

Exelon continues to face an audit of its accounting practices by the Federal Energy Regulatory Commission, for which the utility expects to be charged at least $11 million. The utility did win one lawsuit, when a circuit judge ruled against restitution for millions of Illinoisans who bore the costs of taxpayer-funded subsidies, yet state regulators ordered a $38 million refund to cover some direct costs customers sustained from the bribery scheme.

In late September 2023, the Securities and Exchange Commission (SEC) charged Exelon, ComEd, and Pramaggiore with fraud associated with the multiyear scandal. The utilities agreed to pay a $46.2 million penalty, but complaints against the former CEO will be litigated. According to an SEC official, "Pramaggiore's remarks to investors about ComEd's lobbying activities hid the reality of the long-running political corruption scheme in which they were engaged." To clarify the underlying principle, that official added, "When corporate executives speak to investors, they must not mislead by omission."[56]

Commonwealth Edison claims to be reborn and reformed, but little fundamentally has changed. Executives continue to make political contributions, hire lobbyists, and plead for rate hikes.

Chapter VI

Swaying Elections

FirstEnergy and ComEd are not isolated examples of corrupt monopolies bribing their ways to bailouts. A growing number of utilities also are paying to ensure their sympathizers become their regulators and to block their competitors. If we are to retard fraud and encourage innovation, let's first review a few other power scandals.

FLORIDA

Florida Power & Light (FP&L), the state's largest electric utility, which serves more than twelve million customers, has been accused of opening its checkbook to elect sympathetic legislators . . . and to squash its critics.[1] When a Democratic state senator proposed a law that could reduce the utility's sales, for instance, the power corporation's CEO, Eric Silagy, directed two of his vice presidents, "I want you to make his life a living hell . . . seriously."[2]

To maintain secrecy, that executive used a pseudonymous Yahoo email address to hire a consultant who recruited a political neophyte with the same surname as the utility-critical incumbent. Pitched as a progressive alternative, that ghost contender, as the utility hoped, split the Democratic vote in the Miami-area district, causing the sitting senator to lose his 2020 reelection by only 32 votes out of more than 215,000 cast. After the campaign, the trumped-up candidate, who never campaigned, pleaded guilty to receiving a $50,000 bribe to run, and the Republican victor went on to support FP&L's interests.[3]

The key schemer was Frank Artiles, a former Republican state senator turned scandal-prone influence peddler and bribe offerer.[4] He had resigned from the Florida Senate in 2017 after using a racial slur against two of his

Black colleagues and referring to a female senator as a "bitch" and a "girl." Demonstrating a further lack of discretion, Artiles spent campaign funds to hire as "consultants" a former Hooters "calendar girl" and a Playboy "Miss Social" model, neither of whom had political experience.[5]

When he served as a state senator, Artiles chaired the Communications, Energy, and Public Utilities Committee and pushed numerous pro-utility bills, one of which allowed FP&L to get around a Florida Supreme Court ruling and to charge its Florida customers for exploratory natural-gas fracking in Oklahoma.[6] The senator had received more than $30,000 in reported political contributions from state-based utilities, as well as nearly $2,000 for travel to Daytona Beach and Disney's Epcot theme park.[7]

Artiles inadvertently revealed his campaign scheme when he boasted during an election-night party at Irish restaurant Liam Fitzpatrick's that his ghost candidate had siphoned just enough votes away from the incumbent Democrat who had challenged FP&L's benefits. "That's me. That's all me," he crowed as attendees expressed shock. "He was so loud," complained one. "Why would he just say that out loud?" asked another. "The crowd just kind of shakes its head because he's drinking, and he's very cocky, he's proud, right? And I think he just couldn't help himself. He had to brag."[8]

After the *Miami Herald* published an account of Artiles's arrogance, the former senator called others who were at the bar and demanded they sign affidavits attesting he had not said what was reported. One attendee admitted fear, saying, "He's a bully. I was scared for sure."[9]

Federal agents responded by raiding Artiles's Palmetto Bay home, and prosecutors in March 2021 charged him with three felony campaign-finance charges.[10] The state attorney added a felony charge for offering some $50,000 to the no-party candidate and for trying to "confuse voters and influence the outcome" of a state Senate election.[11] After prosecutors described Artiles as the "mastermind" of the "ghost candidate scandal," a jury in late September 2024 found him guilty on three counts of campaign finance violations, and he was sentenced to sixty days in county jail.[12] While the former legislator dabbed away tears, the judge also restricted him from all pollical work: "No consulting, no fundraising, nothing."[13]

Miami-Dade officials also discovered that a dark-money group—named Grow United and "headquartered" out of a UPS mailbox in Denver—had implemented Artiles's "siphoning strategy" that hurt FP&L critics and aided pro-utility candidates. FP&L denied any role in the ghost-candidate scheme, asserting, "Any report or suggestion that we had involvement in, financially supported, or directed others to support any 'ghost' candidates during the 2020 election cycle is patently false."[14]

Yet prosecutors and journalists revealed the utility funneled at least $3 million to Grow United and that Silagy personally coordinated with it and other dark-money organizations.[15] According to an analysis by Floodlight, a nonprofit investigative newsroom, utility-paid consultants in 2020 advanced a total of three spoiler candidates, allowing three Republican power-company supporters to win their Senate races. As a result, the GOP retained its majority in the forty-member Florida Senate, and FP&L enjoyed sympathetic lawmakers.[16]

One day before the ghost-candidate scheme became public and FP&L's share price dropped dramatically, CEO Silagy, according to a group of angry investors, used insider information to unload 62,480 shares of the utility's stock and pocket $5.4 million.[17]

The *Miami Herald* further reported that 2020 was not FP&L's first venture into dark-money electioneering. The newspaper found that the "multibillion-dollar behemoth" in fall 2018 bankrolled $200,000 to Broken Promises, as well as $13.9 million to Mothers for Moderation, to siphon votes away from a Democrat challenging a utility-friendly Republican incumbent.[18]

Trying to limit more damaging disclosures, NextEra, FP&L's parent company, commissioned an internal investigation and later hired an outside law firm to examine the allegations. It shocked no one that utility executives claimed to have found no wrongdoing, stating creatively, "Based on information in our possession, we believe FPL would not be found liable for any of the Florida campaign finance law violations as alleged in the media articles."[19] The utility, however, refused to release the results of its audits.

Much of the evidence associated with the ghost-candidate scandal came to light amid a power struggle within Matrix, a hard-charging political consulting firm hired by FP&L. One of the Matrix combatants conducted an internal review of the election scheme, found "potential unlawful conduct," and compiled a cache of documents—including checks, bank statements, and internal ledgers—that showed FP&L was invoiced for Grow United's incorporation filing fees and other expenses. According to the *Orlando Sentinel*, "consultants who were controlling Grow United billed FP&L in September 2020 for millions of dollars shortly before they started moving money through it."[20]

By 2022, monopoly-friendly regulators, confirmed by monopoly-friendly legislators, allowed FP&L to help itself to more than $1 billion in unanticipated corporate-tax savings rather than pass those benefits on to customers.[21] The utility's legislative friends also forced the replacement of a FP&L critic with a former utility lobbyist at the helm of the Office of Public Counsel, a supposedly independent state agency that is to represent consumers in rate cases.[22]

Florida Power & Light and NextEra Energy for many years had been big spenders on lobbying and political initiatives. As early as 2009, FP&L opposed four Florida Public Service Commission members who voted against a rate increase. After what was described as "behind-the-scenes lobbying," state senators voted to not confirm those regulators for new terms. The *Miami Herald* reported that the utility used "people inside and outside the company to investigate those state utility regulators, challenge their impartiality, and post negative comments about them and the governor on the internet." When the commission's new term began, utility-supported commissioners approved a record $4.9 billion rate increase and made it easier for FP&L to add additional costs and fees to customer bills.[23]

In recent years, largely because of the Supreme Court's *Citizens United* decision, FP&L has funneled increasingly larger amounts through shadowy groups that don't reveal their donors but exert substantial influence on elections and public policy. The utility first dipped its toes into these dark-money pots in 2016, when it funded groups to oppose a state constitutional amendment that would have allowed wider sales of rooftop solar systems. NextEra Energy had invested far more than most utilities in wind and solar projects, yet it fought to block consumers from generating their own power.[24] As part of its campaign against the ballot measure, the utility helped finance a competing constitutional amendment designed to confuse voters.[25] According to a Florida Supreme Court justice, "Let the pro-solar energy consumers beware. Masquerading as a pro-solar energy initiative, this proposed [alternative] constitutional amendment, supported by some of Florida's major investor-owned electric utility companies, actually seeks to constitutionalize the status quo . . . [and] it may actually have the effect of *diminishing* some rights of solar energy consumers."[26]

FP&L accelerated those referendum tactics in 2019, when it opposed another constitutional amendment, known as the energy-choice measure, that would have broken up utility monopolies and allowed consumers to choose among numerous electricity providers. CEO Eric Silagy feared the petition drive as an existential threat and stated, "We're going to be very actively engaged."[27]

According to the *Orlando Sentinel*, FP&L also leveraged funds from affiliated organizations; the Associated Industries of Florida—the corporate-lobbying group whose biggest donors are FP&L, US Sugar, Walt Disney World, and HCA Healthcare—contributed to its own dark-money nonprofit that then forwarded some $1.2 million to Grow United.[28]

As FirstEnergy did in Ohio to oppose a popular referendum, Floridian hired guns launched a multipronged campaign, headlined by blockers harassing, and allegedly assaulting, the petition's signature gatherers. They pushed community leaders that utilities had supported to speak out against the pro-competition proposition. Through Matrix, they also gave some $2.8 million to a front group, cleverly named Floridians for Affordable Reliable Energy, that supported the state's civil rights groups, such as the Urban League, to oppose the energy-choice referendum.[29] Those organizations, moreover, filed an amicus brief arguing the ballot measure would "significantly increase electricity costs for seniors, low-income households, minority communities, average citizens, and small businesses in Florida."[30]

Most effectively, utility consultants engaged high-priced lawyers that convinced the Florida Supreme Court the proposal was misleading and should not be placed on the ballot.[31] According to an overwhelmed organizer of the petition drive, power monopolies "just practice total warfare. They don't leave a single stone unturned because of the resources they can muster."[32]

On the legislative front, according to media reports, FP&L and its allies drafted and promoted a bill that would retard homeowners with rooftop solar from selling their excess power back to the utility; that legislation, moreover, allowed utilities to impose new fees on the owners of solar collectors.[33] The utility monopoly's interests were clear—the company makes money based on investments in its own generators and power lines but not from solar panels generating electricity on someone else's roof. A first-term Republican senator introduced this anti-solar measure and the next week received a $10,000 campaign contribution from the utility giant.[34]

As these schemes became scandals, FP&L faced a public-relations problem. One reputable news outlet went so far as to write, "Florida's utility giant seems to get what it wants at all costs—whether it be by backing dirty political tricks to sway elections, using its power to bully dissenters, or buying favorable news coverage."[35]

FP&L-backed Matrix responded by trying to control news coverage. According to media reports, the heavy-handed consultants launched a smear campaign against the *Miami Herald* reporter who wrote a story about the company's behind-the-scenes work for the anti-solar legislation.[36] They also spied on a Jacksonville-based columnist who wrote critically of FP&L, and they prepared a seventy-two-page dossier of surveillance photos and personal information on the journalist.[37] They even paid a veteran ABC News freelance producer to pose unwelcome questions to politicians critical of the utility.[38]

When several Florida newspapers announced they would not be intimidated by such tactics and would continue reporting on FP&L's political schemes and scandals, a company spokesperson threatened, "That is your choice, but rest assured, we will hold you accountable if that continues to happen."[39]

The utility's intermediaries, moreover, acquired control of the *Capitolist*—a Tallahassee-based, conservative-bent, snarky-toned, online news site—to advance favorable coverage of the power corporation. The *Capitolist* attacked FP&L's critics, with one headline declaring, without any proof, "Documents suggest Florida's largest companies are secretly sabotaging efforts to protect power lines from hurricane damage."[40] At the direction of a top FP&L executive, the website posted a hit piece just three days before the 2018 election against the Democratic gubernatorial candidate, who was in a tight race with utility-supportive Ron DeSantis. The utility's pugilistic CEO then ordered his staffers, "Promote the @&;amp;!!! out of this" defamatory article.[41]

One of the state's major newspapers reported that "Silagy was secretly running things at *Capitolist*,"[42] while another revealed that "FPL quietly took over a Florida news site and used it to bash critics."[43] The *Capitolist*'s founder—who received $12,000 per month funneled through a network of utility-financed shell companies—confessed to the deceit. "Because 'media' is supposed to be 'objective' and pay-to-play is 'icky' to the larger corporations," he wrote, it's important to look like "we're legit." Claiming to be more effective than traditional public relations, he added, controlling the *Capitolist* allowed FP&L to shape its message without anyone knowing the messenger.[44]

As FP&L's controversies rose, its CEO, Eric Silagy, abruptly retired after more than a decade leading the company. His boss—NextEra's chairman—acknowledged, but underplayed, Silagy's scandals by calling the previous twelve months "a year of distractions (and) challenges." Investors subsequently launched class action alerts claiming, "FPL's surreptitious orchestration of political misconduct exposed it to substantial legal and reputation risk."[45] One journalist suggested "FPL's chief brawler" left a legacy of low trust.[46]

NextEra's executives had long felt big was better, that they needed to expand to thrive. In May 2018, they completed a $6.5 billion deal to buy Gulf Power, which supplied electricity to much of Florida's Panhandle, and they obtained ownership interests in two power plants from the Southern Company. Another target was Jacksonville Electric Authority (JEA), controlled by the city on the Atlantic coast of northeastern Florida. Buying this provider of electricity, water, and sewer services would have locked the state's entire east coast into FP&L's service territory.

A purchase became more likely in 2015, when Lenny Curry defeated the Democratic incumbent to become Jacksonville's mayor. The conservative first-termer expressed support for privatizing government functions and a particular interest in selling the city's century-old municipal utility. NextEra, based in Palm Beach County, was willing to spend some $11 billion on the purchase, but it understood the city's sales decision would be based as much on politics as on economics.[47]

NextEra and FP&L tried several public-relations maneuvers. The utility conglomerates, for instance, hired Curry's former chief administrator and strategist to grease the wheels within city government.[48] They employed another consultant to attend private meetings with JEA executives and plan the municipal utility's privatization.[49] FP&L lobbyists also handed out favors, such as sponsoring a private-plane trip for Jacksonville's mayor, Lenny Curry, and JEA's leader, Aaron Zahn, to an Atlanta Braves' playoff game.[50]

To advance the sale, according to a federal indictment, JEA executives "falsely and fraudulently" projected the public utility to be in a "death spiral."[51] Matrix, FP&L's public-relations consultants, also tried to undermine public confidence in the public utility, allegedly creating a short-lived organization, "Fix JEA Now," that claimed the city-owned utility was "broken" and suffered a "record of failure."[52]

Perhaps most brazenly, operatives supported by FP&L tried to lure a prominent critic of the JEA sale to leave the Jacksonville City Council, which had to approve any purchase. They used Grow United, the same dark-money group that advanced ghost candidates in state Senate elections, to create a $250,000-a-year job for the councilman to lead an organization advancing drug decriminalization across the country, an issue he was passionate about, as evidenced by his introducing legislation to legalize marijuana in Jacksonville. The only hitch was that the public servant would need to resign from the City Council. The *Orlando Sentinel* revealed that the offer had little to do with medical marijuana and a lot to do with ensuring FP&L sidelined critics and obtained enough votes to win the JEA sale. The councilman, who had never heard of the purported organization, responded, "I said, 'Man, I'm not doing that.'"[53]

JEA's own leaders—CEO Aaron Zahn and CFO Ryan Wannemacher—added to the sordidness by crafting in 2018 an "exorbitant" golden parachute for when the sale became finalized.[54] As that bonus scheme became a scandal and the "tide of public opinion was shifting," JEA executives, according to bankers advising the deal, tried to speed up the merger even though rushing would result in a negative outcome for the public utility and the city of Jacksonville.[55]

Finally embarrassed, JEA's board, on the day before Christmas 2019, voted unanimously to stop the sale,[56] and federal prosecutors in March 2022 charged Zahn and Wannemacher with conspiracy and wire fraud for scheming to enrich themselves through the municipal utility's privatization.[57] A jury in March 2024 found Zahn guilty, but Wannemacher innocent. As the verdicts were read, Zahn, who faces up to twenty-five years in prison, could be heard crying.[58]

ALABAMA

Matrix also did behind-the-scenes work for Alabama Power, a subsidiary of Southern Company, which wanted to stop regulatory hearings on its electricity rates, the most expensive in the Southeast. When Terry Dunn, a Tea Party conservative, won a seat on the Alabama Public Service Commission, he said a utility lobbyist promised he could hold his roughly $100,000-a-year job if he remained a team player. "They didn't take me serious," complained Dunn, who began investigating Alabama Power's practices and finances.[59]

In response, the power monopoly and its consultants provided millions to a dark-money group that attacked Dunn in the right-wing press and online, falsely accusing the conservative regulator of opposing the use of coal. They placed another attack ad in an online news outlet that claimed, "Democrats Embrace Republican Public Service Commissioner Terry Dunn," and they pushed the *Alabama Political Reporter* to assert that Dunn was "a radical environmentalist" who finds "companies like Alabama Power a convenient political target."[60] Such attacks gained traction in the deeply red state of Alabama. Dunn subsequently lost his reelection by nineteen percentage points, prompting him to observe, "Southern Company and Alabama Power run the state of Alabama. They work off intimidating. You gotta bow down and kiss the ring."[61]

SOUTH CAROLINA

SCANA Corporation's CEO, Kevin Marsh, pleaded guilty, and was sentenced to two years in prison, for defrauding ratepayers and investors about the costs of constructing two reactors.[62] Despite soaring building expenses, the utility's Virgil C. Summer nuclear expansion never produced a single watt of electricity. That economic disaster, known as the "Nukegate scandal," was made possible by SCANA-advanced legislation that forced customers to pay up front for a project that failed to materialize.[63]

The Base Load Review Act shifted the risks of utility construction from companies to consumers. For decades, from the time of Sam Insull, power monopolies sold bonds and issued shares to cover building costs for generators and power lines, and they incorporated such borrowing expenses into their rate requests when the units began producing power. But because financiers had grown skeptical of over-budget nuclear projects, utilities sought a different source of financing, a pay-as-you-go tool in which they would be compensated as the plants were designed and built. The mechanism went by the odd acronym "CWIP," for "construction work in progress."[64] And it made consumers into unwitting investors.

In South Carolina, the CWIP bill was crafted by SCANA's former general counsel, then a lawyer at a politically influential law firm with offices next to the capitol complex. Understanding the power of doublespeak, his draft legislation began "An act to protect South Carolina ratepayers," but the fine print revealed a utility subsidy without spending caps or penalties if construction costs exceeded expectations.[65]

To obtain the Base Load Review Act, power companies rewarded supportive legislators with more than $510,000 in reported campaign contributions, and unknown amounts of dark-money payments. They also hired a slew of consultants, lobbyists, and publicists. That combination prompted the Speaker of the South Carolina House to say this about utility-experienced executives: "When you're in the General Assembly, you have a need to be able to trust the people in authority." It also convinced the Senate president pro tempore to dramatically parrot SCANA's argument for building new power plants: "We don't need blackouts like in Baghdad here in South Carolina."[66]

The governor's chief of staff, in contrast, labeled the CWIP legislation "probably the clearest case [of] a special interest using all of its power and leverage to get something passed." He added, "The bill was entirely industry driven—in the drafting of it, in the advocacy of it, in terms of putting pressure on legislators."[67]

SCANA, and its South Carolina Electric & Gas Company subsidiary, argued CWIP would secure billions of dollars and spread-out power-plant payments. Critics asserted the use of other people's money would prompt utility executives to take big bets on risky projects. Lawmakers largely ignored the vastly outspent opponents and pushed the bill from introduction to passage in a record seven days, with only 6 of 104 House members objecting.[68]

The risks with the Virgil C. Summer project were huge. South Carolina Electric & Gas (SCE&G) and South Carolina Public Service Authority (known as Santee Cooper) contracted in 2008 with Westinghouse to build two reactors, using an unconventional, but much-hyped, design that relied on prefabricated parts and modular construction. The two reactors would have been America's first in some thirty years, and utility executives predicted they would lead the country into a nuclear renaissance.

When construction began in 2013, setbacks and postponements occurred almost immediately. Parts arrived with manufacturing defects. The more than five thousand laborers working at the site lacked an integrated construction schedule, causing costly confusion. Mechanical and electrical blueprints often proved to be flawed, resulting in "incorrect parts, thousands of engineering changes, and billions of dollars in wasted money."[69]

Delays prompted deceptions. SCE&G and Santee Cooper, for instance, hired Bechtel to audit the project, and those consultants found fifty instances where Westinghouse had used false completion dates. Yet at the demand of a utility attorney, Bechtel scrubbed away its conclusion that the reactors would not be completed in time to collect a $2 billion federal tax credit. State commissioners also relied on that false finding to approve another $800 million rate increase, one of nine hikes that rubber-stamp regulators imposed to defray the utilities' rising costs.[70]

Other coverups were almost comical . . . as well as dangerous. When a quality assurance manager shut down a fabrication plant because of problems with welds and lax safety rules, a more senior utility executive, demanding that construction continue, threw a letter opener at the engineer's head, missing his ear by only a few inches and crashing into a plate-glass window.[71]

Investigators subsequently found that Kevin Marsh deceived investors and regulators in "earning calls, presentations, and press releases" by claiming reactor construction was on track. Just a few months before the project collapsed, the executive declared, "We're excited about where we are."[72]

Stephen Byrne, the utility's executive vice president, added to the ruse, telling Wall Street analysts in late 2012 that V. C. Summer's "construction is progressing well." He asserted the Base Load Review Act allowed the utility to obtain numerous rate increases, saying, "We continue to be pleased that the mechanism is working as designed."[73]

As an example of efforts to keep regulators from diving too deeply into the project's poor finances, the power companies provided Georgia Commissioner Lauren "Bubba" McDonald with $22,000 in meals, lodging, golf outings, and other gifts. One SCANA lobbyist in 2014 served as campaign treasurer for two pro-utility commissioners seeking reelection. Going the extra mile, another lobbyist arranged for a regulator's granddaughter to sing the national anthem at an Atlanta Braves baseball game. Trying valiantly, if unconvincingly, to defend such lavish practices, a commissioner protested, "It is the height of cynicism in our political process—and a complete lack of confidence in our elected officials—to believe that their votes are influenced by dinners or efforts to persuade."[74]

As the scandal unfolded, a SCANA employee admitted corporation executives "got on our jet airplanes and flew around the country showing the same damn construction pictures from different angles and playing [their] fiddles" while the project "was going up in flames."[75] According to the US Securities and Exchange Commission, which charged Marsh with securities violations, "The false statements and omissions enabled SCANA to boost its stock price, sell more than $1 billion in bonds, and obtain regulatory approval to raise customers' rates."[76]

Marsh pleaded guilty in federal court to defrauding ratepayers and was sentenced to two years in prison.[77] When asked if he would do it again, the unrepentant former CEO said, "Absolutely, I would make the same decision. I feel as strongly today—probably even stronger today than I did back in 2008—that this is the solution for us, for a clean energy future."[78]

Stephen Byrne—who also pleaded guilty to multiple charges, including conspiracy to commit mail and wire fraud—had a different take. Rather than defend his actions, he cooperated with federal and state agents, prompting a judge to slightly reduce his sentence to fifteen months in prison. The engineer apologized for his deceptions, saying, "I failed the nuclear industry. What we hoped would be a nuclear renaissance—we put the brakes on it."[79]

Summer's building costs had soared from an estimated $9.8 billion to at least $25 billion. With construction only 30 percent complete, Westinghouse filed for bankruptcy in March 2017, and the utilities abandoned the project a few months later. Because of CWIP, however, ratepayers continued to face higher rates, an estimated $2.3 billion over the next two decades.[80]

The *Post and Courier*, the main daily newspaper in Charleston, South Carolina, tracked the scandal and calculated corruption's on-the-ground costs. Rate increases, it reported, led to an extra $40,000 a year in electricity expenses for the Charleston Animal Hospital, enough to have saved 107 dogs and cats. They reached $1.2 million for the city of Charleston, enough to have paid starting salaries for twenty-six police officers.[81]

After interviewing more than fifty experts and scandal participants, the journalists issued apt observations about the corruption: "Flush with cash, utilities tried to build plants with unproven technology; they launched projects with unfinished designs and unrealistic budgets; they misled regulators and the public with schedules that promised bogus completion dates; they hid damning reports from investors and the public; they tried to silence critics and whistleblowers."[82]

MICHIGAN

Consumers Energy, Michigan's largest utility, has long been active politically, often supporting its supporters and castigating its critics. According to media reports, it contributed heavily to the opponent of a well-known power-corporation foe, who ended up losing his election. It targeted the wife of a utility skeptic who had filed a complaint with the IRS about Consumers Energy misusing tax-exempt organizations for political purposes; she lost her primary for a state House seat.[83]

The power corporation also gave millions to a dark-money group, named Citizens for Energizing Michigan's Economy, that paid for a barrage of ads against a Republican representative who had pushed "energy choice" policies and criticized the utility's election spending as "an outrageous shell game that lends itself to corruption."[84] That lawmaker explained, "Utilities have a 90-percent monopoly by the pleasure of the state, and the utility lobbyists use money compelled from ratepayers' pockets to influence the outcome of elections that determine who their regulators will be." When he lost the Republican primary, the politician added, "They hung my bloody hide on the wall as a warning to any other legislator who might dare to take on their monopoly privileges. The fact they were able to take out the one person who was their most vocal critic will only make things worse."[85]

Consumers Energy, moreover, used its vast resources to criticize competition, particularly from consumers installing their own solar collectors. In 2012, it attacked a constitutional amendment, Proposal 3, that would have required Michigan to obtain 25 percent of its electricity from renewable sources by 2025. Consumers and DTE Energy put up more than $12 million to defeat that initiative and deviously called their own referendum the "Clean Affordable Renewable Energy (CARE) for Michigan." Like several of their colleagues mentioned above, Michigan utilities hired campaign organizers to argue deceptively before minority churches and low-income communities that the pro-solar amendment would undermine the state's existing clean-energy goals, as well as increase electricity costs across the Great Lakes state.[86]

As the utility's dark-money payments became scandals, Consumers Energy in 2018 reached a settlement to stop giving money to political advocacy groups, with its publicists repeating their bland mantra: "We at Consumers Energy stand for the people of Michigan." Yet only a year later, that settlement appeared to be another deceit, whereby utility officials essentially said, "Just kidding." The moratorium, executives now claimed, didn't apply to the parent corporation, CMS Energy, which obviously controls Consumers Energy. One Republican senator who won reelection despite the power corporation's opposition, called the utility's tactics "misleading and disingenuous."[87]

LOUISIANA

Entergy could get a prize for creating the best appearance of public support. The Louisiana-based power corporation wanted to build a $210 million natural gas plant in eastern New Orleans, but community activists said it was not needed, that cheaper upgrades to transmission wires would satisfy electricity demands, and that the project would pollute surrounding neighborhoods. So the utility hired a public relations company, a Los Angeles–based firm appropriately called "Crowds on Demand," to hire actors to speak favorably of the project at regulatory hearings.[88]

Those were colorful events, with some seventy "citizens" showing up in bright orange shirts and holding printed signs that read, "Jobs Giving Community" and "Power Station = Jobs." Little did regulators know these "power-plant supporters" were paid sixty dollars each time they wore their orange shirts to a meeting. After each hearing, they also enjoyed free pizza and a round of drinks at the nearby Dave & Buster's.[89]

A few actors received an extra $200 "speaking fee" if they read prewritten speeches provided by the PR firm. One of those talking points stated, "We've had public meetings for two years now and talked this power station to death. The objections are far outweighed by the benefits." Another read, "Entergy has been more than fair opening this process for public input. I see no reason to belabor this any further. Our only option to address the power disruptions is to proceed with the new plant. There is no Plan B."[90]

The performers had to sign nondisclosure agreements, not to speak with reporters, and never to admit they were paid. Yet according to one "citizen" who broke that pledge, "They paid us to sit through the meeting and clap every time someone said something against wind and solar power." Another observed, "It was very shady, very secretive, especially when we got paid. They literally paid us under the table."[91]

Orange-shirted actors arrived early and filled the hearing room's seats, meaning power-plant opponents showing up on time could not enter. "The fact that people were locked out of meetings is bad enough," complained one critic. "But if you're locked out because there are people who are being paid to sit in there and fill it up so that you can't get in, that's even worse."[92]

Performers were not the only ones being paid to speak up for Entergy's gas plant. At least nine of the witnesses represented nonprofit organizations that had received utility contributions. Like other power corporations, Entergy regularly made "charitable donations" to "buy" support for its proposals from cash-strapped nonprofits and civic groups. The CEO of the local YMCA, which had received $25,000 for adult education services, testified, "Entergy is a faithful corporate partner and puts great thought into all of the efforts that they get behind in our community." The head of the United Way, which obtained $1 million, didn't even mention the gas plant while lavishing praise on the utility, saying, "United Way is grateful to Entergy—to call Entergy a partner in our fight to build better and brighter futures for all."[93]

Entergy denied it had anything to do with the fake grassroots support, a practice known as astroturfing. Yet the New Orleans City Council eventually hired a law firm to investigate and found the power corporation had signed a contract for Crowds on Demand to "turn out 75 supporters, 10 of whom would speak at the meeting."[94] When that information became public, the utility admitted, "We should have been more diligent, and we should have known." A councilwomen called the practice "disturbing" and "morally reprehensible."[95]

Entergy paid a $5 million fine, but regulators approved the power plant.[96]

ARIZONA

Like FirstEnergy, Arizona Public Service Company (APS) doubled down on coal, purchasing in 2013 a larger share of the massive Four Corners generating unit, which required at least $400 million of additional emissions controls. Arizona might be the nation's sunniest state, but its energy mix was only 4 percent solar and more than 40 percent coal.[97]

APS liked that disparity, since it feared losing sales to solar collectors installed by consumers. To protect its expanding coal investments, the utility launched a coordinated campaign against renewable energy.

In 2012, when two pro-solar members of the Corporation Commission, which regulates the state's utilities, were up for reelection, APS executives saw an opportunity to defeat them and block competition. They criticized those regulators for endorsing "net metering," an existing policy that allowed owners of solar collectors to sell their excess power back to utilities. Net metering long had been a minor concern for the utility, but its popularity was soaring, with some five hundred new customers a month cutting into APS's profits.[98]

The debate became a battle between Republican supporters of solar energy—led by one of Arizona's conservative icons, Barry Goldwater Jr.—and Republican defenders of APS. One pro-solar organization ran television advertisements portraying a utility-backed candidate for the regulatory commission as a Pomeranian "lap dog to APS," yet the power monopoly spent significantly larger sums, accusing, with no proof, a pro-solar candidate of crooked financial dealings.[99]

Pointing to a corporate policy against participating in elections of regulators, APS executives denied any role in the inflammatory advertisements and mailers, or any coordination with Save Our Future Now, the anti-solar dark-money group. Yet journalists for the *Arizona Republic* revealed those claims to be false.[100]

Two years later, in 2014, APS executives fretted that the utility-supportive and solar-critical chair of the Corporation Commission had termed out and would retire. To maintain regulatory support, APS and its parent company, Pinnacle West Capital Group, accelerated their campaign efforts, giving almost $11 million to several front organizations that turned around and contributed to the pro-utility campaign.[101] According to press reports, clean-energy supporters were vastly outspent, and the APS's preferred replacement candidate won his race.[102]

Not long after that election, the supposedly independent regulators approved a $95 million *per year* increase in consumer payments to the power monopoly.[103] The Corporation Commission's new chair also pushed to reduce the state's clean-energy target, although his efforts became tainted after reporters revealed he had been holding improper ex parte meetings with APS's chief executive officer.[104]

The utility certainly enjoyed the regulators' largesse, while the CEO, Don Brandt, enhanced his personal pocket. Having been given stock as part of his pay package, as reported in Arizona newspapers, he sold nearly four hundred thousand shares, which had risen in value substantially with those rate increases.[105]

When confronted by journalists, Brandt and other utility executives continued to deny any spending to elect sympathetic regulators. Yet behind the scenes, according to journalist-obtained notes, they talked about hiding their involvement: "Reputationally, we fight this with third-party advocates."[106]

Benefiting regulators also were not particularly forthcoming about their dark-money receipts. One claimed to have no knowledge of the utility's involvement. Another became agitated, declaring, "The idea that it's impossible that we have broad support is insulting. The idea that we could be bought is insulting."[107]

APS, in a bipartisan fashion, sought to curtail oversight or criticism of its political contributions. When a liberal commissioner declared it unsavory for a regulated monopoly to spend its customers' money to elect its regulators, calling dark-money payments "a legal form of corruption," the power corporation spent $1.7 million of that very dark money to defeat her.[108] When a conservative regulator filed a subpoena to obtain information on APS's election expenditures, the power corporation sued him.[109]

In 2018, APS paid almost $40 million to beat back a clean-energy ballot initiative, Proposition 127, that called on utilities to obtain 50 percent of their energy from renewable sources by 2030. Much of that spending, as happened in Ohio, went toward "blockers," individuals hired to prevent the collection of signatures needed to place the pro-solar measure on the ballot. Also funded were "signing bonuses" of up to $7,500 for signature gatherers who quit, as well as social-media ads and robocalls alleging the remaining petition circulators were dangerous felons. Without evidence, initiative opponents also issued reports claiming the pro-solar measure would double the average Arizonan's electricity bill. That layered barrage pushed the ballot measure down to defeat.[110]

Sensing corruption, the FBI and Arizona's attorney general launched investigations into the utility's spending on commission races. According to a whistleblower, APS coordinated with the Corporation Commission's chairman, Gary Pierce, on campaigns against pro-solar candidates. Company documents show the utility supported the Arizona Free Enterprise Club, which spent $450,000 in 2014 to elect two APS allies to the commission. Other media reports showed that this Arizona Free Enterprise Club spent $733,000 to help the campaign of the chief regulator's son to be secretary of state.[111] Gary Pierce apparently saw no conflict of interest with such political contributions; he refused to recuse himself from votes that imposed new fees on rooftop solar customers; and he blocked the commission's debate over deregulation, which would have stripped APS of its power-generation monopoly.[112]

Noting such subterfuge, David Pomerantz, of the watchdog Energy and Policy Institute, said it well: "APS has been pretty exceptional at how brazen they've been about trying to dominate the entire political system in Arizona."[113]

The list of power scandals, unfortunately, grows. While such corruption allows utility monopolies to profit, at least temporarily, it challenges the rule of law, enables inefficiency, and blocks innovation. It requires reform.

Chapter VII

Cut Corruption

Corruption is corrupting, as it degrades public trust in our basic institutions. "Once corruption takes hold," observed a prosecutor, "democracy itself becomes a charade."[1]

As revealed in the preceding tales of power corruption, the rise of fraud within the giant utility industry also causes severe, if often ignored, economic and environmental harm. It boosts electricity rates, raises taxes, and enables outmoded generators to spew additional pollution. To minimize such negative outcomes, we need more than revelations. We need reforms that enhance transparency and block utility racketeering.

Bribery should be seen as bad for business, in part because it blocks efficiency and innovation. Although this book recounts numerous examples of utilities obtaining big wins, at least in the short term, from their scandalous actions, fraud ultimately reduces business wealth by diverting managers from more important responsibilities. Corruption also fosters arrogance, which prompts poor decisions; Chuck Jones, who faces multiple felony charges, mistakenly assumed he could bribe his way out of his own mismanagement.

Americans rank corruption as their greatest fear, surpassing nuclear war, economic collapse, pollution, volcanic eruptions, zombies, and loved ones dying.[2] Fraud particularly frightens financiers. According to Morningstar Research Services LLC, "When investors see that executives have misled either consumers or regulators, they get nervous about what else executives might be doing to mislead investors."[3]

Utility leaders certainly have the means (state-guaranteed revenue), motive (additional profits), and opportunity (captured regulators) to lie and scheme. Although Sam Insull clearly demonstrated the potential for scandal, power monopolists don't need to cross the line to corruption because their income is assured, they produce a product everyone wants, and they face little to no competition. So why bribe and racketeer?

One motivation for corruption's modern rise could be Wall Street's fierce demand for short-term profits, pushing some executives to use unsavory means to show immediate financial gains. Another incentive could be Supreme Court actions that make it easier to hide political payments and avoid prosecutions. Yet from the scandals discussed in this book, I argue power corruption increasingly results from simple economics; having mismanaged their investments toward antiquated and uneconomic generators, more and more utility executives scheme for subsidies and frequently resort to crime.

Tradition-bound monopolies worry modern technologies will prompt retail customers to seek alternative power supply options, leaving them with declining sales and earnings.[4] Such backward-looking colossi reject the future and defend the past. It's no coincidence that on the same day in February 2024, FirstEnergy retreated from its forward-looking climate goal and a state court arraigned two of its top executives for fraudulently bailing out the outmoded.[5]

Unwilling to innovate and unable to earn money in open markets, struggling power corporations and their Wall Street investors tend to view political payments as their most effective investments. A leading financial newsletter, for instance, predicted "FirstEnergy's nuclear bailout would be a win for bondholders," the hedge funds and pooled investors that envisioned a bonanza if they could convince legislators or regulators to supply subsidies.[6]

To be clear, there's no crime in gambling on troubled companies. It happens a lot in the financial markets. After the Supreme Court's *Citizens United* decision, corporations also can legally spend vast sums secretly on elections. But utilities increasingly cross the line between aggressive electioneering and bribery, between sleazy lobbying and outright criminality, and between brass-knuckle politics and racketeering. Scandal-prone monopolies may claim that their dark-money payments are nothing more than companies "supporting policy initiatives that matter to our customers, employees, communities, and shareholders," but juries are finding such disbursements to be illegal payoffs.[7]

To also be clear, corruption could be technology and fuel agnostic. No doubt today's scandals feature utilities wanting to protect their old investments—usually coal-fired and nuclear generators—and to block modern competitors—usually wind and solar. Yet as we work to restrict power corruption during a transition from old to modern technologies, we cannot ignore—and we need to block—"clean" monopolies acting fraudulently.

Many Americans, according to surveys, express frustration—even cynicism—toward corporate lobbying and campaign financing. They complain large companies—particularly monopolies with state-guaranteed revenue—game the system with dark money and racketeering to influence elections, legislation, and regulations. A growing number feel judges and legislators have toppled ethical guardrails and made it easier for bosses to be crooked.[8]

Criticism of subsidy-seeking utilities spans economic and ideological divides. Conservative industrialists, who consume large amounts of electricity, complain about high costs and poor service from backward-looking monopolies. Liberal climate activists assert that extending the life of dirty generators causes unnecessary pollution. Taxpayers and ratepayers feel bailouts raise taxes and rates, while free marketeers protest corporate welfare.

Yet exposing scandals is hard. FBI agents and prosecutors—as well as enterprising investigative reporters—took years to untangle the webs of players and payments in Ohio, Illinois, and other states. These diligent officials slowly and painstakingly flipped suspects to become informants, wiretapped conversations of the sleazy, dug through obtuse records, and decoded the phone and message exchanges of conspirators.

Exposés do have impacts, but reform requires perseverance. It took Ohio legislators eight months after the Speaker and several lobbyists were arrested to eliminate the bailout for troubled nukes. (And even then, as noted above, they made that change only after federal regulators began to penalize power corporations selling state-subsidized electricity into wholesale markets.) Perhaps not yet sufficiently embarrassed by their scandals, Buckeye politicians still have not reversed HB 6's other provisions that underwrote dirty coal plants and overturned clean-energy programs. The Ohio Manufacturers Association estimated Ohioans by early 2024 had paid $500 million on coal bailouts and would be charged an additional $450 million by 2030.[9]

Revelations of past abuses also don't guarantee future ethical behavior. The Ohio judge overseeing Larry Householder's trial hoped the Speaker's twenty-year term would convince "lobbyists, law firms, consultants, and strategists" to stand up to legislators "receiving millions of dollars while advancing bailout legislation."[10] Yet several years after Larry's sentencing, Ohio lawmakers still have not strengthened the state's ethics or campaign-finance laws. They may have ousted Householder, but his shameful approach remains. The subsequent House Speaker, as mentioned before, voted against Larry's ouster, supported as the Republican caucus's policy director someone who worked closely with the Householder racketeering enterprise, and blocked efforts to repeal the OVEC coal subsidies. Such ongoing conduct prompted one journalist to ask about Ohio officials, "What does that tell you about their combined sense of ethics?"[11]

Utility scandals, in fact, offer cautionary insights into state legislatures, often run by part-time politicians prone to special interests wanting special treatments. As costs of election campaigns soar, bribery's temptations rise, as do examples of secret money and corrupt intent molding elections, legislation, and regulations.

Power fraud also is a wake-up call on dark money, showing how corporations secretly use vast sums to bribe and racketeer. Moreover, it demonstrates how the Supreme Court's curbing of anti-corruption tools leads to criminal malfeasance in states across the country.

How do we curb power corruption? One key is transparency.

Let's begin by shining a light on dark money. The Supreme Court's *Citizens United* decision, obviously, impacts more than electric utilities, yet the power industry's abuses should serve as leverage to reform political-contribution rules in ways that end unlimited and untraceable spending.

Anti-corruption prosecutors focus their wrath on dark money, claiming utility scandals would not have happened without it. Said one government lawyer, "The millions paid [via dark-money groups] are akin to bags of cash; unlike Political Action Committee contributions, they were not regulated, not reported, not subject to public scrutiny."[12] Another called these secretive organizations "the perfect money-laundering tool."[13] And Neil Clark brashly declared, "Let's call it what it is—pay to play"; the former Ohio lobbyist fretted that big monopolies already awash with guaranteed profits, such as electric utilities, progressively use undisclosed payments to control regulatory and legislative debates.[14]

Since the current Supreme Court is unlikely to outright overturn its pro-corporation decisions, one reform would be to distinguish utilities, which are government-sanctioned monopolies, when it comes to reporting and limiting secret spending. That argument reflects the suggestion by former Justice Anthony Scalia that state-granted monopolies should be treated differently than other corporations under campaign finance laws.[15] Another adjustment would be for state and federal regulators, who swear to oversee power-corporation finances, to require the regular disclosure of *all* utility political payments.

While most politicians may be hesitant to give up dark-money receipts, reforms would be popular. Ninety percent of Americans complain about Big Money's influence in politics, and more than three-quarters favor a constitutional amendment to overturn *Citizens United*.[16] The public also would support Congress demanding stronger disclosure and trace-back requirements, empowering the Federal Elections Commission to confront dark money's illegal coordination with candidates, enhancing the oversight powers of the Federal Energy Regulatory Commission (FERC) and the Securities and Exchange Commission, and establishing the right of voters to know who is spending money to influence their vote.

Anthony Kennedy, the retired Supreme Court associate justice who authored the majority 5-4 opinion in that 2010 *Citizens United* case, assumed unrestrained political payments would still be disclosed, allowing voters to determine who funded which candidates. In delivering the court's opinion,

Kennedy wrote that the public should "see whether elected officials are 'in the pocket' of so-called moneyed interests."[17] As evidenced by utility scandals across the country, however, neither legislators nor regulators implemented the justice's call for transparency, and Kennedy later admitted "disclosure is not working the way it should."[18]

Power-corporation bribery makes other parts of Kennedy's opinion also seem naive. The justice argued "that independent expenditures, including those made by corporations, do not give rise to corruption or the appearance of corruption.... The fact that [donors] may have influence over or access to elected officials does not mean that these officials are corrupt.... The appearance of influence or access, furthermore, will not cause the electorate to lose faith in our democracy."[19]

The four justices in the minority disagreed and insightfully warned of probable corruption by politically active corporations, unions, and other well-heeled organizations. John Paul Stevens wrote that the majority decision represented "a rejection of the common sense of the American people, who have recognized a need to prevent corporations from undermining self-government." A brief by the then–solicitor general, now Supreme Court justice Elena Kagan, predicted a "pay-to-play" government that conforms to the wishes of deep-pocketed individuals and corporations able "to afford the ante."[20]

A subsequent analysis by Public Citizen found that the Supreme Court's campaign-finance rulings "unleashed torrents of outside spending by unregulated groups . . . and led to a massive increase in anonymous political spending."[21] Election-related payments associated with just Ohio races for the US Senate soared from $45,000 in 2004, to $3.5 million in 2010, to more than $54 million in 2016, to almost $441 million in 2024.[22]

When examining politicking and corruption, most journalists have focused on how the Supreme Court's *Citizens United* ruling revolutionized campaign financing, equating corporations with people and money with speech.[23] Yet the justices did much more in other decisions to enable fraud, particularly by restricting political corruption to "quid pro quo" activities and the "direct exchange of an official act for money."[24] Limiting illegal corruption to this most extreme form of bribery made it harder to prosecute subornation. The chief justice further claimed that spending to "garner influence over or access to elected officials or political parties" wasn't necessarily graft but rather was a needed exercise of First Amendment rights. The dance of "ingratiation and access . . . are not corruption," he declared, but are "a central feature of democracy."[25]

A few years after issuing such opinions, the Supreme Court went even further, overturning a variety of bribery convictions, including of former Virginia governor Bob McDonnell and his wife, who accepted tens of thousands of dollars from a Richmond executive trying to have the state help promote a tobacco-based dietary supplement.[26] The justices also threw out corruption verdicts against two allies of New York governor Andrew Cuomo in relation to a graft-plagued economic development effort in Buffalo.[27] Donald Trump, in his first term, took up the leniency banner by pardoning thirteen public officials convicted of corruption.[28] And in its June 2024 *Snyder* decision, the Supreme Court further weakened federal anti-corruption laws by siding with the former mayor of Portage, Indiana, who had been convicted of accepting $13,000 from a trucking company weeks after it received a $1.1 million city contract; the conservative majority argued the payment was a legal "gratuity" rather than an illegal "bribe."[29]

Turning a blind eye to bribery is a relatively new phenomenon. Throughout most of the twentieth century, observed one attorney, "lawmakers criminalized the everyday palm-greasing and back-scratching of an earlier era, outlawing improper gratuities, conflicts of interest, extortion, and racketeering. They created robust campaign-finance laws, independent regulatory commissions, and comprehensive civil-service systems."[30]

Large bipartisan majorities abhor the results of the Supreme Court's recent deregulation of political money and lobbying. A 2023 survey found that the second most common word describing American policymaking was "corrupt."[31] In the twenty-five years since the Roberts court opened the political-contribution floodgates and restricted corruption cases, trust in government fell by a third, reaching a dismal 16 percent. According to one legal analyst, "The court's decisions have increased the time and complexity of corruption investigations and bred caution and uncertainty among prosecutors, who worry that even in cases that seem clear-cut, a conviction is no longer guaranteed to survive judicial scrutiny."[32]

A few states responded to power scandals by pushing back on the high court's removal of restrictions. Illinois, as noted above, approved the Climate and Equitable Jobs Act that creates an independent ethics committee. Arizonans in November 2022 approved a ballot measure, with over 70 percent approval, requiring public disclosure of big-dollar payments to dark-money political groups trying to influence state and local campaigns.[33]

While this book argues for reinstating and enhancing anti-corruption provisions, the Supreme Court could do the opposite and continue, or even increase, its march toward scandal. Some court observers fear the current justices could find schemes like Larry Householder's to be legal, while others worry a president could undercut justice by pardoning more convicts. Kate Shaw, a professor at the University of Pennsylvania, commented, "The court seems to be inching toward the idea that this kind of corrupt conduct is actually constitutionally privileged."[34] The guilty executives in the Commonwealth Edison case, in fact, had their sentencings postponed, hoping the high court would further constrict the definition of corruption.

We also need to shine a very bright light on each utility's political expenditures, requiring mandatory and regular disclosures. The definition of political spending must be fulsome and include payments to outside consultants, dues to pro-utility associations, political action committee and dark-money contributions, and salaries and expenses for utility staff working to advance legislation and regulations. Political spending also should include the contributions power corporations give to charities in exchange for their supportive testimony, as well as for utility "goodwill" advertising intended to improve a company's image. Since regulated businesses enjoy monopoly control over their service territories, rather than advertise to compete for customers, they "seek to improve their reputation in ways that increase their political standing, leading to regulatory outcomes that grow profits."[35]

All such political expenditures, moreover, must be borne by shareholders, not ratepayers. The reasoning is straightforward: Why should a government-sanctioned monopoly charge its customers for high-priced lobbyists and election payments to obtain expensive bailouts and higher rates that harm those very customers? Posed another way, why should powerful utilities block an individual's freedom and force consumers to cover political persuasion campaigns they disagree with?

The Energy and Policy Institute described the current practice well: "Unlike other companies, regulated monopoly utilities can force customers to fund their political expenditures through the rate-collection process, effectively turning them into a conscripted army of millions of small-dollar donors. That provides an almost limitless open spigot of money that pours first into utility accounts, and then into our politics." Instead, requiring monopolies to charge investors for their politicking would "force utilities to at least choose between spending their profits on political advocacy and delivering it to shareholders in the form of dividends."[36]

Multistate holding companies also should no longer shield their political expenditures from single-state regulators. Part of the FirstEnergy scandal, for example, was that the holding company quietly charged its subsidiaries' customers across multiple states to fund its Ohio-based bribery campaign.[37]

FERC and several states claim to oppose the allocation of political expenses to consumers, yet their regulations are riddled with loopholes. A utility's ratepayers, rather than its investors or shareholders, regularly get charged for the monopoly's political activities and subsidy seeking.

In 2022, utility commissions in fourteen states encouraged FERC to tighten its accounting requirements to ensure utilities do not charge consumers for lobbying expenses. That request focused on trade association dues, a large portion of which is devoted to influencing government officials. Estimates of those payments vary, but some analysts suggest utilities annually spend almost $100 million on such fees.[38]

In 2023, Connecticut, Maine, and Colorado passed legislation prohibiting power corporations from charging their customers for efforts to sway political outcomes. Banned are consumer payments to dark-money organizations, trade associations, lobbyists, and public relations specialists. These utility-accountability laws do not prohibit such actions, but they require power monopolies to use monies from shareholders rather than ratepayers and to file annual and detailed reports on their political-influence spending.[39]

Beyond stemming the growing flood of secret political payments and protecting consumers from being charged for utility lobbying, how can we block power corruption? How can we erode the political power of fraudulent monopolies? Since there's no silver bullet, allow me to offer several, admittedly diverse, measures designed to reduce racketeering:

- Impose real penalties on corrupt executives, corporations, politicians, and regulators. Since those found guilty of utility crimes have tended to be shameless and to express limited, if any, remorse, their colleagues will think twice about corrupt actions only if the fraudsters face strict jail time, and not in country club prisons. Individuals who break the law and the public trust can't be excused because they were rich, traveled on corporate jets, or soaked up genuflections from political supplicants. Penalties for guilty corporations, moreover, need to sting.
- Provide rigor and transparency to the selection of regulators. When governors do the picking, as happens in Ohio, make sure the nominating committee does not include former utility executives or lobbyists; also require regulated utilities to disclose all payments to the governor and recommended candidates. When hopeful commissioners face elections, as happens in Arizona, voters should have the right to know who power corporations are underwriting to be their overseers.
- Tighten recusal standards for utility regulators, far too many of whom have become shills for power monopolies. Noting FirstEnergy's bribe, for example, Sam Randazzo should have been forced, at the least, to abstain from cases impacting the giant utility. In fact, regulators should have no associations with the regulated; being more specific, if you lobbied, worked, or consulted for—as well as obtained contributions from—a utility, you cannot be an independent commissioner.
- Refund, with full interest and stiff penalties, all revenue found to be illegally obtained. When utilities keep funds that courts rule their collection to be unlawful, they're incentivized to turn toward bribery and racketeering, knowing their questionable receipts cannot be fully clawed back. Public

utility commissions and FERC should utilize their statutory authorities to fine rule-breaking power companies.
- Block kickbacks, such as those Sam Randazzo negotiated between well-connected industrials and utilities. Also prohibit "riders," the flow-through mechanisms used by power corporations to obtain additional revenue without full regulatory reviews. Further, require commissioners to conduct regular and comprehensive rate cases in which they fully audit and reveal a utility's finances.
- Reinstate anti-corruption provisions the Supreme Court eliminated or weakened. Recognize that corruption extends beyond pay-to-play schemes.
- Enhance ethics compliance. The blocking of bailouts needs to be accompanied by anti-corruption measures that prevent future fraud. As an example, the Illinois scandal prompted the creation of an independent ethics monitor, increased public participation in setting a utility monopoly's goals, and accelerated transparency of power-corporation spending.[40]
- Restrict gerrymandering. The rigging of district maps to guarantee partisan supermajorities curtails checks and balances, and it enables the growing corruption infecting state governments. One Ohio legislator commented, "With deeply gerrymandered districts, Republican politicians feel invincible and are more beholden to special interest groups and corporations than they are to their own constituents." HB 6 was a manifestation of this lack of accountability.[41]
- Have utilities earn profits based on their actual performance rather than their gross investments. While power monopolies crave guaranteed revenues, their incomes should be tied to measurable standards, such as increased efficiency, enhanced reliability, reduced pollution, improved customer service, or economic development in distressed communities.
- Rather than subsidize, move poorly performing utilities into bankruptcy and ensure failing executives feel the consequences of their mismanagement. Block utilities from using insolvency to avoid the impacts of their malfeasance, such as when FirstEnergy tried to unload its coal-ash and nuclear-waste responsibilities.
- Restore provisions of the Public Utility Holding Company Act to better regulate monopolies controlling multistate subsidiaries. Increase coordination among federal and state regulators to ensure multistate utilities don't escape oversight.
- Don't let the big fish swim away. The *Orlando Sentinel*, which investigated Florida Power & Light, appropriately complained that "the penny ante players" often pay the prosecutorial price, "not the people at the top—the elected officials or powerful interests who were making all this happen." No doubt Ohio and Illinois prosecutors caught some big fish, but climbing the food chain is both hard and needed.[42]

- Frame subsidies for what they are—corruption-based tax increases. In fact, they're regressive charges that hit hardest at moderate- and low-income consumers who, too frequently, can't afford the bailout's higher costs and face electricity disconnections.
- Protect whistleblowers who report corruption and misrepresentations. Insider information often is needed to identify fraud and bribery.
- Broadcast corruption trials. Revelatory audio and video recordings would increase public pressure for both justice and reform.
- Make part-time state legislators, who often need other employment or funds to make ends meet, less vulnerable to bribes. Such jobs, for instance, could become full-time, and financial-disclosure requirements should be made stricter.
- Level the legal field and support independent watchdogs. Deep-pocketed monopolies should not enjoy hordes of highly paid regulatory lawyers and consultants while citizen and consumer advocates endure limited budgets. At a minimum, as recommended above, shareholders, not ratepayers, should cover the costs of utility attorneys and "expert" witnesses.
- Don't pick technologies. Power monopolies, despite claiming to support free markets, seek bailouts for their preferred projects, mostly coal and nuclear units. Those subsidies distort markets and make it hard for emerging entrepreneurs to compete.
- Support independent and investigative reporting. Power corruption often gets revealed by persistent journalists willing and able to follow leads, ask tough questions, and withstand pressure from well-heeled utilities and their public-relation hacks. Expose news outlets controlled by power monopolies.
- Enforce antitrust rules on power utilities that dominate markets and block competitors. Like that focused on tech and labor markets, aggressive antitrust enforcement is needed on what conservative scholars call "the country's most entrenched monopolies: public utilities that control access to our nation's electric grid."[43]
- Enhance competitive markets. Regulators and legislators can enable innovators by removing barriers to their development. In Ohio, for instance, Randazzo's discriminatory restrictions on the siting of wind turbines should be overturned. Power corporations, moreover, should not swallow up now-competitive businesses, such as electric vehicle charging stations. Put simply, to enhance efficiency and modernization, monopolies should shrink rather than expand.

Although revelations of utility scandals open the door for such reforms, none will be achieved easily, largely because today's monopolies still hold substantial resources to protect their status quo. Change gets even harder as electricity policy becomes debated on a cultural battlefield. Consider, for instance, how proponents of coal burning rally fervently to oppose financial trends and preserve a way of life.

Cultural warriors often put their politics above their pocketbooks. When a private-power corporation in West Virginia, for instance, wanted to close an outmoded coal-fired generator, state commissioners—who have included the coal association's former president, a FirstEnergy lobbyist, and a politician pledged to end what she perceived as a "war on coal"—approved a subsidy that would have the state's consumers pay $3 million a month to keep the aged plant burning three million tons of coal annually. Republican governor Jim Justice, whose family fortune comes from mining the black rock, weighed in by holding up a lump and proclaiming, "I owe my life to this right here."[44]

Corruption charges, moreover, can prompt partisan backlash. In May 2023, the US Department of Justice cited Jim Justice's son and his coal companies with 130 environmental violations and sought $5 million in civil penalties. Repeating a theme from the presidential campaign, the National Republican Senatorial Committee, noting Governor Justice was running for a Senate seat, accused Democrats of "weaponizing the federal government . . . [and] a complete abuse of power."[45]

Utilities caught being corrupt often deliver cleverly crafted claims of reform. After a jury found senior executives guilty of bribery, for instance, Exelon's chairman asserted the utility had "taken robust action to aggressively identify and address deficiencies, including enhancing our compliance governance and our lobbying policies to prevent this type of misconduct from ever happening again."[46]

Power corporations also tend to ignore corruption's breadth and suggest their racketeering results solely from a few bad apples. Again, an Exelon spokesman blamed "a small number of senior ComEd employees and outside contractors [for] orchestrating this misconduct, and they no longer work for the company."[47]

Many utility "corrections," moreover, are toothless and short-lived. In Ohio, a supposedly "transparent" FirstEnergy rejected a shareholder resolution calling for the disclosure of its direct and indirect political expenses. At Arizona Public Service (APS), a new CEO committed to stop electioneering payments that support the utility's preferred regulators, but, as public attention shifted, an investor group quietly claimed APS's "First Amendment right" to participate secretly and extensively in elections, referendums, and policy debates.[48]

Electricity monopolies have long enjoyed significant resources, largely because they receive government-guaranteed profits from consumers who have little choice from where to buy their electricity. Since utilities recognize their fortunes are tied to decisions by commissioners, they have consistently tried to influence them and control the flow of information, what Nobel Prize–winning economist George Stigler called "regulatory capture."[49]

Yet a rising number of power corporations want more. Rather than just obtain assured returns on their investments, they seek bailouts for their bad business decisions and investments in now-outmoded technologies. To obtain such subsidies, they're often crossing the line into corruption, with the results being reduced trust in public and private institutions, higher costs, blocked innovation, and more unnecessary pollution. Since fraud-obtained subsidies are won by the powerful overcoming the popular, it can be said that utility corruption pollutes democracy.

Scandals spread as electricity economics evolves. Since the days of Sam Insull, power companies have profited by earning returns on their investments in ever larger and more expensive generators, yet today's old-technology units—mainly nuclear reactors and coal-fired plants—have trouble competing in open markets as well as ramping up and down in response to fluctuating electricity demand. Those outmoded generators face new competition from remarkable recent advances—including, as mentioned in the first chapter, sensors, smart meters, controls, smaller-scale generators, advanced turbines, microgrids, and battery storage—that offer lower-cost power as well as increased reliability. Some of these innovations enable entrepreneurs, and even individuals, to produce and manage their own power and circumvent electricity monopolies.

It's a rare utility representative who admits this obvious, but usually unspoken, truth about modern technologies. In September 2023, however, a consultant for APS confessed "that one of the dangers to utility shareholders from the increasing growth of the prosumer [consumers using technological improvements to control their own electricity use] is that the investments made by the prosumers with their own money may supplant investments that the utility may otherwise have been able to make and earn a return on, for the benefit of their shareholders."[50] To avoid such a fate, monopolists increasingly try to block prosumers, more and more with corruption.

Shelves of studies debate the outline of our energy future. I don't pretend to predict what technologies and companies will emerge and thrive, but I do hope to have convincingly suggested that a shift to modernization requires transparency and legality. Said another way, since today's growing power corruption provides economic lifelines to outmoded generators, blocking fraud opens the door to energy advances.

Efficient and modern technologies thrive in fair markets, while outdated and dirty power plants rely on bailouts. Utility monopolies increasingly bribe public officials to subsidize those uneconomic units, and they resort to racketeering to block competition. Good government and energy innovation have become linked.

Notes

CHAPTER I

1. Marty Schladen, "Swanky D.C. Dinners between FirstEnergy Execs and Householder Led to Corrupt Scheme," *Ohio Capital Journal*, January 24, 2023.
2. "Deferred Prosecution Agreement," *United States of America v. FirstEnergy Corp.* (S.D. Ohio, Western Division, July 20, 2021).
3. Federal prosecutors charged that FirstEnergy paid some $60 million, and other entities added approximately $4 million, to secure and protect a $1.3-billion bailout.
4. Jessie Balmert, "Columbus Lobbyist Neil Clark, Accused in HB 6 scandal, Died by Suicide, Autopsy Confirms," *The* [Cincinnati] *Enquirer*, June 8, 2021.
5. "Deferred Prosecution Agreement," *FirstEnergy Corp.*
6. Ryan Randazzo, "APS Acknowledges Spending Millions to Elect Corporation Commission Members, after Years of Questions," *The Republic*, March 29, 2019.
7. Mario Alejandro Ariza, "Florida GOP Operative Admits Role in 'Ghost' Candidate Scheme That Defeated Utility-Targeted Dem," *Floodlight*, April 12, 2024.
8. John F. Wasik, *The Merchant of Power* (New York: St. Martin's Press, 2006).
9. Richard Munson, *From Edison to Enron* (Westport, CT: Praeger Publishers, 2005).
10. Samuel Insull, "The Obligations of Monopoly Must Be Accepted," speech on January 7, 1910, at a dinner at the Congress Hotel, Chicago.
11. Richard F. Hirsh, *Power Loss* (Cambridge: Massachusetts Institute of Technology, 1999).
12. Hon. Richard D. Cudahy and William D. Henderson, "From Insull to Enron: Corporate (Re)Regulation After the Rise and Fall of Two Energy Icons," *Energy Law Journal*, Vol 26:35; 2005.
13. "Rich Men and Corrupt Politics," *New York Times*, March 6, 1927.
14. M. L. Ramsey, *Pyramids of Power: The Story of Roosevelt, Insull, and the Utility Wars* (New York: Bobbs-Merrill, 1937).

15. T. J. Brennan et al., *A Shock to the System: Restructuring America's Electricity Industry* (Washington, DC: Resources for the Future, July 1996).

16. Burton Berry, "Mr. Samuel Insull," Insull Collection at Loyola University Chicago (unpublished but copyrighted in 1962 by Samuel Insull Jr.).

CHAPTER II

1. "Utilities," *Last Week Tonight with John Oliver*, HBO, May 16, 2022.

2. Jake Zuckerman, "FirstEnergy Asks Its Fired Former CEO to Return the $56 Million It Paid Him," *Ohio Capital Journal*, July 28, 2022.

3. US Department of Justice, "FirstEnergy Nuclear Operating Company to Pay $28 Million Relating to Operation of Davis-Besse Nuclear Power Station," press release, January 20, 2006.

4. J. E. Dyer, Nuclear Regulatory Commission regional administrator, to Howard Bergendahl, vice president–nuclear at FirstEnergy Nuclear Operating Company, May 3, 2002.

5. NRC statement in letter from Union of Concerned Scientists to John Grobe, chairman of Davis-Besse 0350 Panel, July 3, 2002.

6. US-Canada Power System Outage Task Force, "Final Report on the August 14, 2003, Blackout in the United States and Canada," April 2004.

7. FirstEnergy, "FirstEnergy to Sell Competitive Natural Gas and Hydro Assets to LS Power Equity Partners," press release, January 19, 2017.

8. Testimony of Steven Staub, January 24, 2023.

9. Ohio Senate, Testimony by Anthony J. Alexander, October 4, 2007.

10. David Roberts, "This Ohio Utility Has an Innovative Plan to Save Coal Power: Force Customers to Buy It," *Vox*, September 3, 2015.

11. Kathiann Kowalski, "Why Attention to Detail Matters in the Government's HB 6 Corruption Trial," Energy News Network, February 6, 2023.

12. Tom Sanzillo and Cathy Kunkel, "FirstEnergy: A Major Utility Seeks a Subsidized Turnaround," Institute for Energy Economics and Financial Analysis, October 2014.

13. Testimony of Steven Staub, FirstEnergy's vice president and treasurer, January 24, 2023.

14. Marty Schladen, "Swanky D.C. Dinners between FirstEnergy Execs and Householder Led to Corrupt Scheme, Prosecutors Say," *Ohio Capital Journal*, January 24, 2023.

15. Tom Knox, "Dynegy CEO: Re-Regulation in Ohio Would Help 'the Weakest in the Herd,'" *Columbus Business First*, August 7, 2015.

16. Carl Surran, "FirstEnergy Appears to Have Few Friends in Bailout Bid," *Seeking Alpha*, April 9, 2018.

17. FirstEnergy investment call with analysts, *Q4 2014 FirstEnergy FactBook*, February 17, 2015.

18. "Deferred Prosecution Agreement," *United States of America vs. FirstEnergy Corp.* (S.D. Ohio, Western Division, July 20, 2021).

19. Moody's, "FirstEnergy Generation, LLC—Moody's Downgrades FirstEnergy Solutions' Probability of Default Rating to D-PD following Bankruptcy Filing; Will Withdraw Ratings," April 3, 2018.

20. Laura A. Bischoff and Jessie Balmert, "'A Giant Lobbying Firm That Runs a Utility': FirstEnergy's Involvement in Ohio Politics Dates Back Decades," *Columbus Dispatch*, October 31, 2021.

21. Julie M. McKinnon, "Consumers' Counsel Quits amid Criticism," *The Blade*, November 6, 2003.

22. Testimony of Maureen Willis, agency director, OCC, before the Ohio Senate Energy and Public Utilities Committee, January 23, 2024.

23. John Finnigan, "Utility Nepotism: FirstEnergy Shops for Rates from Sister Company, Leaves Customers with the Bill," *LinkedIn* (blog), September 9, 2015.

24. *FirstEnergy Service Company v. PJM Interconnection, LLC*, complaint filed before the US Federal Energy Regulatory Commission, Docket no. EL14-55-000, May 23, 2014.

25. Dan Haugen, "FirstEnergy Wants to Put the Brakes on Ohio's Efficiency Mandate," Energy News Network, November 21, 2012.

26. Julia Pyper, "Gov. Kasich Vetoes Continued Freeze on Ohio Clean Energy Mandates," gtm [Greentech Media], December 27, 2016.

27. Rob Kelter, "Environmental Lawyer: Ohio Is Overlooking Energy Efficiency," *The Blade*, May 7, 2024.

28. As will be discussed in subsequent chapters, Sam Randazzo had run an industrial energy–users association that opposed Ohio's energy efficiency and renewable energy standards. A federal grand jury would charge Randazzo with embezzling funds from that organization.

29. John Funk, "Ohio Wind Law Crippling Wind Development, $4.2 Billion Boost to Ohio Economy," cleveland.com, May 24, 2017.

30. Jeff St. John, "PJM Says It Doesn't Need FirstEnergy's Nuclear Plants for Grid Reliability," gtm, April 30, 2018.

31. Robert Walton, "Dynegy Offers Natural Gas Alternative to FirstEnergy, AEP Plant Subsidy Proposals," *Utility Dive*, January 13, 2016.

32. Dick Munson, "Rubber-Stamp Regulators: Ohio Gives FirstEnergy Another Go-Ahead," *Energy Exchange*, May 11, 2016.

33. John Finnigan, "Ohio Failed to Protect Customers and Markets—So Federal Regulators Came to the Rescue," *Energy Exchange*, May 2, 2016.

34. Kathiann M. Kowalski, "Advocates Weigh In with Federal Regulators on FirstEnergy Plan," Energy News Network, June 24, 2016.

35. Ibid.

36. John Funk, "FirstEnergy Customers Would Pay Equivalent of Extra Monthly Electric Bill for Up to Eight Years," cleveland.com, June 23, 2016.

37. Kathiann M. Kowalski, "Timeline: FirstEnergy Bet on Coal, Nuclear and 'Bailouts,'" Energy News Network, April 23, 2018.

38. Kathiann M. Kowalski, "FirstEnergy 'Bailout' Raises Questions of Corporate Separation," Energy News Network, October 18, 2015.

39. Staff Writer, "FirstEnergy Keeps Raking in the Money," *Columbus Dispatch*, May 28, 2017.

40. Public Utilities Commission of Ohio, "Fifth Entry on Rehearing" (Approval of Distribution Modernization Rider in the FirstEnergy Electric Security Plan), case no. 14-1297-El-SSO, October 12, 2016.

41. Ibid. See also Ohio Public Utilities Commission, "PUCO Adopts Agreement on FirstEnergy Tax/Grid Modernization," press statement, July 17, 2019.

42. Gavin Bade, "Re-Regulation on the Horizon? State Plant Subsidies Point to Looming 'Crisis' in Organized Power Markets," *Utility Dive*, October 20, 2016.

43. Asim Hague text to Michael Dowling, June 19, 2019. See also Kathiann Kowalski, "Former PUCO Chair Texted He Knew FirstEnergy Charge Was Likely Unlawful, but Company Would Keep Money Anyway," Energy News Network, May 20, 2022.

44. Asim Hague to Michael Dowling, June 19, 2019. See also reporting by Kowalski, "Former PUCO Chair Texted He Knew."

45. FERC Letter to FirstEnergy Corporation approving the final audit report covering the period January 1, 2015, to September 30, 2021, under Docket No. FA19-1-000.

46. Kathiann M. Kowalski, "Utility and Fossil Fuel Influence in Ohio Goes Beyond Passage of Bailout," *Eye on Ohio*, n.d.

47. Kathiann M. Kowalski, "New Ohio 'Bailout' Request Shakes Up Nuclear/Carbon Debate," Energy News Network, March 2, 2017.

48. Tom Knox, "Cooper Tire CEO: Power Proposals 'a Political Gift' to AEP and FirstEnergy," *Columbus Business First*, January 19, 2016.

49. Chuck Jones (guest columnist), "FirstEnergy's 'Powering Ohio's Progress' Rate Plan Is about Preserving Vital Power Plants for Ohio Customers," cleveland.com, August 2, 2015.

50. St. John, "PJM Says It Doesn't Need FirstEnergy's Nuclear Plants."

51. Cathy Kunkel, "FirstEnergy Witness Does to Ohioans What He Did to West Virginians," Institute for Energy Economics and Financial Analysis, September 16, 2015.

52. Kowalski, "Utility and Fossil Fuel Influence in Ohio."

53. Earthjustice Press Room, "Federal Energy Regulatory Commission Denies FirstEnergy's Request to Transfer Pleasants Plant Ownership," January 13, 2018.

54. Document prepared by FirstEnergy's lawyers for the deposition of company vice president of strategy Joseph Storsin in a civil lawsuit filed by FirstEnergy shareholders. (Exhibit JD 0046 in FE_CIV_SEC_0730350). Reported by Jeffrey Tomich, "FirstEnergy Utility Gave to Pro-Trump Dark Money Group," *E&E News by Politico*, March 29, 2022.

55. Donald Shaw, "Trump's Top Bundler Pleaded the Fifth in Ohio Bribery Case," *Sludge*, July 23, 2024.

56. "Deferred Prosecution Agreement," *FirstEnergy Corp.*, 23. Chuck Jones's text message, at 6:50 p.m., continued, "I mentioned memo (to the president) and he said, 'I'm well aware of the memo. It's coming, We're on it.' . . . Told POTUS Ohio loves him, and he could be a big help. Then Secret Service dragged me out by both arms."

57. Debunking Lewandowski's denial was an email from Michael Rubino (a Trump campaign veteran who worked with Lewandowski) to Michael Dowling (FirstEnergy VP) on June 22, 2017, with subject: "Contract for Lewandowski Strategic Advisors," which the subsequent note said was attached, along with an invoice. See also Eric Wolff, Josh Dawsey, Ben White, and Daniel Lippman, "Lewandowski Pressed Trump on Aid to Coal Industry," *Politico*, August 25, 2017. Additionally, the document prepared by FirstEnergy's lawyers for the deposition of company vice president of strategy Joseph Storsin asserts, "Through its engagement with Avenue Strategies LLC, FirstEnergy hired Corey Lewandowski, a close advisor to then-President Trump, to further the federal solution effort."

58. Michael Dowling email, quoting Lewandowski, to Charles Jones. Subject: DOE Team, May 2, 2017.

59. Neil S. Clark, *What Do I Know? I'm Just a Lobbyist* (48 Hour Books, 2021).

60. FirstEnergy Newsroom, "FirstEnergy Announces 2018 Financial Results," February 19, 2019.

61. FirstEnergy Investor Relations, "FirstEnergy Announces Transformational $2.5 Billion Equity Investment," January 22, 2018.

62. Gavin Bade, "Perry: Economics Not 'the Issue' for FirstEnergy Emergency Evaluation," *Utility Dive*, April 9, 2018.

63. Dave Anderson, "FOIAs Reveal FirstEnergy Meeting with Rick Perry, 30+ Corporate Jet Flights to D.C. since Trump's Inauguration," Energy and Policy Institute, June 8, 2018.

64. Josh Siegel, "Coal Plant Operator Unaware of Possible Trump Move to Keep Plants Open," *Washington Examiner*, February 9, 2018.

65. Brady Dennis and Juliet Eilperin, "Trump Administration Rolls Back Obama-Era Rule Aimed at Limiting Toxic Wastewater from Coal Plants," *Washington Post*, August 31, 2020.

66. "Obscure Coal CEO Rains Money on Trump," *St. Louis Post-Dispatch*, July 22, 2017.

67. Darren Sweeney, "FERC Decision Seen as More Detrimental to FirstEnergy than AEP," *S&P Global*, April 29, 2016.

68. Timothy Cama, "Lewandowski Slams 'Deep State' Regulators for Rejecting Perry Coal Plan," *The Hill*, January 9, 2018.

69. Quote by Rep. Joe Barton (R-TX). See Darrell Proctor, "FERC: There Is No Grid Emergency," *Power*, June 13, 2018.

70. Scott DiSavino and Valerie Volcovici, "FirstEnergy Seeks Emergency Lifeline for U.S. Nuclear, Coal Plants," Reuters, March 29, 2018.

71. Dick Munson, "FirstEnergy's 202(c) Request Is a Bigger Deal Than You Think," *pv magazine*, April 26, 2018.

72. Coming out of bankruptcy in July 2020, FirstEnergy Solutions became Energy Harbor, an independent company that owned numerous generators and sold power into wholesale markets. FirstEnergy itself focused on the transmission and distribution of electricity, both of which were regulated monopolies; it continued to own two coal-fired power plants in West Viriginia. With its stock price low, FirstEnergy obtained investments from Carl Icahn, a billionaire activist investor and

corporate raider, and Blackstone, both of which obtained seats on FirstEnergy's board of directors.

73. Statement by Howard A. Learner, executive director, Environmental Law & Policy Center, "ELPC Statement on FirstEnergy Solutions Bankruptcy," April 1, 2018. See also Kathiann M. Kowalski, "Coal, Nuclear Cleanup Costs Central to FirstEnergy's Rejected Bankruptcy Plan," Energy News Network, April 11, 2019.

74. FirstEnergy Form 10-K to the US Securities and Exchange Commission, for fiscal year ended December 31, 2021.

75. US Bankruptcy Court, Northern District of Ohio, Eastern Division, in re: FirstEnergy Solutions Corp., et al., "Notice of Resignation and Termination of Audit and Accounting Services," case no. 18-50757, October 2, 2019.

76. FirstEnergy Solutions Corp. et al., Debtors, case no. 18-560757, August 29, 2019, Alan M. Koschik, US bankruptcy judge.

77. Patrick Fitzgerald, "FirstEnergy Solutions Exits Bankruptcy as Energy Harbor," *Wall Street Journal*, February 27, 2020.

78. Laura Bischoff and Jessie Balmert, "House Bill 6 Corruption Case: Who Is John Kiani?" *Columbus Dispatch,* February 14, 2023.

79. PR Newswire, "FirstEnergy Solutions Successfully Completes Financial Restructuring, Emerges as Energy Harbor," February 27, 2020.

80. Testimony of Steven Staub, January 24, 2023.

81. Statement of Abid Qureshi, a partner at the law firm Akin, made before bankruptcy judge Koschik during a court hearing on October 21, 2021.

82. Dave Anderson, "Who Knew about Bribes Paid during FirstEnergy Solutions' Bankruptcy and House Bill 6 Bailout Campaign?" Energy and Policy Institute, November 16, 2021.

83. Statement by Stephen Burnazian as testified by Juan Cespedes. Reported by Jake Zuckerman, "Nuclear Exec Would Have Made $100 Million from Sale of Plants at Heart of Bribery Trial, Lobbyist Says," cleveland.com, February 16, 2023.

84. Laura Bischoff and Jessie Balmert, "Householder Trial: Jurors Dropped into World of Dark Money, Energy, High-Stake Politics," *Columbus Dispatch*, January 30, 2023.

85. Jeremy Pelzer, "Cleveland Businessman Tony George Was Go-Between for FirstEnergy, Ex-House Speaker Larry Householder over Nuclear Bailout," cleveland.com, August 24, 2022. See also "Joint Motion to Amend Interlocutory Appeal by Adding the Attached Deposition Transcripts of FirstEnergy Assistant Controller Tracy Ashton," before the Public Utilities Commission of Ohio, August 19, 2022; Ashton here revealed that George was identified as "Individual B" in "Deferred Prosecution Agreement," *FirstEnergy Corp.*

86. Schladen, "Swanky D.C. Dinners."

87. Jessie Balmert and Laura A. Bischoff, "Householder Never Repaid Political Consultant for Florida Home Repairs, Legal Bill," *Columbus Dispatch*, February 22, 2023. See also Jake Zuckerman, "Who Paid the Bribes? Plot Hole Grows after Householder Conviction, as FirstEnergy Execs Remain Unscathed," cleveland.com, March 12, 2023.

88. Householder-Borges trial transcript R.217, tr.7641-42.

89. IRS Form 990 for Partners for Progress, Inc., for tax year 2017. Daniel M. McCarthy was listed as the group's principal officer. FirstEnergy would provide all of Partners for Progress's resources, as well as 95 percent of Generation Now's funding—almost $61 million of the group's $64 million—with the rest coming from labor unions representing workers at the reactors, American Electric Power, and coal producers.

90. The "Deferred Prosecution Agreement" states, "Although Partners for Progress appeared to be an independent 501(c)(4) on paper, in reality, it was controlled in part by FirstEnergy Corp. executives, who funded it and directed its payments to entities associated with public officials." . . . "FirstEnergy Corp. exclusively funded Partners for Progress through payments from FirstEnergy Service, which totaled approximately $25 million between 2017 and 2019, approximately $15 million of which was wired to Generation Now. FirstEnergy Corp. executives directed Partners for Progress to make payments in 2018, 2019, and 2020, including payments to Generation Now, which helped conceal FirstEnergy Corp. as the source of the payments from the public." *FirstEnergy Corp.*

91. "Brief for Plaintiff-Appellee United States," *United States of America v. Matthew Borges* (US Court of Appeals for the Sixth Circuit, May 23, 2024).

92. Testimony by Juan Cespedes on February 13, 2023, about October 10, 2018, meeting.

93. Testimony by Juan Cespedes, February 13, 2023.

94. Andrew Tobias and Jake Zuckerman, "How an FBI Agent Says Householder, Conspirators Personally Enriched Themselves in Corruption Scheme," cleveland.com, February 9, 2023.

95. Quote attributed to Jeff Longstreth, Householder's top political aide. Reported by Jake Zuckerman, "Ousted FirstEnergy CEO Chuck Jones Again Asserts His Innocence, after Householder Guilty Verdict," cleveland.com, March 11, 2023.

96. Laura Bischoff, "FirstEnergy Pumped $1M into Backing DeWine, Records Show," *Dayton Daily News*, March 5, 2021.

97. Charles Jones to Samuel Randazzo, December 2018. Reported by Jeremy Pelzer, "Texts Shed Additional Light on How Sam Randazzo Was Named PUCO Chair, Worked to Help FirstEnergy," cleveland.com, August 22, 2022.

98. Jessie Balmert and Laura A. Bischoff, "Unanswered Questions: How Ohio's Top Utility Regulator Got Caught Up in Pay-to-Play Scandal," *Cincinnati Enquirer*, April 16, 2024.

99. The State of Ohio, Summit County, "Draft Indictment for: Engaging in a Pattern of Corrupt Activity with Specifications . . . ;" February 9, 2024. See also "Bill of Particulars," *State of Ohio v. Samuel C. Randazzo et al.* (February 24, 2024).

100. FirstEnergy initially tried to suggest the $4.3 million was simply the balance due from Randazzo's previous contracts, but FirstEnergy's "Deferred Prosecution Agreement" admits, "FirstEnergy Corp. paid $4.3 million dollars to Public Official B [Sam Randazzo] through his consulting company in return for [Randazzo] performing official action in his capacity as PUCO Chairman to further FirstEnergy Corp.'s interests relating to passage of nuclear legislation and other specific FirstEnergy Corp. legislative and regulatory priorities, as requested and as opportunities arose." *FirstEnergy Corp.*, 24.

101. Charles Jones to Samuel Randazzo, December 19, 2018.
102. Marty Schladen, "Ohio Gov. Mike DeWine Stands behind Aide While She Stays Mum about Bribery Scandal," *Ohio Capital Journal*, March 11, 2024.
103. "Bill of Particulars," *State of Ohio*.
104. Text messages between Chuck Jones and Sam Randazzo, December 19, 2018. See also FirstEnergy's "Deferred Settlement Agreement," 43.
105. Ohio Public Utilities Commission, "Commissioner Appointment Process," https://puco.ohio.gov/about-us/resources/commissioner-appointment-process.
106. Untitled and undated document, beginning, "Publicly available documents suggest that PUCO applicant Sam Randazzo has opaque, undisclosed financial ties to FirstEnergy that should be fully examined and made public." Uploaded in 2019 by Westlaw, associated with Thomson Reuters. That statement contradicts DeWine's later claim that Randazzo's ties to FirstEnergy were well known before the governor nominated Sam.
107. Jake Zuckerman, "Former DeWine Aide Warned Governor about Utility Regulator before the FBI Raided His Home," *Ohio Capital Journal*, April 4, 2022.
108. Kathiann M. Kowalski, "Ohio Clean Energy Groups Will Seek Recusals from PUCO Nominee," Energy News Network, February 13, 2019.
109. Zuckerman, "Former DeWine Aide Warned Governor"; Jake Zuckerman, "FirstEnergy Paid $4.3 Mil to Top Energy Regulators and Reaped the Benefits, Court Docs State," *Ohio Capital Journal*, July 23, 2021.
110. Chuck Jones text to Michael Dowling, January 30, 2019.
111. Michael Dowling text to Chuck Jones, January 30, 2019.
112. Chuck Jones message to Michael Dowling, January 31, 2019, 12:35 p.m.
113. Michael Dowling message to Chuck Jones, January 31, 2019, 12:33 p.m.
114. Ibid.
115. Jake Zuckerman, "Before Appointing Now-Indicted Sam Randazzo, Gov. DeWine Was Warned. Twice," cleveland.com, December 4, 2023.
116. John Funk, "How a Longtime Critic of Clean Energy Became Ohio's Top Utility Regulator," Energy News Network, March 9, 2020.

CHAPTER III

1. John Funk, "FirstEnergy to Seek 'Zero Emission Credits' for Its 2 Ohio Nukes," cleveland.com, February 21, 2017.
2. Lobbyist Neil Clark suggested it was Housholder, without talking to the team of consultants, who "buckled" to AEP and Duke by adding coal subsidies to the subsidy bill.
3. Larry Pearl, "FirstEnergy Nears Proposal to Decouple Ohio Utility Revenues, Electricity Consumption: CEO," *Utility Dive*, November 5, 2019; Jeffrey Tomich, "FirstEnergy Could Reap $355M from Scandal-Plagued Law," *E&E News*, October 1, 2020.
4. Ohio Common Cause prepared a timeline of the HB 6 scandal. "'A Cycle of Corruption': A Timeline of the Householder/HB6 Scandal" can be found at

https://www.commoncause.org/ohio/resource/a-cycle-of-corruption-a-timeline-of-the-householder-hb6-scandal.

5. Paul Sotkiewicz (president of E-Cubed Policy Associates), "The Market and Financial Position of Nuclear Resources in Ohio," American Petroleum Institute, May 28, 2019.

6. Jeff Barge, "Personal View: There's Still Time to Say No to Ohio's Costly Nuclear Bailout," *Crain's Cleveland Business*, July 21, 2019.

7. Remarks of Dave Griffing, vice president, government affairs, FirstEnergy Solutions, to the Energy and Natural Resources Committee of the Ohio House of Representatives, May 8, 2019.

8. Testimony by Michael Haugh, on behalf of the Office of the Ohio Consumers' Counsel, before the House Senate Energy and Public Utilities Committee, June 29, 2019.

9. Comment by Andre Porter, then-chairman of the Public Utilities Commission of Ohio. Reported by Randy Lilleston, "Ohio PUC Chair Rebukes Utilities: 'Stop Trying to Scare Ohioans,'" *Utility Dive*, August 19, 2015.

10. Robert Walton, "Dynegy Offers Natural Gas Alternative to FirstEnergy, AEP Plant Subsidy Proposals," *Utility Dive*, January 13, 2016.

11. John Finnigan, "FirstEnergy's Bailout Campaign Is Filled with All Kinds of Wrong. Please Let a Failed HB 6 Be the End of It," *Environmental Defense Fund Energy Exchange*, July 16, 2019.

12. McKinsey & Company, "JobsOhio and the Long-Term Innovative Revitalization of a State's Economy," October 6, 2022.

13. Laura A. Bischoff, "Columbus Utility Gave $900K to Groups Linked to HB6 Scandal," *Dayton Daily News*, December 2, 2020.

14. While HB 6 was introduced in the House on March 12, 2019, with the Clean Air Program language, a substitute with OVEC language was not introduced until May 23, 2019. However, the initial Senate version, introduced on May 30, 2019, did not have the Clean Air Program language. See the Ohio Legislature, House Bill 6 Status, https://www.legislature.ohio.gov/legislation/133/hb6/status.

15. Leah Cardamore Stokes, *Short Circuiting Policy* (Oxford: Oxford University Press, 2020).

16. Jake Zuckerman, "Ohioans Spent $211 Million Subsidizing Two Coal Plants over Last Two Years," *Ohio Capital Journal*, January 12, 2022.

17. Christopher Mahila (with PUCO) to Marie Fagan (with London Economics), September 8, 2020. See also "Initial Comments to Protect Consumers from AEP's Coal Plant Charges by Office of the Ohio Consumers' Counsel," before the Public Utilities Commission of Ohio, case no. 18-1004-EL-RDR, November 12, 2021.

18. Marty Schladen, "Analysis: Paying to Warm the Planet. Corrupt Utility Law Forces Ohioans to Make Climate Worse," *Ohio Capital Journal*, September 19, 2023.

19. Householder also faced four convictions for alcohol-impaired driving; see Athens News Staff, "Will Revelations about Householder Affect Nov. Election?," *Athens News*, September 5, 2000. In his memoir, Neil Clark, to get back at an unappreciative Householder, seemed to suggest he was the source of those "anonymous" charges.

20. Staff Writer, "State Audit Blasts Perry County," *Columbus Dispatch*, March 6, 2008.

21. Such an endorsement had its downside since that previous Speaker, Cliff Rosenberger, resigned in April 2018 amid an FBI investigation of his "relationships with lobbyists and donors."

22. Taped conversation of Neil Clark, as presented in court, February 14, 2023.

23. Dave Ghose, "Bill Seitz and Ryan Smith: The Diplomat and the Street Fighter," *Columbus Monthly*, October 25, 2016.

24. Testimony of Juan Cespedes, February 13, 2023.

25. FirstEnergy disclosures were in response to a class action RICO lawsuit filed by Ohio ratepayers. The utility admitted that "between August 1, 2019, and October 2019, FirstEnergy Service Company, as directed by FirstEnergy Solutions Corp. a/k/a Energy Harbor, wire transferred $25,738,591 from FirstEnergy Solutions Corp. to Generation Now. FirstEnergy further admits that on October 10, 2019, FirstEnergy Service Company wire transferred $10,000,000 to an entity, which FirstEnergy understands then wire transferred $10,000,000 to Generation Now and that on October 18, 2019, FirstEnergy wire transferred $10,000,000 to an entity, which FirstEnergy understands then wired $3,000,000 to Energy Now on October 22, 2019."

26. Terry Smith, "Should Anyone Be Surprised by Householder's Downfall?" *Ohio Capital Journal*, August 11, 2020.

27. Rick Rouan, Jessi Balmert, and Jackie Borchardt, "How Dark Money Fueled Larry Householder's Campaign for Ohio House Speaker," *Cincinnati Enquirer*, July 29, 2020.

28. Ibid.

29. Testimony of Juan Cespedes, February 14, 2023.

30. Testimony of FBI Special Agent Blane Wetzel, February 2, 2023, discussing Householder-Jones messages of November 7, 2018.

31. FirstEnergy's "Deferred Prosecution Agreement," 25.

32. Test messages between Juan Cespedes and Robert Klaffky, January 7, 2019.

33. Laura Bischoff, "Former Ohio House Speaker Householder Looking to Return to Power," *Dayton Daily News*, March 12, 2017.

34. Jake Zuckerman, "Householder Trail: Email Shows Lobbyists Circulated Draft Legislation for House Bill 6 Months before Bill Was Public," cleveland.com, February 2, 2023.

35. Testimony of Juan Cespedes, February 14, 2023.

36. Householder-Borges Trial transcript Id., 6811-15.

37. Householder-Borges Trial transcript R.302, Ex.15, 12253.

38. A bit more than 80 percent of FirstEnergy's value is owned by institutional stockholders such as pension and mutual funds.

39. Statement by Micah Derry, state director, Americans for Prosperity—Ohio.

40. Jessie Balmert and Laura Bischoff, "Householder Never Repaid Political Consultant for Florida Home Repairs, Legal Bills," *Columbus Dispatch*, February 22, 2023.

41. Marty Schladen, "Federal Judge Blasts Householder as a 'Bully,' Sentences Him to 20 Years," *Ohio Capital Journal*, June 30, 2023.

42. John Caniglia, "Documents Offer Rare View of Pressure Larry Householder Exerted in House Bill 6 Scandal," cleveland.com, December 31, 2020.

43. Sandy Theis, "Householder Trial Update #4," Common Cause Ohio, February 7, 2023.

44. Comment by Rep. Rick Carfagna (R-Genoa Township). Reported by Anna Staver, "'Next Level Pressuring': Latest Emails Texts Show Republican Push for $1B Nuclear Bailout," *Columbus Dispatch*, December 30, 2020.

45. Staver, "'Next level pressuring.'"

46. Laura A. Bischoff and Jessie Balmert, "Lobbyist: DeWine Got $3M from FirstEnergy but Householder 'Went to War' for Them," *Columbus Dispatch*, February 15, 2021.

47. Federal prosecutors' sentencing memorandum for defendant Matt Borges, case no. 20-CR-77, June 23, 2023.

48. FBI recording of Neil Clark, July 2019.

49. Opening statement by assistant US attorney Emily Glatfelter, January 23, 2023.

50. "United States' Trial Brief," *United States of America v. Larry Householder et al.* (US District Court, S.D. Ohio, case no. 20-CR-177, January 6, 2023). Reported by Dave Anderson, "Feds Reveal More Secret Pass-Throughs for FirstEnergy Money in Larry Householder Racketeering Case," Energy and Policy Institute, January 10, 2023.

51. Sarah Kleiner, "An Ohio Legislator Defied FirstEnergy Lobbyists. Then a 'Dark Money' Group Helped Sink Her Bid for Congress," The Center for Public Integrity, May 22, 2018.

52. "Strings Attached: How Utilities Use Charitable Giving to Influence Politics and Increase Investor Profits," Energy and Policy Institute, December 2019.

53. Notes on Josh Rubin's advice as recorded by Michael Dowling, December 2018.

54. Testimony of Juan Cespedes, February 24, 2023.

55. David Roberts, "Ohio Just Passed the Worst Energy Bill of the 21st Century," *Vox*, July 27, 2019.

56. Statement of John Judge, Energy Harbor's president and CEO, May 14, 2022. FirstEnergy Solutions was renamed Energy Harbor when it emerged from bankruptcy in February 2020.

57. Text messages by Larry Householder and Michael Dowling, July 21, 2019, presented at trial. Reported by Associated Press, "'Boom': FirstEnergy Exec Text Revels in Landing State Plane," February 2, 2023.

58. Staff Writer, "The More You Learn, the Worse House Bill 6 Looks," *Columbus Dispatch*, August 2, 2019.

59. Nathanael Johnson, "How a $60 Million Bribery Scandal Helped Ohio Pass the 'Worst Energy Policy in the Country," *Grist*, January 26, 2022.

60. Comment by Ty Pine. Reported by Tribune News Service, "FirstEnergy Paid $300k to Nonprofit Tied to Huffman," *limaohio.com*, April 23, 2024.

61. Mike Dowling text to Chuck Jones, May 30, 2019. Reported by Andrew J. Tobias, "Matt Huffman Downplayed Ties to Dark Money Group. New Records Show It Paid Thousands to His Political Team," cleveland.com, May 19, 2024.

62. Quote by Juan Cespedes as reported by Jake Zuckerman, "Huffman Denies Raising Dark Money, Despite Claims from FirstEnergy Lobbyists," cleveland.com, April 24, 2024.
63. Jake Zuckerman, "FirstEnergy Paid $300,000 to a Dark Money Org That a Lobbyist Tied to Senate President Matt Huffman," cleveland.com/*Plain Dealer*, April 23, 2024.
64. *Cincinnati Enquirer*, "FirstEnergy's Ties to DeWine Administration," July 28, 2021.
65. Text by Chuck Jones to a coal executive, FirstEnergy's "Deferred Prosecution Agreement," November 10, 2019, 41.
66. Michael Dowling text message to Charles Jones, January 28, 2019.
67. The Public Utilities Commission of Ohio, in the Matter of the Application of Ohio Edison Company et al., "Entry," November 21, 2019.
68. Chuck Jones text message to Sam Randazzo, November 22, 2019.
69. Jake Zuckerman, "Former DeWine Aide Warned Governor about Utility Regulator before the FBI Raided His Home," *Ohio Capital Journal*, April 4, 2022.
70. Chuck Jones text message, March 4, 2020. Referenced in FirstEnergy Deferred Prosecution Agreement, 43.
71. Andrew J. Tobias, "Former Top Ohio Utility Regulator Was Involved with Writing Tainted Nuclear Bill, Emails Show," cleveland.com, January 11, 2021.
72. Testimony by Juan Cespedes. Reported by Marty Schladen, "Householder Co-Defendant: Campaign Checks Were 'Specially Tied' to $1.3B Bailout," News 5 Cleveland, February 14, 2023.
73. Emails and texts from Tully and Randazzo, released by the Ohio General Assembly in response to an FBI subpoena seeking records on HB 6. See Schladen, "Householder Co-Defendant." It should be noted that all these efforts for secrecy failed as investigators and journalists discovered fraud.
74. After leaving the Ohio House of Representatives, where part of his HB 6 drafting cut renewable-energy initiatives, Tully became board president of Utility Scale Solar Energy Coalition of Ohio and then-director of state affairs for Savion, which delivers utility-scale solar and energy-storage project development.
75. "Columbus Judge Places Hold on $8 Million of Sam Randazzo's Assets," *Crain's Cleveland Business*, August 13, 2021.
76. Tobias, "Former Top Ohio Utility Regulator Was Involved."
77. Interview with author, March 28, 2024.
78. David DeWitt, "Rampant 'Good Old Boys' Corruption Is Robbing Ohioans Blind," *Ohio Capital Journal*, January 26, 2023. Dan McCarthy, DeWine's legislative director and former FirstEnergy lobbyist, texted Michael Dowling, FirstEnergy's chief lobbyist, that he was sending the executive a pen, which DeWine used to sign HB 6 into law.
79. John Funk, "FirstEnergy Solutions Moves to Ditch Union Contracts for Bailed Out Plants, Drawing Democrats' Ire," *Utility Dive*, August 5, 2019.
80. Ibid.

81. Dave Anderson, "FirstEnergy Front Group Paid Convicted Lobbyist Matthew Borges' Firm to Attack Cleveland Public Power," Energy and Policy Institute, June 29, 2023.

82. Matt Evans, president of (and former president of external relations for) Boich Companies, which co-owned with FirstEnergy the largest underground coal mine in Montana. As evidence of the influence web, the Boich Companies' spokesman was Mike Dawson, who served as media aide to Mike DeWine when he served in the US Senate; as a FirstEnergy lobbyist; as husband to Laurel Pressler Dawson, DeWine's longtime chief of staff; and as recipient of a $10,000 loan from Sam Randazzo.

83. Ty Pine email to Matthew Gregorits (with image), July 24, 2019.

84. Text messages between Chuck Jones and Michael Dowling, May 14, 2021.

85. Morgan Trau, "New Texts Show FirstEnergy Allegedly Working with Gov. DeWine to Pass House Bill 6," *Ohio Capital Journal*, June 20, 2024.

86. "Bill of Particulars," *State of Ohio v. Samuel C. Randazzo, et al.*, in the Court of Common Pleas, Summit County, Ohio.

87. Comment by Jeff Williams. Laura Bischoff, "'Jaw Dropping': Ex-FBI Agent Describes Ohio Corruption Case on House Bill 6," *Columbus Dispatch*, July 31, 2023.

88. Quote by Bill Siderewicz. Reported by Ron Selak Jr., "Plug Pulled on Third Lordstown Power Plant," *Tribune Chronicle*, August 21, 2019.

89. Andy Chow, "Nuclear Power Plant Bailout Opponents Criticize Company's Stock Buyback," Statehouse News Bureau, May 13, 2020. Katherine Blunt and Andrew Scurria, "Bribery Probe into a Nuclear Plant Bailout Examines Facilities' Owner," *WSJ Pro Bankruptcy*, October 14, 2020.

90. Andrew Tobias, "With Ohio Bailout Law Secured, FirstEnergy Solutions Successor Moves to Increase Share Buybacks by $300 Million," cleveland.com, May 12, 2020.

91. Ron Selak Jr., *Tribune Chronicle*, August 21, 2019.

92. *Ohio Channel*, "Third Consideration of HB 6, Ohio Senate, July 17, 2019."

93. Dave Anderson, "FirstEnergy Dark Money Payments Included over $550,000 for 'Consumers' Group's Campaign against Cleveland Public Power," Energy and Policy Institute, June 29, 2023.

94. Ibid.

95. Randy Ludlow, "Feds: Householder Pay-to-Play Scheme Extended beyond House Bill 6," *Columbus Dispatch*, July 22, 2020.

96. Initially, a referendum needs at least one thousand signatures of registered voters, as well as a summary of the referendum submitted to the attorney general. If the AG accepts that summary within ten days, referendum supporters need enough signatures to equal 6 percent of the votes cast for governor in the previous election.

97. Comment by Matt Borges. Reported by Jake Zuckerman, "FBI Agent Testifies in Corruption Trial That Lobbyist Matt Borges Gave GOP Consultant $15,000, Asked Him to Keep Talks Secret," cleveland.com, February 6, 2023.

98. Comment by Jeff Longstreth. Reported by Jessie Balmert and Laura A. Bischoff, "Corrupt Scheme or Politics As Usual? Trial of Ex-Ohio House Speaker Larry Householder Begins," *Columbus Dispatch*, January 16, 2023.

99. Jessie Balmert and Laura Bischoff, "Power Grab: How Larry Householder Delivered an Unpopular Bailout for FirstEnergy," *Columbus Dispatch*, February 19, 2023.

100. Recording of Householder by the FBI at a September 2019 dinner. Reported by Balmert and Bischoff, "Corrupt Scheme or Politics as Usual?"

101. Affidavit in Support of Criminal Complaint filed July 17, 2020, in *United States of America v Larry Householder et al.*, case no. 1:20-MJ-00526, in the US District Court for the Southern District of Ohio ("Charging Affidavit").

102. Jessie Balmert and Laura A. Bischoff, "House Bill 6 Trial: FirstEnergy Counted on Matt Borges to Influence Ohio AG Dave Yost," *Columbus Dispatch*, February 3, 2023.

103. Indictment filed July 30, 2020, in "Indictment," *United States of America v. Larry Householder et al.*, case no. 1120CR077 (US District Court, S.D. Ohio).

104. Matt Borges to Melissa Hoeffel of Roetzel & Andres law firm. Referenced during testimony of FBI Special Agent Blane Wetzel, February 2, 2023.

105. Interview with author, March 8, 2024.

106. Balmert and Bischoff, February 19, 2023.

107. Message sent by Jeff Longstreth to SLH (Speaker Larry Householder), June 12, 2009.

108. Ibid.

109. Interview with author, March 8, 2024.

110. Comments by Michael Roberson of Advanced Micro targeting, as reported by Marty Schladen, "Stalking, Assault Alleged in Repeal Fight over Corrupt Utility Bailout in Ohio," *Ohio Capital Journal*, February 21, 2023.

111. Ohio Attorney General News Releases, "AG Yost Tells Petition Disruptors to 'Knock It Off' Following Reports of Harassment," September 30, 2019.

112. Neil Clark recorded conversation, July 24, 2019.

113. Indictment filed July 30, 2020. Amanda Garrett, "Part 4: Householder Directs Dirty Campaign to Save Bailout as Millions Flow," *Akron Beacon Journal*, August 5, 2020.

114. Juan Cespedes text to Jeff Longstreth, July 2019.

115. Interview with the author, March 4, 2024.

116. "Motion to Quash Subpoena Issued to Timothy Burga," *United States of America vs. Larry Householder, et al.*, in the US District Court for the Southern District of Ohio, Western Division, case no. 1-20-CR-077 (January 30, 2023).

117. Interview with author, March 4, 2024.

118. Interview with author, March 8, 2024.

119. Testimony of Anna Lippincott, February 13, 2023.

120. Marty Schladen, "Ohio Sec. of State Frank LaRose Won't Discuss Householder Connections," *Ohio Capital Journal*, June 29, 2023; Marty Schladen, "LaRose Says He Doesn't Remember Conversations with Players in Ohio Racketeering Scandal," *Ohio Capital Journal*, July 27, 2023.

121. Criminal Complaint, *United States of America v. Matthew Borges*, July 17, 2020. Borges promised a second payment of $10,000 at the signature deadline.
122. Testimony of Juan Cespedes, February 14, 2023.
123. Anna Staver, "'It's Terrifying': FBI Tipster Who Wore Wire in Larry Householder, Matt Borges Case Talks," *Columbus Dispatch*, March 10, 2023.
124. *United States of America v. Matthew Borges* (US District Court S.D. Ohio, case no. 1:20-MJ-00526, Criminal Complaint, July 17, 2020). Reported by Jeremy Pelzer, "Meet the Man Who Helped the FBI Expose Ohio House Speaker Larry Householder's Alleged $60M Bribery Scheme," cleveland.com, July 24, 2020.
125. Householder-Borges Trial transcript Ex.616C,12554.
126. Garrett, "Part 4."
127. Bischoff, "'Jaw Dropping.'"
128. Editorial Board, "Ad Invokes Spurious Chinese Invasion of Ohio to Try to Head Off HB 6 Referendum," cleveland.com, August 28, 2019.
129. The text for a TV ad that ran in August 2019 read, "They took our manufacturing jobs. They shuttered our factories. Now they're coming for our energy jobs. The Chinese government is quietly invading our American electric grid, intertwining themselves financially in our energy infrastructure. Now, a special interest group, boosting Chinese financial interests, is targeting Ohio's energy, taking Ohio money, exporting Ohio jobs, even risking our national security. They're meddling in our elections."
130. Garrett, "Part 4."
131. Andrew J. Tobias and Jake Zuckerman, "FBI Agent Describes Borges' Efforts to Lobby Ohio Attorney General Dave Yost on HB6," cleveland.com, February 3, 2023.
132. Testimony of Juan Cespedes, February 14, 2023.
133. If the referendum obtained enough signatures, Householder intended to kill it by introducing new legislation that would clarify HB 6 was a tax bill. In its "Deferred Prosecution Agreement," page 39, FirstEnergy admitted it gave more money to Generation Now "knowing and with the intent that the money was in return for Public Official A's [Householder's] efforts to defeat the ballot referendum and ensure House Bill 6 became law, to include special official action for alternate legislation if the ballot referendum received enough signatures to get on the ballot."
134. Matt Borges text to Juan Cespedes, June 26, 2019.
135. Dave Yost News Releases, "Summary Language Rejected for Proposed House Bill 6 Referendum," August 12, 2019.
136. Comment by Michael Roberson of Advanced Micro Targeting, as reported by Schladen, "Stalking, Assault Alleged in Repeal Fight."
137. According to a Yost spokeswoman, after prosecutors indicted Borges, the attorney general donated the $10,000 to a human trafficking organization that helps survivors.
138. Marty Schladen, "Ohio AG Yost Says He Won't Explain His Role in Bailout Scandal Because of Other Cases," *Ohio Capital Journal,* May 29, 2024.
139. Jeremy Pelzer, "House Bill 6 Referendum Effort Is Dead after Group Drops Lawsuit Appeal," cleveland.com, January 22, 2020; Marty Schladen, "Corruption

Trial Texts: Ohio AG Yost Didn't Speak Out Against Bailout Because of Utility Support," *Ohio Capital Journal*, February 3, 2023.

140. Interview with author, March 8, 2024.

141. Interview with author, March 12, 2024.

142. Closing Statement by Assistant US Attorney Matthew Singer, March 7, 2023.

143. Larry Householder text to Charles Jones, revealed during Householder trial testimony, March 2, 2023.

CHAPTER IV

1. Laura A. Bischoff, "'Jaw Dropping': Ex-FBI Agent Describes Ohio Corruption Case on House Bill 6," *Columbus Dispatch*, July 31, 2023.

2. In the US District Court for the Southern District of Ohio, *United States v. Larry Householder, Jeffrey Longstreth, Neil Clark, Matthew Borges, Jean Cespedes, and Generation Now*, case no. 1:20-MJ-00526. Sixty-one million dollars of that $64 million came from FirstEnergy and its subsidiaries.

3. "Ohio House Speaker Larry Householder Arrested in $60 Million Bribery Case," *Columbus Dispatch*, July 21, 2020.

4. FirstEnergy Newsroom, "FirstEnergy, Local IBEWs Received Industry Recognition for Efforts to Serve Customers, Protect Jobs in Ohio," March 6, 2020.

5. Marty Schladen, "Analysis: Bribery Scandal Shows How Ohio Politics Is Polluted with Dark Money," *Ohio Capital Journal*, March 15, 2023.

6. Patrick Wilson, "Four Types of Scandals Utility Companies Get Into with Money from Your Electric Bills," *Richmond Times-Dispatch* and *ProPublica*, October 10, 2020.

7. Dave Yost News Releases, "AG Yost Adds Jones, Dowling, Randazzo as Defendants in Amended FirstEnergy Racketeering Lawsuit," August 5, 2021.

8. Dave Yost News Releases, "Former PUCO Chairman, Former FirstEnergy Executives Indicted on Public Corruption Charges," February 12, 2024.

9. Press release by US Attorney's Office, Southern District of Ohio, July 22, 2021: "Within 60 days of today's filing, FirstEnergy must pay $115 million to the United States and $115 million to the Ohio Development Service Agency's Percentage of Income Payment Plus Plan, a program that provides assistance to Ohioans in paying their regulated utility bills."

10. FirstEnergy's "Deferred Prosecution Agreement," 15. US Attorney's Office, Southern District of Ohio press release: "FirstEnergy Charged Federally, Agrees to Terms of Deferred Prosecution Settlement," July 22, 2021.

11. US Attorney's Office, Southern District of Ohio, "Purported 501(c)(4) Admits to Being Used to Conceal Corrupt Payments Related to Passage of Legislation," February 19, 2021; US Securities and Exchange Commission, Form 8-K for FirstEnergy, July 21, 2024. In that document FirstEnergy acknowledges it will not soon be clear of the deferred criminal case, that the US Attorney's Office for the Southern District of Ohio is not yet dropping the charge of honest service fraud.

12. "Notice of (I) Pendency and Proposed Settlement of Stockholder Derivative Actions; (II) Settlement Fairness Hearing: and (III) Motion for an Award of Attorneys' Fees and Litigation Expenses," *Employees Retirement System of the City of St. Louis et al. v. Charles Jones et al. and FirstEnergy Corp.* (US District Court, S.D. Ohio, Eastern Division, May 16, 2022).

13. Patrick Williams, "FirstEnergy CEO Says Company May Have to Put 'Money on the Table' to Move Past Scandal," *Akron Beacon Journal*, April 26, 2024.

14. Agreement entered into between the Office of the Attorney General and the Office of the Summit County Prosecutor and FirstEnergy; Exhibit 99.2, August 12, 2024. Marty Schladen, "Ohio Attorney General Dave Yost Settles with FirstEnergy for $20 Million," *Ohio Capital Journal*, August 14, 2024.

15. Jeremy Pelzer, "FirstEnergy Makes $20 Million Deal with AG Dave Yost's Office to Avoid HB6 Prosecution, Drop Company from Civil Lawsuits," cleveland.com, August 13, 2024.

16. Ethan Howland, "FirstEnergy to Pay $100M to Settle SEC HB 6 Bribery Investigation," *Utility Dive*, September 13, 2024.

17. Householder was expelled from the House on a 75-to-21 vote.

18. Opening statement by assistant US attorney Emily Glatfelter, January 23, 2023.

19. Testimony of Larry Householder, March 2, 2023.

20. Ibid.

21. Householder attorney Mark Marein, January 31, 2023.

22. Morgan Trau, "Lead Householder Juror Explains Why Trial 'Left Sour Taste' in His Mouth," *Ohio Capital Journal*, May 18, 2023.

23. Two jurors were dismissed after testing positive for COVID-19, and the trial was delayed five and a half days. Jurors wore N-95 masks and tested regularly for the virus.

24. US Attorney Kenneth L. Parker, in "Jury Convicts Former Ohio House Speaker, Former Chair of Ohio Republican Party of Participating in Racketeering Conspiracy," press release from US Attorney's Office, Southern District of Ohio, March 9, 2023.

25. Laura Bischoff and Jessie Balmert, "'You Were a Bully': What Judge Said to Ex-Ohio Speaker Larry Householder," *Columbus Dispatch*, June 29, 2023.

26. Interview with author, April 30, 2024.

27. Brief for Plaintiff-Appellee United States, filed by US Attorney Kenneth L. Parker and Assistant US Attorney Alexis J. Zouhary, August 26, 2024. Reported by Jim Provance, "Convicted Speakers Bribery Scheme Not Politics As Usual, Prosecution Argues," *The Blade*, August 26, 2024.

28. Jessie Balmert, "Lawyer: Ex-Ohio Speaker Larry Householder Seeks Pardon from President-Elect Trump," *Cincinnati Enquirer*, November 12, 2024.

29. Morgan Trau, "Attorney: Ex-Ohio Speaker Larry Householder Using Trump 'Connections' to Try to Get Out of Prison," *Ohio Capital Journal*, November 18, 2024.

30. Dave Yost News Releases, "Ex-Ohio House Speaker Larry Householder Indicted on 10 State Felony Counts," March 25, 2024.

31. Jessie Balmert, "New Charges Could Block Ex-Ohio House Speaker Larry Householder from Public Office," *Cincinnati Enquirer*, March 25, 2024.

32. Testimony of Juan Cespedes, February 13, 2023.

33. Staff reports, "Sticky Fingers 101: How Members of OSU's Student Government Financed a Night on the Town," *Scene*, February 22, 2001.

34. Jeremy Pelzer, "Ohio House Speaker Larry Householder, Allies Got More than $60 Million in FirstEnergy Bribes to pass HB6, Feds Claim," cleveland.com, July 21, 2020.

35. Testimony of Jeff Longstreth, February 22, 2023; Paula Christian, "'I Handled the Money': Householder Aide Pleads Guilty to Racketeering, Testifies in Public Corruption Trial," WCPO of Cincinnati, February 22, 2023.

36. Julie Carr Smyth, "Ex-Ohio GOP Chair, Lobbyist Matt Borges Shows Remorse, Gets 5 Years for Role in $60M Bribery Scheme," AP, June 30, 2023.

37. Laura A. Bischoff, "Borges, Charged in $60M Bribery Scheme and Once Ohio GOP Leader, Owned and Paid Off IRS Debts," *Dayton Daily News*, August 24, 2020.

38. Recording of Matt Borges, presented by prosecutors in their closing arguments, March 7, 2023.

39. Testimony of Matt Borges, June 30, 2023.

40. Jessie Balmert, "Columbus Lobbyist Neil Cleark, Accused in HB 6 Scandal, Died by Suicide, Autopsy Confirms," *Cincinnati Enquirer*, June 8, 2021.

41. An FBI agent, Jeff Wiliams, commented, "Many of us have speculated about this [blue T-shirt] but we've come to the same conclusion that it appears to be a shot at Mike DeWine." Reported by Bischoff, "Jaw Dropping."

42. Jessie Balmert, Jackie Borchardt, and Anna Staver, "Florida Authorities Investigated Death of Ohio Lobbyist Neil Clark, Indicted in Bribery Scandal," *Cincinnati Enquirer*, March 16, 2021.

43. Comment by William Ireland as reported by John Caniglia, "From Powerbroker to Pariah: House Bill 6 Allegations Devastated Lobbyist Neil Clark, Friends Say," cleveland.com, July 2, 2021.

44. Neil S. Clark, *What Do I Know? I'm Just a Lobbyist* (48 Hour Books, 2021).

45. Ibid.

46. John Caniglia, "'The Companies Drove the Bus': Neil Clark's Book Details His Views on House Bill 6, FirstEnergy and What He Told FBI Agents," cleveland.com, July 2, 2021.

47. Testimony of Larry Householder, March 1, 2023.

48. Clark, *What Do I Know?*

49. Common Cause Ohio, "A Brief History of Ohio Corruption," February 1, 2023.

50. Laura A. Bischoff, "Super Lobbyist Neil Clark and Federal Investigations: What's Going On?" *Dayton Daily News*, August 6, 2020.

51. Clark, *What Do I Know?*

52. Ibid.

53. Ibid.

54. Recordings of Neil Clark, presented by prosecutors in their closing arguments, March 7, 2023. The rambling lobbyist also spoke at length about his grandmother's meatball recipe.

55. Jim Provance, "Randazzo Suicide Note Made No Mention of Guilt or Innocence in Scandal," *The Blade*, April 13, 2024.

56. Marty Schladen, "Money Paid, Favors Done. Messages Detail Relationship between Ohio Regulator and Energy Executives," *Ohio Capital Journal*, August 8, 2023.

57. Samuel C. Randazzo letter to the Honorable Michael D. DeWine, November 20, 2020. Reported by Mark Williams, "Powerful Ohio Utilities Regulator Steps Down Following FBI Search of His Home," *Columbus Dispatch*, November 20, 2020.

58. "Deferred Prosecution Agreement," *United States of America v. FirstEnergy Corp.*, case no. 1:21-cr-86. A subsequent disclosure added that Randazzo acted as a public servant "at the request or for the benefit of FirstEnergy as a consequence of receiving such [$4.3 million] payment." "Schedule 1 of Waiver and Amendment No. 2 to Credit Agreement" (November 17, 2020).

59. FirstEnergy 10-K report to the SEC for the fiscal year ending December 31, 2020.

60. Marty Schladen, "Judge Slams Former Ohio Regulator for Not Giving Details about How He Spent $4.3M in Utility Money," *Ohio Capital Journal*, May 18, 2023.

61. Dave Yost News Releases, "Attorney General Yost Seizes Randazzo's Assets to Preserve Them for Collection," August 13, 2021.

62. Supreme Court of Ohio, *The State Ex Rel. Yost v. FirstEnergy Corp.*, Opinion 2022-1286, January 16, 2024.

63. Ibid. Demonstrating the linked ties among Ohio politicos, Justice Joe Deters recused himself, noting he had been, as state treasurer, boss of convicted felon Matt Borges. Justice Pat DeWine, however, kept his place on the bench although his father, the governor, had signed the bribery-for-bailout bill.

64. Slip Opinion No. 2024-Ohio-101, Ohio Supreme Court, January 16, 2024. See also "Statement from AG Yost on Court's Decision to Uphold Request to Freeze Randazzo's Assets," January 16, 2024; and Jessie Balmert, "Ohio Can Freeze Ex-PUCO Leader Sam Randazzo's Assets, State Supreme Court Rules," *Cincinnati Enquirer*, January 16, 2024.

65. Before PUCO, "Joint Motion to Amend Interlocutory Appeal by Adding the Attached Deposition Transcripts of FirstEnergy Assistant Controller Tracy Ashton," August 19, 2020.

66. *State of Ohio v. Samuel C. Randazzo et al.* See also Jeremy Pelzer, "Ex-Ohio Utility Regulator Sam Randazzo Negotiated Secret Deals Long before FirstEnergy Payments Started, Prosecutors Say," cleveland.com, April 22, 2024.

67. Hearing of the Ohio House Select Committee on Energy Policy and Oversight, September 16, 2020.

68. "Bill of Particulars," *State of Ohio v. Samuel C. Randazzo et al.* See also Pelzer, "Ex-Ohio Utility Regulator Sam Randazzo Negotiated Secret Deals." That article also notes, "Randazzo used the same tactic to embezzle more than $1.2 million of a $9.9 million 'side deal' that American Electric Power, a Columbus-based utility, reached with IEU-Ohio in 2015."

69. "Bill of Particulars," *State of Ohio*.

70. Jessie Balmert, "Ex-Ohio Utility Regulator Sam Randazzo Could Face Discipline for Breaking Attorney Rules," *Columbus Dispatch*, March 19, 2024.

71. Dan Testa, "Top Ohio Regulator Resigns after FirstEnergy Discloses $4M Consultant Payment," *S&P Global Market Intelligence*, November 20, 2020.

72. *USA v. Samuel Randazzo* (US District Court, S.D. Ohio, Western Division, case no. 1:23CR 114 Forfeiture Allegation, November 29, 2023).

73. Ibid.

74. Jessie Balmert and Laura A. Bischoff, "Unanswered Questions: How Ohio's Top Utility Regulator Got Caught Up in Pay-To-Play Scandal," *Cincinnati Enquirer*, April 16, 2024.

75. "Bill of Particulars," *State of Ohio*.

76. Jim Provance, "FirstEnergy Tried to Get Attorney General to Block Referendum, Prosecutors Claim," *The Blade*, February 3, 2023. Not long after the scandal broke, Yost donated FirstEnergy's $24,000 to charities.

77. Testimony of Matt Borges, February 3, 2023. According to Borges, Yost "would be out front [in opposition to HB 6] if not for [FirstEnergy] support and [Borges's] involvement."

78. Jessie Balmert and Laura A. Bischoff, "Ohio AG Announces Indictments for Ex-FirstEnergy Execs, Randazzo in House Bill 6 Scandal," *Cincinnati Enquirer*, February 12, 2024. As noted before, however, Yost eventually signed a $20 million settlement with FirstEnergy, a figure well below what some journalists, and the utility's own consultants, expected.

79. "Draft Indictment for: Engaging in a Pattern of Corrupt Activity with Specifications, . . . ," The State of Ohio, Summit County (February 9, 2024).

80. "Indictment for Engaging in a Pattern of Corrupt Activity, . . ." The State of Ohio, Summit County (February 12, 2024). Reported by Marty Schladen, "Ohio Indictments Provide a Better Picture of Squalid Relationships That Spurred Massive Scandal," *Ohio Capital Journal*, February 14, 2024.

81. FirstEnergy, in its deferred prosecution agreement, admitted that its 2015 amendment to Randazzo's consulting contract "coincided with and was made in exchange for [Randazzo's] industrial group withdrawing its opposition to a 2014 PUCO Electric Security Plan settlement package involving FirstEnergy Corp.'s Ohio electric distribution subsidiaries." Referenced in PUCO, "In the Matter of the 2020 Review of the Delivery Capital Recovery Rider of Ohio Edison Company et al.," case no. 20-1629-EL-RDR.

82. Samuel Randazzo email to Anne Vogel (aide to Governor DeWine), July 29, 2020.

83. Transcript of FirstEnergy earnings call with financial analysts, July 23, 2020.

84. "In the Matter of FirstEnergy Corp., Order Instituting Cease-and-Desist Proceedings . . . ," United States of America before the Securities and Exchange Commission, September 12, 2024.

85. "Defendants Jones and Dowling's Motion to Compel Second Rule 30(B)(6) Deposition of FirstEnergy," case no. 2:20-cv-03785-ALM-KAJ (July 22, 2022). FirstEnergy did not disclose publicly the $4.3-million payment until after the FBI

raided Randazzo's condo in November 2022, which was about one month after the utility fired Jones and Dowling.

86. Jim Mackinnon, "FirstEnergy Fires CEO Chuck Jones after 2 Plead Guilty in Householder Bribery Scheme," *Akron Beacon Journal*, October 29, 2020.

87. FirstEnergy Form 10-Q quarterly report to the US SEC, June 30, 2022.

88. "Deferred Prosecution Agreement," *United States of America v. FirstEnergy Corp.* (US District Court, S.D. Ohio, Western Division, July 20, 2021).

89. "Appendix A: Statement of Facts," page 21, *United States of America v. FirstEnergy Corp.* (US District Court, S.D. Ohio, Western Division, Forfeiture Allegation, case no: 1:21-cr-000896-TSB Doc #1, signed by Steven E. Strah, President & CEO, FirstEnergy Corp., July 20, 2021).

90. *United States of America v. Matthew Borges* (US District Court, S.D. Ohio, Criminal Complaint, case no. 1:20-MJ-00526), 26: "Checks to Generation Now from [account] #4788 were signed by the Senior VP and CFO Company A Service Co., who is now the President of Company A Corp. [Steven E. Strah]."

91. Email from Michael Dowling to Steven Strah et al., April 15, 2019.

92. "Attorney General Yost Statement on Next Steps in HB 6 Scandal," March 10, 2023.

93. Jake Zuckerman, "No Easter Vacation for Indicted FirstEnergy Lobbyist, Judge Rules," cleveland.com, March 18, 2024.

94. Andrew J. Tobias and John Caniglia, "FirstEnergy Fires CEO, Two Other Executives, amid Federal Investigations over Nuclear Bailout Bill," cleveland.com, October 29, 2020.

95. Ibid.

96. *Securities and Exchange Commission v. Charles E. Jones*, US Securities and Exchange Commission, Litigation Release no. 26105 (September 12, 2024). See also Patrick Williams, "SEC Sues Ex-FirstEnergy CEO Jones: Conspiracy Charged Brought against Him, Ex-Exec Dowling," *Akron Beacon Journal*, September 13, 2024.

97. Jeremy Pelzer, "Forensic Experts Are Working to Recover Texts Deleted by Ex-FirstEnergy CEO Chuck Jones after He Was Fired," cleveland.com, January 28, 2022.

98. Julie Carr Smyth and Samantha Hendrickson, "Fired FirstEnergy Execs Indicted in $60 Million Ohio Bribery Scheme; Regulator Faces New Charges," AP, February 12, 2024.

99. US Attorney, S.D. Ohio, press release, January 17, 2025, "Grand Jury Indicts 2 Former FirstEnergy Executives in Racketeering Conspiracy Involving More Than $60 Million in Bribery Schemes." See also Jack Zuckerman, "Indicted FirstEnergy CEO Told Executive to Lie to Investigators About Consulting Contract, Feds Say," cleveland.com, January 17, 2025.

100. Kathiann M. Kowalski, "Ohio Budget Amendments: Another Utility 'Bailout' and a Rollback of Wind Setbacks," Energy News Network, June 21, 2017.

101. Jeremy Pelzer, "Energy Harbor Seeks Option of Turning Down HB6 Nuclear Bailout Money," cleveland.com, December 21, 2020.

102. Ohio Manufacturers' Association's initial brief before the PUCO in case no. 21-477-EL-RDR. See also "HB6 Enabled Coal Company That Donated to Householder Bribery Fund to Keep Overcharging for Coal," Checks & Balances Project, November 12, 2023. Another reference is from Kathiann M. Kowalski, "Coal Company Got Big Payback from HB 6," Energy News Network, November 13, 2023.

103. Jake Zuckerman, "Coal Bailout from Scandal-Tainted House Bill 6 Is Here to Stay, Ohio House Speaker Jason Stephens Signals," cleveland.com, March 28, 2023.

104. Morgan Trau, "House Leadership Protects Scandal-Ridden House Bill 6, Blocking Repeal Effort," *Ohio Capital Journal*, June 22, 2023.

105. Marty Schladen, "Critics Take Aim at HB 6 Coal Subsidies," *Ohio Capital Journal*, February 24, 2021.

106. Comment by Kim Bojko for the Ohio Manufacturers' Association, reported by Kathiann M. Kowalski, "Ohio Ratemaking Reform Bill Would Give More Favors to Utilities, Critics Say," Energy News Network, May 17, 2024.

107. Comment by Rep. Casey Weinstein, reported by Kowalski, ibid.

108. Mark Williams, "Ohio Regulators OK $100 Million in Consumer Subsidies for 2 Aging Coal-Fired Power Plants," *Columbus Dispatch*, August 23, 2024.

109. Kathiann M. Kowalski, "Consequences Continue as Bill at Center of Ohio Utility Corruption Scandal Marks Fifth Anniversary," *Ohio Capital Journal*, June 23, 2024.

110. Kathiann M. Kowalski, "Ohio Regulatory Judge Steps Back from FirstEnergy's HB 6 Cases after Subpoenaed Records Reveal His Role," Energy News Network, March 7, 2022.

111. Kathiann M. Kowalski, "FirstEnergy Says Ohio Law at Center of Corruption Probe Protects It from Ratepayer Lawsuits," Energy News Network, December 1, 2001.

112. Ohio Citizen Action, "Randazzo Influence Remains at PUCO," March 31, 2021.

113. Interviews with the author, July 1, 2024.

114. "FirstEnergy Charged Federally, Agrees to Terms of Deferred Prosecution Settlement," US Attorney's Office, Southern District of Ohio, July 22, 2021; "Deferred Prosecution Agreement," *United States of America v. FirstEnergy Corp.*, case no. 1:21-cr-86. The company agreed to pay $115 million within sixty days to the US Treasury and $115 million to a program of the Ohio Development Service Agency that assists low-income electricity users. None of the funds can be recovered from ratepayers, nor can the utility use the penalty as a tax deduction; SEC, Form 8-K from FirstEnergy, August 12, 2024.

115. Laura A. Bischoff and Jessie Balmert, "FirstEnergy Charged in Ohio Bribery Scheme, Agrees to Deferred Prosecution Settlement for $230 Million," *Cincinnati Enquirer*, July 22, 2021.

116. Dan Well, "FirstEnergy Rises after $230 Million Settlement with Justice Department," *The Street*, July 22, 2021.

117. John Caniglia, "Judge Questions FirstEnergy Settlement with Shareholders, Demanding to Know How Deal Came About," cleveland.com, February 11, 2022.

118. Jim Mackinnon, "'Who Paid the Bribe?' Federal Judge Tells FirstEnergy Lawyer to Name Names in HB6 Scandal," *Akron Beacon Journal*, March 9, 2022.

119. John Caniglia, "'Who Paid the Bribes?' Federal Judge Demands Info on House Bill 6 in Hearing over FirstEnergy Shareholders' Litigation," cleveland.com, March 9, 2022.

120. Laura Bischoff and Jessie Balmert, "Prosecutors Recommend 16 to 20 Years in Prison for Ex-Ohio House Speaker Larry Householder," *Columbus Dispatch*, June 22, 2023.

121. Kathiann M. Kowalski, "Dark Money Helped Utilities Subsidize Coal Plants, Delaying Climate Action at Ratepayers' Expense," *Ohio Capital Journal*, May 3, 2022.

122. Marty Schladen, "FirstEnergy Seeks $1.4 Billion More from Ohio Ratepayers. Watchdog Objects," *Ohio Capital Journal*, November 7, 2023.

123. FirstEnergy Press Release, "FirstEnergy Reaches Agreement to Resolve Department of Justice Investigation," July 22, 2021.

124. Andrew J. Tobias, "FirstEnergy Fights Release of Reports Documenting Internal Investigation of House Bill 6 Scandal," cleveland.com, May 16, 2024.

125. In the US District Court for the Southern District of Ohio, Eastern Division, in re FirstEnergy Corp. Securities Litigation, Order & Opinion, May 6, 2024.

126. Before PUCO, In the Matter of the Review of Ohio Edison Company et al., March 17, 2024.

127. Jake Zuckerman, "Regulators Block Deposition of FirstEnergy's Former Ethics Chief," *Ohio Capital Journal*, July 29, 2022.

128. Federal Energy Regulatory Commission, "Audit of FirstEnergy Corporation and its Subsidiaries," docket no. FA19-1-000 (February 4, 2022).

129. Kathiann M. Kowalski, "FirstEnergy's Transparency Pledge Clashes with Ongoing Actions," Energy News Network, April 19, 2021; "State's Brief in Opposition to Defendant Dowling's Motion for Permission to Travel," *State of Ohio v. Michael J. Dowling* (Court of Common Pleas, Summit County, Ohio, March 7, 2024).

130. Amanda Chu, "'We Don't See a Pathway' to Coal Phaseout by 2030, Says US Utility," *Financial Times*, July 4, 2024.

131. Brian Tierney statement during an earnings conference call, August 2, 2023. FirstEnergy hired Tierney in June 2023; he previously served as global head of portfolio operations and asset management for Blackstone, the infrastructure group, and he spent twenty-three years at Ohio-based American Electric Power.

132. Jake Zuckerman, "FirstEnergy's CEO and SVP Ordered $64 Million Bribery Scheme, Shareholders Say," *Ohio Capital Journal*, March 24, 2022; Adding to the intrigue, Steven Strah, FirstEnergy's CEO who signed the Deferred Prosecution Agreement that depicted Chuck Jones as the scheme's architect, "looked to Chuck Jones as a mentor and friend for 20 years. They worked together. Their families vacationed together. They attended each other's parents' funerals." Reported by Jake Zuckerman, "An Ousted FirstEnergy CEO Signed a Deal Blaming His Mentor for a Bribery Scheme. He Said the Feds Never Talked to Him," cleveland.com, August 1, 2024.

133. US District Court for the Southern District of Ohio, Eastern Division, re FirstEnergy Corp Securities, no. 2:20-cv-03785.

134. "Defendants Charles Jones and Michael Dowling's Motion for Protective Order," in FirstEnergy Corp. Securities Litigation, April 17, 2023. Magistrate judge Kimberly Jolson denied the motion on May 19, 2023. Initial filing reported by Marty Schladen, "Fired FirstEnergy Executives Team Up with Others Suing to Get FE Report on Ohio Scandal," *Ohio Capital Journal*, July 13, 2023.

135. "Order Approving Stipulation and Consent Agreement re FirstEnergy Corp. under IN23-2." Federal Energy Regulatory Commission, December 20, 2020. See also "Federal Regulators Fine FirstEnergy $3.86M for Omitting House Bill 6 Payments from Audit," *Akron Beacon Journal*, January 3, 2023.

136. David Pomerantz, "Ohio Bill Would Bar Utilities from Charging Customers for Politics," Energy and Policy Institute, September 6, 2023. See also New Jersey's Board of Public Utilities' "Board Orders" for April 12, 2023.

137. Ethan Howland, "FirstEnergy Agrees to Pay $3.9M for Failing to Tell FERC about Energy Bill Bribery Payments," *Utility Dive*, January 3, 2023. The Energy and Policy Institute's David Pomerantz, in *Getting Politics Out of Utility Bills* (2023), called the penalty "a rounding error compared to the $90 million that FirstEnergy attempted to illegally take from customers."

138. Kaylee Lindenmuth, "PUC Suspends, Will Investigate FirstEnergy Rate Increases," ABC 27, WHTM, April 25, 2024. In contrast, New Jersey regulators in February 2024 approved a substantially smaller—$85 million—base rate hike, and West Virginia commissioners in March 2024 adopted a $105 million rate hike.

139. Kathiann M. Kowalski, X post, April 18, 2024; and Williams, "FirstEnergy CEO Says. . . ."

140. Kathiann M. Kowalski, "HB 6 Updates: More Bill Charges on the Way While Cases Continue," Energy News Network, September 5, 2024.

141. "FirstEnergy to Revamp Decision Making, Continues Cooperating with Crime Commission," *Congwer*, October 27, 2023.

142. Office of the Ohio Consumers' Counsel, "FirstEnergy Wants the PUCO to Increase Your Electric Bill," referring to PUCO case 23-301.

143. Tony Geftos, "Davis-Besse Public Utilities $54M Devaluation to Cost Taxpayers," WTVG, December 18, 2023.

144. Jake Zuckerman, "FirstEnergy Exec Was Fired Amid Bribery Probe after His Daughter Pitched a $44k/Month Contract, Records Show," cleveland.com, August 23, 2024. During the securities lawsuit against FirstEnergy, Chack invoked his Fifth Amendment right against self-incrimination more than one hundred times. Chack has not been criminally accused.

145. Jake Zuckerman, "Another Ex-FirstEnergy Lobbyist Pleads the Fifth in Investigation, Citing Self-Incrimination Risks," cleveland.com, November 14, 2024. Article addresses Justin Biltz, FirstEnergy's director of state and regulatory affairs until 2021.

146. *Today in Ohio*, the daily news podcast of cleveland.com and the *Plain Dealer*. August 23, 2024.

147. Dan Clark, "FirstEnergy Corp. Fires 2 Top Attorneys amid Federal Corruption Probe," *ALM/Law.com*, November 10, 2020.

148. Marty Schladen, "Former Associate Testifies That Ex-Ohio GOP Chair Borges Paid to Spy on Bailout Repeal Effort," *Ohio Capital Journal*, February 15, 2023.

149. Testimony of Juan Cespedes, February 13, 2023.

150. Ibid. See also Schladen, "Former Associate Testifies."

151. "Brief for Plaintiff-Appellee United States," *United States of America v. Matthew Borges* (US Court of Appeals for the Sixth Circuit, May 23, 2024).

152. Jessie Balmert and Laura Bischoff, "After House Bill 6 Victory, Householder Worked to Solidify Power," *Columbus Dispatch*, February 8, 2023.

153. Householder-Borges Trial transcript R.302, Ex.15,12253.

154. "Bill of Particulars," State of Ohio, Summit County (February 9, 2024).

155. Ethan Howland, "With FERC Approval in Hand, Vistra Poised to Close on $6.3B Energy Harbor Buy," *Utility Dive*, February 20, 2024. Energy Harbor's primary assets were three nuclear reactors—Beaver Valley, in Pennsylvania, and Davis-Besse and Perry, in Ohio.

156. Energy Harbor website, accessed on February 15, 2023.

157. Vistra Corp News Releases, "Vistra Completes Energy Harbor Acquisition," March 1, 2024.

158. Laura A. Bischoff, "Columbus Utility Gave $900K to Groups Linked to HB6 Scandal," *Dayton Daily News*, December 2, 2020.

159. Lisa Barton (AEP's chief operating officer) to Michael Dowling (FirstEnergy's senior vice president), March 18, 2019.

160. Mark Williams, "Despite Fresh Indictments, Ohio Consumers Still Paying $500,000 a Day for House Bill 6," *Columbus Dispatch*, February 13, 2024.

161. United States of America Before the Securities and Exchange Commission, "In the Matter of American Electric Power, Inc." January 17, 2025.

162. Jake Zuckerman, "Coal Plant Subsidies from Pay-for-Play Legislation Have Cost Ohioans $173 Million," *Ohio Capital Journal*, August 18, 2022.

163. Clark, *What Do I Know?* The *Dayton Daily News* reported that DeWine met that day—October 10, 2018—with FirstEnergy executives at an RGA fundraiser at the Columbus Club. According to the RGA's tax filing, FirstEnergy Solutions the very next day contributed $500,000.

164. Laura Bischoff, "Ohio Superlobbyist Neil Clark's Tell-All Book Has Statehouse Insiders Abuzz," *Columbus Dispatch*, July 2, 2021.

165. Clark, *What Do I Know?* See also "United States' Sentencing Memorandum for Defendant Larry Householder," US District Court, Southern District of Ohio (June 22, 2023).

166. Jessie Balmert, "FirstEnergy Gave $2.5M to GOP Governors' Dark Money Group Backing DeWine's 2018 Bid," *USA Today Network*, April 19, 2024. See also Henry J. Gomez and Ruby Cramer, "A New Group Is Attacking an Ohio Democrat from the Left. A Republican Is behind the Group," BuzzFeed News, May 2, 2018.

167. Mike DeWine text to Chuck Jones, October 13, 2018.

168. Michael Dowling text to Charles Jones, October 16, 2018. Trau, "Gov. DeWine Deflects Questions." See also Jake Zuckerman, "'Call Mike DeWine on the $500k:' Governor's Text Sparked Dark Money Payment, Texts Show," cleveland.com, June 16, 2024.

169. Ibid.

170. Jake Zuckerman, "DeWine Says He Didn't Know about Nearly $4 Million in Dark Money FirstEnergy Spent to Back His Bid for Governor," cleveland.com, April 23, 2024. It appears FirstEnergy's first payment to State Solutions, for $500,000 (and labeled "DeWine"), was made the morning after the gubernatorial candidate met with utility executives at the exclusive Columbus Club.

171. Comment by University of Cincinnati professor David Niven as reported by Marty Schladen, "Ohio Gov. DeWine Said He Didn't Know of Millions of FirstEnergy Support. Is That Plausible?" *Ohio Capital Journal*, April 29, 2024.

172. Ibid.

173. Charles E. Jones email to John Wilder (of Bluescape Group), April 14, 2018.

174. Trau, "Gov. DeWine Deflects Questions."

175. Zuckerman, "'Call Mike DeWine on the $500k.'"

176. Morgan Trau, "New Texts Allegedly Show Ohio Lt. Gov. Jon Husted Leading FirstEnergy's Push for House Bill 6," News 5 Cleveland, June 21, 2024.

177. Brent Larkin, "Gov. DeWine's Longstanding FirstEnergy Ties Imperil His Political Future," cleveland.com, January 3, 2021.

178. Mike Dawson also worked as spokesperson for Boich Companies, a coal mining and marketing company that benefited substantially from HB 6. Boich's CEO gave $25,000 to open bank accounts for the dark-money group supporting Team Householder. Boich Companies and FirstEnergy have long co-owned Montana's largest underground coal mine. Laurel Dawson is no longer DeWine's chief of staff—the position she held when he was governor and previously as a US representative and US senator—but she maintains a state job advising the governor.

179. Andrew J. Tobias, "Former FirstEnergy Exec's Secret Advice in Handwritten Note: Keep DeWine in the Dark," cleveland.com, February 13, 2024.

180. Marty Schladen, "Further Questions about DeWine Administration's Involvement in Ohio Bribery Scandal," *Ohio Capital Journal*, April 4, 2024. The journalist added, "It might have been of interest to DeWine to know that his chief of staff's lobbyist husband was having such talks with the governor's PUCO chairman."

181. Jessie Balmert, "DeWine's Adviser Knew about a $4.3M Payment to Randazzo. She Isn't Answering Questions," *Columbus Dispatch*, March 4, 2024. Laurel Dawson had been DeWine's chief of staff when he served in the US House of Representatives and the US Senate.

182. Julie Carr Smyth and Mark Gillispie, "Utility Regulator Targeted by FBI Saw a Whirlwind Rise," Associated Press, November 21, 2020.

183. Laura A. Bischoff and Jessie Balmert, "DeWine on House Bill 6: 'We All Make Mistakes. Every Call I Make as Governor Is Not Right,'" *Columbus Dispatch*, February 15, 2024.

184. Jessie Balmert, "Ohio Gov. Mike DeWine's Chief of Staff Laurel Dawson Changes Roles," *The Enquirer*, May 20, 2021.

185. Marty Schladen, "FirstEnergy Admits It Controlled Dark Money Group Started by DeWine Aide," *Ohio Capital Journal*, July 23, 2021.

186. Marty Schladen, "DeWine Refuses to Explain Aide's Role in Bailout Scandal," *Ohio Capital Journal*, February 17, 2021; Jeremy Pelzer, "Gov. Mike DeWine Names Ex-Aide Who Led FirstEnergy-Funded Dark Money Group to Ohio State Racing Commission," cleveland.com, May 31, 2023.

187. Text by FirstEnergy vice president Michael Dowling to Partners for Progress Treasurer Michael Vanburen, as reported by Marty Schladen, "FirstEnergy Exec Tried to Keep DeWine Aide's Name Off of $10M Transaction," *Ohio Capital Journal*, February 8, 2023.

188. Laura A. Bischoff and Jessie Balmert, "'Chuck. Can U Call Me?' Mike DeWine Texted to FirstEnergy CEO, Looking for Campaign Help," *Cincinnati Enquirer*, June 17, 2024.

189. Editorial, "Lobbyist Wrong Choice," *The Blade*, October 16, 2023.

190. Governor DeWine email to Sam Randazzo, June 9, 2019.

191. Jessie Balmert and Laura A. Bischoff, "FBI Subpoenaed Records Detail Ex-PUCO Chairman Sam Randazzo's Influence on Energy Policy," *Columbus Dispatch*, August 2, 2022.

192. Michael Dowling text to Chuck Jones, June 4, 2019.

193. David DeWitt, *Ohio Capital Journal*, January 26, 2023.

194. Editorial: "Gov.'s Integrity Suspect," *The Blade*, February 17, 2024.

195. Karen Kasler, "DeWine Learned of FirstEnergy Payment to Former PUCO Chair before He Resigned," Statehouse News Bureau, July 26, 2021.

196. Marty Schladen and Morgan Trau, "Ex-FirstEnergy Executives, Ohio Utility Regulator Charged by State in Bailout and Bribery Scandal," *Ohio Capital Journal*, February 12, 2024.

197. *The Blade* Editorial Board, "Gov.'s Integrity Suspect," February 17, 2024.

198. Karen Kasler, "DeWine on Former PUCO Chair Sam Randazzo: 'I Wish We Hadn't Appointed Him,'" WOSU/Statehouse News Bureau, February 14, 2024.

199. Zuckerman, "DeWine Says He Didn't Know."

200. Bischoff and Balmert, "DeWine on House Bill 6: 'We All Make Mistakes.'"

201. David DeWitt, "How Citizens United Cleared the Way for the Biggest Political Bribery Scandal in Ohio History," *Ohio Capital Journal*, April 25, 2024. See also Josh Rultenberg, "Lt. Gov. Jon Husted Says He Has 'No Idea' Why Former FirstEnergy Execs Want Him to Talk," *Spectrum News*, December 1, 2021.

202. Trau, "Gov. DeWine Deflects Questions."

203. Morgan Trau, "New Texts Show FirstEnergy Allegedly Working with Gov. DeWine." Statement by State Rep. Casey Weinstein.

204. Ibid.

205. US Attorney David M. DeVillers, July 21, 2020.

206. Jeremy Pelzer, "Gov. Mike DeWine Calls for Repeal of House Bill 6, Reversing His Position from the Day Before," cleveland.com, July 23, 2020.

207. Randy Ludlow, "DeWine Gives $19,755 in Campaign Cash from HB 6 Figures to Food Banks," *Columbus Dispatch*, September 18, 2020.

208. "Subpoena to Produce Documents, Information, or Objects or to Permit Inspection of Premises in a Civil Action," November 17, 2023, case no. 2:20-cv-03785-ALM-KAJ.

209. Morgan Trau, "FirstEnergy VP Dowling plans to call DeWine and Husted to the Stand in Corruption Trial," News 5 Cleveland, June 20, 2024.

210. Statement by Dayton Mayor Nan Whaley, a Democrat challenging DeWine in the 2022 election.

211. Mike Dowling text message to Chuck Jones.

212. Jake Zuckerman, "FirstEnergy Made Secret $1 Million Payment for 'Husted Campaign' in 2017, Documents Show," cleveland.com, April 10, 2024.

213. Michael Dowling text to John Kiani, July 16, 2019. Reported by David DeWitt, "Ohio Gov. Mike DeWine and Lt. Gov. Jon Husted are Dripping with the Stink of Public Corruption," *Ohio Capital Journal*, February 16, 2024. See also Jake Zuckerman, "FirstEnergy Paid $2.5 Million Secret Payment to Nonprofit Backing DeWine in 2018, New Records Show," cleveland.com, April 22, 2024.

214. Trau, "New Texts Allegedly Show Ohio Lt. Gov. Jon Husted."

215. Zuckerman, "'Call Mike DeWine on the $500k.'"

216. Morgan Trau, "Ohio Lt. Gov. Husted Denies Knowledge of Corruption Scheme in Wake of FirstEnergy Texts," *Ohio Capital Journal*, July 1, 2024.

217. Zuckerman, "'Call Mike DeWine on the $500k.'"

218. Rultenberg, "Lt. Gov. Jon Husted Says He Has 'No Idea.'"

219. Morgan Trau, "Ohio Lt. Gov. Husted Denies Knowledge."

220. Jake Zuckerman, "Lt. Gov. Husted Says He Has No Memory of Name-Drops Detailed in FE Bribery Scandals," cleveland.com, December 8, 2023.

221. Clark, *What Do I Know?*

222. Quote by Ashley Brown, reported in Mario Alejandro Ariza and Kathiann M. Kowalski, "FirstEnergy Gave $1 Million to Boost Ohio Lt. Gov. Husted's Campaign before Scandal, Document Shows," *Ohio Capital Journal*, April 10, 2024.

223. Joel Bailey to Michael Dowling, December 2017.

224. Julie Carr Smyth and Mark Gillispie, "Utility Regulator Targeted by FBI Saw a Whirlwind Rise," AP, November 21, 2020.

225. "Confidential" spreadsheet attached to an email from Laura M. DeNicola to Kristina A. Housley, both with FirstEnergy addresses, January 21, 2020. Housley was executive assistant to FirstEnergy's Mike Dowling.

226. Marty Schladen, "Ohio Lt. Gov. Husted Won't Say if He Knew about $1M Dark-Money Contribution," *Ohio Capital Journal*, April 15, 2024.

227. Jessie Balmert, "FirstEnergy Made $1M Donation through Dark Money Group to Back Jon Husted, Records Show," *Cincinnati Enquirer*, April 20, 2024.

228. Clark, *What Do I Know?*

229. Marilou Johanek, "Ohio's New U.S. Senator Jon Husted Has a History of Connections to Energy and Charter Scandals," *Ohio Capitol Journal,* January 21, 2025.

230. *Scott Sloan Show* with Ohio secretary of state Frank LaRose, Cincinnati's 700WLW, June 28, 2023.

231. Closing Statement by Assistant US Attorney Matthew Singer, March 7, 2003.
232. Ohio Democrats, "LaRose Super PAC Being Run by Former Householder Operative," June 29, 2023.
233. Marty Schladen, "Ohio Sec. of State Frank LaRose Won't Discuss Householder Connections," *Ohio Capital Journal*, June 28, 2023.
234. Text from Chuck Jones as reported by Schladen, "FirstEnergy Exec Tried to Keep DeWine Aide's Name Off."
235. David DeWitt, "Householder and Borges Felony Convictions Just a Start in Stopping Ohio Pay-to-Play Corruption," *Ohio Capital Journal*, March 10, 2023.
236. Schladen, "Ohio Sec. of State Frank LaRose."

CHAPTER V

1. "Deferred Prosecution Agreement," *United States of America v. Commonwealth Edison Company* (July 16, 2020). Other estimates of the utility's benefits include $1 billion from formula rates and up to $2.35 billion from reactor subsidies.
2. "Power Woes Ending Today: ComEd," 5 Chicago, July 15, 2011.
3. Hannah Meisel, "Former ComEd CEO Testifies She Was Unaware of Madigan Allies' Monthly Checks for No Work," NPR Illinois, April 18, 2023.
4. Testimony of Scott Vogt, vice president of ComEd, March 20, 2023.
5. Testimony of Anne Pramaggiore, April 13, 2023.
6. Testimony of State Rep. Bob Rita, assistant majority leader, March 21, 2023.
7. "Emails Detail Madigan's Use of ComEd as Crony Job Service," *Illinois Policy*, December 2, 2020.
8. The day after ComEd executed the outside lawyer's contract, lawmakers overrode the previous governor's (Pat Quinn's) veto of the Energy Infrastructure Modernization Act.
9. Michelle Gallardo, "ComEd Four Trial: Prosecutors Try to Connect Mike Madigan to Various Utility Contracts, Hirings," *ABC Eyewitness News*, March 22, 2023.
10. Jon Seidel and Tina Sfondeles, "A Michael Madigan Associate and Three Others Were Found Guilty on All Counts in a ComEd Bribery Trial," WBEX Chicago, May 2, 2023.
11. Rich Miller, "Details Emerge during ComEd Four Trial," *Illinois Times*, April 27, 2023.
12. Phone conversation between Michael McClain and John Hooker, February 11, 2019.
13. Mike McClain on a wiretapped phone call with Will Cousineau, Madigan's longtime political director, 2018.
14. Tony Arnold and Dave McKinney, "ComEd Charged with Bribery for Steering Jobs, Other Benefits for Speaker Michael Madigan. Speaker Denies the Feds' Claims," WBEZ, July 17, 2020.

15. Jason Meisner and Ray Long, "'ComEd Four' Bribery Trial to Put Focus on Ex-Speaker Madigan's Power, State's Blurry Line between Politics and Crime," *Chicago Tribune*, March 12, 2023.

16. Bob Skolnik and Bob Uphues, "ComEd/Madigan Probe Hits Home in Riverside," *Riverside-Brookfield Landmark*, July 28, 2020.

17. Michelle Gallardo, "ComEd 4 Trial: Former ComEd CEO Anne Pramaggiore Returns to Stand in Bribery Case," ABC 7, April 17, 2023.

18. Testimony of Tom O'Neill, former general counsel of ComEd, March 22, 2023.

19. Hannah Meisel, "Former Top Lawyer Paints Madigan Confidant as 'Double Agent' during Testimony in ComEd Trial," WQAD 8, March 22, 2023.

20. Testimony of State Rep. Bob Rita, assistant majority leader, March 21, 2023.

21. Chuck Neubauer, Better Government Association, and Dan Milhalopoulos, "ComEd Kept Paying Madigan Confidant after Retirement Announcement," WBEZ, November 13, 2019.

22. Hannah Meisel, "Former Speaker Will Stand for His Own Corruption Trial Next Year," *Capital News Illinois*, May 2, 2023.

23. Jon Deidel and Jesse Howe, "Timeline of the ComEd Bribery Scandal," *Chicago Sun-Times*, March 28, 2023.

24. Arnold and McKinney, "ComEd Charged with Bribery for Steering Jobs."

25. "McClain: 'Don't Put Anything in Writing' . . . 'I Think All That Can Do Is Hurt Ya,'" *Capitol News Illinois*, March 29, 2023.

26. Jon Seidel and Tina Sfondeles, "Madigan's Vast Patronage System in ComEd: Jurors See, Hear Federal Evidence," *Chicago Sun-Times*, March 28, 2023.

27. Ray Long, Robert Channick, and Jason Meisner, March 13, 2023.

28. Testimony by Scott Vogt, ComEd's vice president of strategy, energy policy, and revenue initiatives, as reported by Hannah Meisel, "ComEd Exec Testifies Utility Prepared for Bankruptcy Before 2011 Law Threw It a Lifeline," *Capitol News Illinois*, October 25, 2024.

29. Respiratory Health Association, "Future Energy Jobs Act a Big Win."

30. ComEd Exhibit 18-T, "Telephone Conversation between Michael McClain and Anne Pramaggiore," case no. 20 CR 812, May 8, 2018.

31. Exhibit 136-T, "Telephone Conversation between Michael McClain and John Hooker and Anne Pramaggiore," case no. 20 CR 812, February 20, 2019.

32. Ray Long and Jason Meisner, "Exelon Utilities CEO Anne Pramaggiore Abruptly Retires Amid Federal Probe into Illinois Lobbying," *Chicago Tribune*, October 16, 2019.

33. "Deferred Prosecution Agreement," *United States of America v. Commonwealth Edison Company* (US District Court, N.D. Illinois, Eastern Division, July 16, 2020).

34. Matt Masterson, "Federal Judge Dismisses Bribery Charge against ComEd," *WTTW News*, July 17, 2023.

35. US Attorney's Office, Northern District of Illinois, "Former Commonwealth Edison Executives and Consultants Charged with Conspiring to Corruptly Influence and Reward State of Illinois Office," November 18, 2020.

36. Catherine Clifford, "Why Illinois Paid $694 Million to Keep Nuclear Plants Open," CNBC, November 20, 2021.
37. Citizens Utility Board, "The Climate & Equitable Jobs Act," www.citizensutilityboard.org/climate-and-equitable-jobs-act.
38. "The Special April 2021 Grand Jury Charges," *United States of America v. Michael J. Madigan and Michael F. McClain* (US District Court, N.D. Illinois, Eastern Division, March 2, 2022).
39. "Madigan Spokeswoman Issues Statement on ComEd Bribery Scheme," 5 Chicago, July 17, 2020.
40. Opening statement by assistant US attorney Sarah Striker, October 22, 2024.
41. Jon Seidel and Tina Sfondeles, "ComEd Bribery Defendants: No Corruption, Just 'Classic, Honest, Legal Lobbying,'" *Chicago Sun-Times*, March 22, 2023.
42. "Closing Arguments Begin in 'ComEd Four' Trial," *Chicago Tonight*, PBS, April 24, 2023.
43. Meisel, "Former Speaker Will Stand."
44. Ibid.
45. Matt Masterson, "'ComEd Four' Found Guilty of Conspiring to Bribe Former Illinois House Speaker Michael Madigan," WTTW, May 2, 2023.
46. Hannah Meisel, "Government Paints Ex-ComEd officials as 'Grand Masters of Corruption' before Jury Deliberations," *Capitol News Illinois*, April 25, 2023.
47. Michelle Gallardo, "All Defendants Found Guilty on All Counts in 'ComEd 4' Trial surrounding Ex-Speaker Mike Madigan," ABC 7, May 3, 2023.
48. Dave McKinney, "The ComEd Jury Foreman Says Madigan Is a Dangerous Force in Illinois Politics," WBEZ Chicago, May 6, 2023.
49. Gallardo, "All Defendants Found Guilty on All Counts."
50. Dave McKinney, "How the Jurors Reached Their Guilty Verdict in the ComEd Bribery Trial," WBEZ Chicago, May 3, 2023.
51. Jon Seidel and Tina Sfondeles, "A Michael Madigan Associate and Three Others Were Found Guilty on All Counts in a ComEd Bribery Trial," *Chicago Sun Times*, May 2, 2023.
52. Under an indemnity guarantee spelled out in Exelon's bylaws, the company is paying the legal fees—including five attorneys apiece—for both former employees, Anne Pramaggiore and John Hooker. Since Michael McClain and Jay Doherty were ComEd consultants rather than employees, the company did not cover their legal fees. Dave McKinney, "Exelon Paying Legal Bills for Two Former Executives of ComEd Convicted of Bribery," WBEZ Chicago, May 16, 2023.
53. Todd Feurer, "'ComEd Four' Seek Acquittal in Madigan Case after Supreme Court Ruling Narrowing Federal Bribery Laws," *CBS News Chicago*, August 28, 2024. Supreme Court of the United States, *Snyder v. United States*, decided June 26, 2024.
54. Brett Rowland, "Prosecutors Say No Reasons for New Trial in ComEd Four Case," *Washington Examiner*, October 17, 2024.
55. Martina Barash, "Exelon Gets Approval for $173 Million Investor Deal over Scandal," *Bloomberg Law*, September 11, 2023.
56. US Securities and Exchange Commission, "SEC Charges Exelon, Its Subsidiary Commonwealth Edison, and Subsidiary's Former CEO Anne Pramaggiore with

Fraud in Connection with Political Corruption Scheme," press release, September 28, 2023.

CHAPTER VI

1. Mario Alejandro Ariza, "Florida 'Ghost Candidates' Scandal Puts the Entire Utility Sector on Trial," *Mother Jones*, September 18, 2024.
2. Eric Silagy email to John Holley and Daniel Martell, January 7, 2019.
3. Mario Alejandro Ariza and Miranda Green for *Floodlight* and Annie Martin for *Orlando Sentinel*, "Leaked: US Power Companies Secretly Spending Millions to Protect Profits and Fight Clean Energy," July 27, 2022.
4. *Floodlight* reported that Patrick Bainter, the lead political consultant to Florida Senate Republicans, recruited Artiles, saying he "admitted hiring a disgraced ex-senator and approving a dirty trick to recruit a third-party candidate to siphon votes from a South Florida Democrat."
5. Mary Ellen Klas, "Hooters 'Calendar Girl' and Playboy 'Miss Social' Were Artiles' Paid Consultants," *Miami Herald*, March 15, 2022.
6. Mary Ellen Klas, "FPL's Fracking Charge on Customer Bill Is Blasted by Florida Supreme Court," *Miami Herald*, May 19, 2016.
7. Kristen Clark, "Sen. Frank Artiles Apologizes for Using Racial Slurs," *Miami Herald*, March 15, 2022.
8. Ana Ceballos and Samantha Gross, "Disgraced Republican Lawmaker Plants No-Party Candidate in Key Senate Race, Sources Say," *Miami Herald*, March 15, 2022.
9. Annie Martin, "Interviews Examine Artiles Boasts about 'Ghost' Candidate Scheme, Funding for Dark-Money Group," *Orlando Sentinel*, November 17, 2021.
10. Scott Glover, Curt Devine, and Audrey Ash, "Former Florida State Senator Charged in Spoiler Candidate Scheme," CNN, March 18, 2021.
11. Ana Ceballos, Samantha J. Gross, and David Ovalle, "Former Senator Artiles Paid No-Party Candidate More Than $40K, Arrest Warrant Charges," *Miami Herald*, March 18, 2021.
12. Charles Rabin, "Former State Senator Artiles Found Guilty of Campaign Finance and Registration Violations," *Miami Herald*, October 1, 2024. See also Mario Alejandro Ariza, "Ex-Florida Senator Guilty in Election Case Sentenced to 60 Days in Jail," *Floodlight*, November 18, 2024. Coincidently, US District Judge Aileen Cannon dismissed a securities-fraud lawsuit that alleged FP&L made misleading statements about its involvement with ghost candidates. Jim Saunders, "Judge Aileen Cannon Tosses 'Ghost Candidate' Lawsuit by Investors in FPL Parent Company," *Miami Herald*, October 1, 2024.
13. Charles Rabin, "Ex-GOP State Sen. Artiles Sentenced to 60 Days in Scheme to Throw Election against Democrat," *Miami Herald*, November 18, 2024.
14. Statement by FP&L spokesperson David P. Reuter.

15. Annie Martin and Jason Garcia, "Florida Power & Light Execs Worked Closely with Consultants behind 'Ghost' Candidate Scheme, Records Reveal," *Orlando Sentinel*, December 2, 2021.

16. Mario Alejandro Ariza, "Florida GOP Operative Admits Role in 'Ghost' Candidate Scheme That Defeated Utility-Targeted Dem," *Floodlight*, April 12, 2024.

17. Annie Martin, "Former FPL CEO Sold $5.4 Million in Company Stocks as Ties to Political Scandals Become Public," *Orlando Sentinel*, December 17, 2023.

18. Mary Ellen Klas, Nicholas Nehamas, and Ana Claudia Chacin, "'Nightmare Scenario': How FPL Secretly Manipulated a Florida State Senate Election," *Miami Herald*, August 29, 2022.

19. Josh Saul and Will Wade, "NextEra Slides as Florida Executive Departs after Campaign-Donation Probe," *Bloomberg*, January 25, 2023.

20. Martin and Garcia, "Florida Power & Light Execs Worked Closely with Consultants."

21. Jason Garcia, "Florida Power & Light Pocketed $1 Billion in Tax Cuts for Itself. But Now It Can Pass Tax Increases On to Its Customers," Seeking Rents, August 24, 2022.

22. Alissa Jean Schafer, "Amid Connections to Ongoing Election Scandals, NextEra Pours Millions into Florida's 2022 Election Cycle," Energy and Policy Institute, September 8, 2022.

23. Sarah Blaskey, "How FPL Secretly Took Over a Florida News Site and Used It to Bash Critics," *Miami Herald*, August 13, 2022.

24. Mary Ellen Klas and Mario Alejandro Ariza, "Revealed: The Florida Power Company Pushing Legislation to Slow Rooftop Solar," *Floodlight*, December 20, 2021.

25. John Schwartz, "Measure in Florida That Claims to Back Solar Power May Discourage It," *New York Times*, October 27, 2016.

26. Supreme Court of Florida, No. SC15-2150, "Advisory Opinion to the Attorney General Re: Rights of Electricity Consumers Regarding Solar Energy Choice," March 31, 2016.

27. NextEra Energy Q4 2018 Earnings conference call transcript, April 22, 2019.

28. Annie Martin and Jason Garcia, "Big Business-Linked Group Gave Over $1 Million to Dark-Money Entity Promoting 'Ghost' Candidates," *Orlando Sentinel*, November 18, 2021.

29. Mario Alejandro Ariza and Kristi E. Swartz, "Utility Fraud and Corruption Are Threatening the Clean Energy Transition," *Mother Jones*, March 1, 2024.

30. Mario Alejandro Ariza and Kristi Swartz for *Floodlight*, and Adam Mahoney for *Capital B*, "Power Companies Paid Civil Rights Leaders in the US South. They Became Loyal Industry Advocates," *The Guardian*, January 9, 2024.

31. Jeffrey Schweers, "Florida Supreme Court Pulls the Plug on 'Energy Choice' Ballot Initiative," *Tallahassee Democrat*, January 9, 2020.

32. Jason Garcia, "Man behind 'Ghost' Candidate Cash Also Led Dark-Money Group Supporting Florida's Big Utility Companies," *Orlando Sentinel*, October 20, 2021.

33. Mary Ellen Klas and Mario Alejandro Ariza, "Documents Show FPL Wrote Bill to Slow Rooftop Solar's Growth by Hampering Net Metering," *Miami Herald*, December 20, 2021.

34. Klas and Ariza, "Revealed: The Florida Power Company."

35. Editorial, "In FPL's Playbook, Dirty Political Tricks and Propaganda Seem to Be Business as Usual," *Miami Herald*, July 29, 2022.

36. Renzo Downey, "Florida Power and Light Launches Website Attacking *Miami Herald*'s 'Biased' Tallahassee Bureau Chief," *Florida Politics*, January 6, 2022.

37. David Bauerlein, "'Unsettling,' 'Un-American': FPL Consultant Obtained Personal Information, Surveillance Photo of Journalist Nate Monroe," *Florida Times-Union*, June 24, 2022.

38. Miranda Green, Mario Ariza, David Folkenflik, "She Was an ABC News Producer. She Also Was a Corporate Operative," *Morning Edition*, NPR, December 21, 2022.

39. Comment by FP&L spokesperson David Reuter, reported by Nate Monroe, "Florida Power & Light Dominated the State. Now Scandal Darkens Its Future," *Florida Times-Union*, July 26, 2022.

40. Brian Burgess, "Documents Suggest Florida's Largest Companies Are Secretly Sabotaging Effort to Protect Power Lines from Hurricane Damage," *The Capitolist*, April 1, 2019.

41. Sarah Blaskey, "Powerbrokers: How FPL Secretly Took Over a Florida News Site and Used It to Bash Critics," *Miami Herald*, August 13, 2022.

42. Martin and Garcia, "Florida Power & Light Execs Worked Closely with Consultants."

43. Blaskey, "Powerbrokers."

44. Ibid.

45. "NextEra Energy, Inc. (NEE) Class Action Alert: Robbins LLP Reminds Investors of Lead Plaintiff Deadline in Class Action Against NextEra Energy, Inc.," *Business Wire*, June 9, 2023.

46. Nate Monroe, "Commentary: Eric Silagy, FPL's Chief Brawler, Leaves Legacy of High Profits but Low Trust," *Florida Times-Union*, January 25, 2023.

47. David Bauerlein, "NextEra Offered $11 Billion to Buy JEA during Last Year's Sales Negotiations," *Florida Times-Union*, August 26, 2020.

48. Christopher Hong, "Documents Show Curry's Former Chief Administrator, Political Strategist Worked for JEA Bidder," *Florida Times-Union*, May 16, 2020.

49. Ibid.

50. Hannah Lee, "Details of the Ethics Investigation into City Officials, Former JEA CEO, Lobbyists Released," 104.5 WOKV, January 11, 2021.

51. Mike Mendenhall, "The JEA Indictments: Secret Spreadsheets, a False 'Death Spiral,'" *Jacksonville Daily Record*, March 10, 2022.

52. Nate Monroe, "Amid JEA Privatization Controversy, a City Council Member Received a Mysterious Job Offer. A Dark-Money Group May Have Been behind It." *Florida Times-Union*, December 10, 2021.

53. Annie Martin and Jason Garcia, "Operatives Working for FPL Arranged Job Offer to Opponent of Jacksonville Utility Sale, Records Show," *Orlando Sentinel*, December 10, 2021.

54. Ariza and Swartz, "Utility Fraud and Corruption Are Threatening the Clean Energy Transition."

55. Jim Piggott, "JEA Pushed for Accelerated Plan to Sell Utility to Alter the Narrative after Public Backlash, Investment Banker Says," News 4 JAX, March 4, 2024.

56. Christopher Hong, "JEA Spent $10 Million on Its Controversial Efforts to Privatize. Now, the City-Owned Utility Is off the Market," *Florida Times-Union*, December 24, 2019.

57. *United States of America v. Aaron Zahn and Ryan Wannemacher* (US District Court, Middle District Florida, Jacksonville Division, March 2, 2022).

58. Jim Piggott, Tiffany Salameh, and Ariel Schiller, "Former JEA CEO Found Guilty in Federal Fraud, Conspiracy Case; Former CFO Found Not Guilty," News 4 JAX, March 15, 2024.

59. David Folkenflik, Mario Ariza, Miranda Green, "In the Southeast, Power Company Money Flows to News Sites That Attack Their Critics," *All Things Considered*, NPR, December 19, 2022.

60. Ibid.

61. Ibid.

62. US Attorney's Office, District of South Carolina, "Former SCANA CEO Sentenced to Two Years for Defrauding Ratepayers in Connection with Failed Nuclear Construction Project," October 7, 2021.

63. Alex Crees, "The Failed V. C. Summer Nuclear Project: A Timeline," Choose Energy, December 4, 2018.

64. Javon L. Harris, "Santee Cooper, Dominion Energy Bill Mirrors Failed VC Summer Legislation. Here's How," *The State*, March 8, 2024.

65. South Carolina General Assembly, 117th Session, 2007–2008, S. 431, Act No. 16, "An Act to Protect South Carolina Ratepayers. . . ."

66. Tony Bartelme, "Power Failure: How Utilities across the U.S. Changed the Rules to Make Big Bets with Your Money," *Post and Courier*, December 10, 2017.

67. Ibid.

68. Ibid.

69. Ibid.

70. Hearing #16-11554, before the Public Service Commission of South Carolina, "Transcript of Testimony and Proceedings," October 13, 2016.

71. Bartelme, "Power Failure."

72. Tony Bartelme and John McDermott, "SCANA CEO Kevin Marsh Is at the Center of the Nuclear Project's Spectacular Failure. Who Is He?" *Post and Courier*, October 8, 2017.

73. "SCANA Corporation's CEO Discusses Q3 2011 Results—Earnings Call Transcript," *The Street*, October 26, 2011.

74. James Salzer, "Lobbyists Treat PSC Like Royalty," *Atlanta Journal-Constitution*, December 7, 2013.

75. Jeffrey Collins, "Securities Agents Sue 2 SC Utility Execs over Nuclear Fraud," *Seattle Times*, February 27, 2020.

76. US Securities and Exchange Commission, "Litigation Release No. 24751, SCANA Corporation," February 27, 2020.

77. US Attorney's Office, District of South Carolina, "Former SCANA CEO Pleads Guilty to Conspiracy to Commit Mail and Wire Fraud," February 24, 2021.

78. Avery G. Wilks and Andrew Brown, "Ex-SCANA CEO Kevin Marsh Pleading Guilty to Fraud Charges Tied to Failed VC Summer Project," *Post and Courier*, November 24, 2020.

79. Jeffrey Collins, "Executive Gets 15 Months in Prison in Doomed Nuclear Project," AP, March 8, 2023.

80. Crees, "Failed V.C. Summer Nuclear Project."

81. Bartelme, "Power Failure."

82. Ibid.

83. Jay Greene, "Consumers Energy Confirms Affiliated PAC Donated to Rep. Gary Glenn's Election Opponent," *Crain's Detroit Business*, May 25, 2018.

84. Matt Kasper, "Consumers Energy Contributed $43.5 Million over Four Years to Citizens for Energizing Michigan's Economy," Energy and Policy Institute, September 12, 2019.

85. Comment by former State Rep. Gary Glenn, a Williams Township Republican. Jonathan Oosting, "Consumers Energy: Settlement Won't Stop Political Spending by Parent Company," *Detroit News*, February 26, 2019.

86. Matt Kasper, "Michigan's Utilities Have a History of Trying to Block Renewable Energy Increases Like the One That Could Be on the Ballot in November," Energy and Policy Institute, February 12, 2018.

87. Comment by Senator Tom Barrett as reported by Jonathan Oosting, "Consumers Energy: Settlement Won't Stop Political Spending by Parent Company," *Detroit News*, February 26, 2019; Consumers Energy in 2021 put forth a Clean Energy Plan that calls for ending its coal use by 2025 and adding some 8,000 megawatts of solar and 550 megawatts of energy storage by 2040. The utility in 2023 announced another proposal to cut costs for community solar by more than 50 percent. Environmentalists applauded but seemed to give more praise to the Michigan Public Service Commission's decision to cut the utility's proposed rate increase in half and to advance environmental justice and equity programs.

88. Edward Klump, "Entergy: 'Crowds on Demand' Paid Actors to Support Gas Plant," *E&E News*, May 11, 2018.

89. Michael Isaac Stein, "Actors Were Paid to Support Entergy's Power Plant at New Orleans City Council Meetings," *The Lens*, May 4, 2018.

90. Klump, "Entergy: 'Crowds on Demand.'"

91. Stein, "Actors Were Paid to Support Entergy's Power Plant."

92. Ibid.

93. Daniel Tait and David Pomerantz, "Energy Paid Actor Scandal Widens, Nonprofits Used to Support Gas Plant," Energy and Policy Institute, May 11, 2018.

94. Ibid.

95. Stein, "Actors Were Paid to Support Entergy's Power Plant."

96. Patrick Wilson, "Four Types of Scandals Utility Companies Get Into with Money from Your Electric Bills," *ProPublica*, October 10, 2020.

97. Pinnacle West Capital Corporation News Release, "APS Announces Landmark Accord for Four Corners Power Plant; Company Agrees to Purchase Southern California Edison Share of Units 4,5; Close Units 1, 2, 3 if Deal Approved," November 8, 2010.

98. Post by Energy and Policy Institute: https://energyandpolicy.org/renewable-energy-state-policy-attacks-report-2015/arizona-net-metering-attacks.

99. Comment by pro-solar group Tell Utilities Solar Won't Be Killed (TUSK), reported in Ryan Randazzo, "Corporation Commission Chair Says an Imposter E-Mailed His Op-Ed Piece," *The Republic*, August 6, 2014.

100. Laurie Roberts, "APS Executives Up to Their Eyeballs in Political Schemes to Grab More of Our Money," *The Republic*, April 11, 2019. See also APS letter to Docket Control at Arizona Corporation Commission, "Commission's Investigation into the Political Spending of Arizona Public Service Company and Its Affiliates," March 29, 2019.

101. The sum of $1.4 million went to the Cattle Feeders' Association, which held sway over rural voters.

102. APS also gave $3.5 million to Save our Future Now and another $5.9 million to the Arizona Free Enterprise Club, two dark-money groups that boosted two pro-utility Republicans onto the Corporation Commission. See also Ryan Randazzo, "APS Acknowledges Spending Millions to Elect Corporation Commission Members, after Years of Questions," *The Republic*, March 29, 2019.

103. Ibid.

104. Ibid.

105. Jim Small and Jeremy Duda, "Taking Stock: APS's Election Spending Meant Millions for Its CEO," *Arizona Mirror*, September 3, 2019.

106. Roberts, "APS Executives Up to Their Eyeballs."

107. Kristena Hansen, "'Dark Money' Clouds Contentious Arizona Corporation Commission Race," KJZZ Radio, October 16, 2014.

108. Randazzo, "APS Acknowledges Spending Millions."

109. Robert Walton, "Attorneys Tussle over Arizona Regulator's Pursuit of APS Campaign Finance Records," *Utility Dive*, May 30, 2017.

110. Ryan Randazzo, "APS Goes All Out in Fight against Clean-Energy Measure," *The Republic*, June 1, 2018. See also Ryan Randazzo, "APS Parent Company Spent $37.9M Fighting Clean-Energy Measure," *The Republic*, January 17, 2019.

111. Jeremy Duda, "APS Docs Reveal It Funded 2014 'Dark Money' Effort Supporting Commissioner's Son," *Arizona Mirror*, April 1, 2019.

112. Gary Pierce also was alleged to have taken bribes from a private water utility owner, but that prosecution ended in a mistrial in July 2018. See Ryan Randazzo and Michael Kiefer, "Mistrial Declared in Bribery Case Involving Arizona Corporation Commission," *The Republic*, July 17, 2018. That mistrial, according to interviewed analysts, sapped momentum for an APS indictment, including for the utility's 2014 support to Pierce's son, Justin, running to be Arizona's secretary of state. See Duda,

"APS Docs Reveal." See also letter, dated March 29, 2019, from Barbara Lockwood, APS's vice president of regulation, to the Arizona Corporation Commission's docket control.

113. David Pomerantz, "APS' Irrational War against Renewable Energy Policy Creates Big Risks for Investors," *Utility Dive*, September 5, 2018.

CHAPTER VII

1. Closing Statement in FirstEnergy case by assistant US attorney Matthew Singer, March 7, 2023.
2. Chapman University, "Fear Study 2023," https://www.chapman.edu/wilkinson/research-centers/babbie-center/survey-american-fears.aspx; Christopher D. Bader et al., *Fear Itself: The Causes and Consequences of Fear in America* (New York: New York University Press, 2020).
3. Comment by Travis Miller of Morningstar Research Services, in Mario Alejandro Ariza and Kristi E. Swartz, "Utility Fraud and Corruption Are Threatening the Clean Energy Transition," *Mother Jones*, March 1, 2024.
4. David K. Ownes, EVP, Business Operations, Edison Electric Institute, "Facing the Challenges of a Distribution System in Transition," background notes for 2012 EEI Board and Chief Executives Meeting, Colorado Springs, CO, September 12–14, 2012.
5. The Intergovernmental Panel on Climate Change, "The evidence is clear: the time for action is now. We can halve emissions by 2030," April 4, 2022.
6. Nora Colomer, "FirstEnergy Nuclear Bailout Would Be a Win for Bondholders," *Bond Buyer*, July 5, 2019.
7. Patrick Wilson, "Power Play: The Influence of Virginia's Biggest Utility," *Richmond Times-Dispatch* and *ProPublica*, October 10, 2020.
8. Andy Cerda and Andrew Daniller, "7 Facts about America's Views of Money in Politics," Pew Research Center, October 23, 2023.
9. The Ohio Manufacturers' Association, "OVEC Subsidies Dramatically Increase, $100M in the First Half of 2024," February 16, 2024.
10. Judge Timothy Black at sentencing, June 29, 2023.
11. David DeWitt, "Rampant 'Good Old Boys' Corruption Is Robbing Ohioans Blind," *Ohio Capital Journal*, January 26, 2023.
12. Affidavit by US attorney, Southern District of Ohio, July 21, 2020.
13. Andrew Tobias, "FirstEnergy Document Trove Reveals Dark Money's Extensive Influence over Ohio Politics. Here's How It Works," cleveland.com, April 28, 2024.
14. Marty Schladen, "Analysis: Bribery Scandal Shows How Ohio Politics Is Polluted with Dark Money," *Ohio Capitol Journal*, March 15, 2023.
15. Justice Anthony Scalia, Concurring, Citizens United v. FEC, 558.U.S 310. "The Founders' resentment towards corporations was directed at the state-granted monopoly privileges that individually chartered corporations enjoyed." Noting the existing ban on federal contractors making political payments, the Scalia

argument—seeing state-granted monopolies as different from regular companies—could be expanded to ban electioneering by all recipients of such state benefits.

16. "A Survey of Voters Nationwide," Voice of the People, May 2018. See also Greg Stohr, "Bloomberg Poll: Americans Want Supreme Court to Turn Off Political Spending Spigot," *Bloomberg*, September 28, 2015.

17. Supreme Court of the United States, *Citizens United, Appellant v. Federal Election Commission*, no. 08-205 (January 21, 2010).

18. Eliza Newlin Carney, "Citizens United Fuels Movement for Overhaul," *American Prospect*, January 21, 2016.

19. Supreme Court, "Citizens United."

20. "*Citizens United v. Federal Election Commission*, Response Motion to Dismiss or Affirm," Docket Number 07-953 during Supreme Court Term 2007.

21. Taylor Lincoln and Public Citizen Staff, "Ten Years after Citizens United," *Public Citizen*, January 15, 2020.

22. Anna Massoglia, "'Dark Money Groups Have Poured Billions into Federal Elections since the Supreme Court's 2010 Citizens United Decision," *Open Secrets*, January 24, 2023. See also David DeWitt, "How Citizens United Cleared the Way for the Biggest Political Bribery Scandal in Ohio History," *Ohio Capital Journal*, April 25, 2024. See also John Kosich, "Ohio Race for US Senate This Year Rated as Most Expensive in the Country," *News 5 Cleveland*, October 24, 2024.

23. John Cassidy, "Roberts's Law: One Dollar, One Vote," *New Yorker*, April 2, 2014.

24. Supreme Court of the United States, *Snyder v. United States*, decided June 26, 2024. Supreme Court of the United States, *Shaun McCutcheon et al. v. Federal Election Commission*, decided September 28, 2012. See also Congressional Research Service, "Campaign Finance and First Amendment: Supreme Court Considers Constitutionality of Limits on Repayment of Candidate Loans," April 26, 2022.

25. *McCutcheon et al. v. Federal Election Commission*, April 2, 2014. 572 US 185 (2014). This decision, as *Citizens United*, was decided on a 5-4 vote.

26. Eyder Peralta, "Supreme Court Throws Out Former Virginia Gov. Bob McDonnell's Conviction," NPR, June 27, 2016.

27. Robert Barnes, "Supreme Court Overturns Public-Corruption Conviction of Cuomo Aide," *Washington Post*, May 11, 2023.

28. Kedric Payne, "Trump's Legacy of Pardoning Public Corruption," Campaign Legal Center (CLC), January 20, 2021. During his first term, Trump granted clemency to more than two hundred people; see Jessie Balmert, "Lawyer: Ex-Ohio House Speaker Larry Householder Seeks Pardon from President-Elect Trump," *Cincinnati Enquirer*, November 12, 2024.

29. *Snyder v. United States*, no. 23-108, June 26. 2024; John Fritze, "Supreme Court Sides with Mayor Accused of Accepting a Bribe in Latest Ruling to Limit Public Anti-Corruption Laws," CNN, June 20, 2024.

30. Ian MacDougall, "Every Politician Has Got to Have Somebody That's the Hit Man," *New York Times Magazine*, January 25, 2024.

31. Pew Research Center, "Americans' Feelings about Politics, Polarization and the Tone of Political Discourse," September 19, 2023.

32. MacDougall, "Every Politician Has Got to Have Somebody."

33. Mary Jo Pitzl, "Proposition 211: Ballot Measure to Require Disclosure for Political Spending Wins in Arizona," *Arizona Republic*, November 8, 2022.

34. MacDougall, "Every Politician Has Got to Have Somebody."

35. Ibid.

36. David Pomerantz, "Getting Politics Out of Utility Bills," Energy and Policy Institute, January 26, 2023.

37. Matt Kasper, "Legislation Introduced by Rep. Kathy Caster Instructs FERC to Ban Utilities from Using Ratepayer Dollars for Political Activities," Energy and Policy Institute, August 2, 2023.

38. Ethan Howland, "14 States Urge FERC to Tighten Accounting Rules to Prevent Utilities from Recouping Lobbying Expenses," *Utility Dive*, February 23, 2022.

39. Charlie Spatz, "Maine Becomes Third State This Year to Pass Legislation Prohibiting Utilities from Charging Ratepayers for Political Activities," Energy and Policy Institute, June 21, 2023.

40. Citizens Utility Board, "What Is the Climate & Equitable Jobs Act," https://www.citizensutilityboard.org/wp-content/uploads/2021/07/Climate-Equitable-Jobs-Act-CEJA.pdf.

41. Comments by Rep. Michael O'Brien. Quoted in Editorial Board, "HB 6 Scandal Proves It's Time to Shed Light on Dark Money Groups in Ohio," *Akron Beacon Journal*, May 10, 2024.

42. Scott Maxwell, "Florida 'Ghost' Candidate Scandal: Insiders Confess. Masterminds Skate," *Orlando Sentinel*, April 16, 2024.

43. Kent Chandler and Joshua Macey, "Utilities Are America's Real Monopoly Problem and Need Scrutiny," *Bloomberg Law*, September 30, 2024.

44. John Mark Shaver, "Gov. Jim Justice Signs Coal Bills," *WV News*, April 3, 2019. In November 2024, Jim Justice was elected to the US Senate.

45. Kevin Breuninger, "DOJ Sues Son of West Virginia Gov. Jim Justice and His Coal Empire over Millions in Unpaid Fines," CNBC, May 31, 2023.

46. Statement by Exelon CEO Christopher M. Crane, July 17, 2020.

47. "ComEd Reaches Agreement to Resolve Justice Department Investigation," *Business Wire* press release, July 17, 2020.

48. Rachel Leingang, "Investor Group Says APS Subpoena Would Violate First Amendment," *Arizona Capitol Times*, October 7, 2015.

49. George J. Stigler, "The Theory of Economic Regulation," *Bell Journal of Economics and Management Science* 2, no. 1 (Spring 1971). See also Will Kenton, "Regulatory Capture Definition with Examples," *Investopedia*, August 1, 2024.

50. Dan Gearino, "Some Rare, Real Talk from a Utility about Competition with Rooftop Solar," *Inside Climate News*, September 21, 2023.

Bibliography

Bakke, Gretchen. *The Grid: The Fraying Wires between Americans and Our Energy Future*. New York: Bloomsbury USA, 2017.

Bryce, Robert. *A Question of Power: Electricity and the Wealth of Nations*. New York: PublicAffairs, 2023.

Hirsh, Richard F. *Power Loss*. Cambridge: Massachusetts Institute of Technology, 1999.

Hughes, Thomas P. *Networks of Power*. Baltimore: Johns Hopkins University Press, 1993.

Jonnes, Jill. *Empires of Light*. New York: Random House, 2003.

Leonard, Andrew, and Robert Hyman. *America's Electric Utilities: Past, Present, and Future*. Dumfries, VA: PUR Books, 2005.

Mayer, Jane. *Dark Money*. New York: Doubleday, 2016.

McLean, Bethany, and Peter Elkind. *The Smartest Guys in the Room: The Amazing Rise and Scandalous Fall of Enron*. New York: Portfolio Trade, 2003.

Morgan, Richard, and Sandra Jerabek, *How to Challenge Your Local Electric Utility*. Washington, DC: Environmental Action Foundation, 1974.

Munson, Richard. *From Edison to Enron*. Westport, CT: Praeger Publishing, 2005.

Nye, David E. *Electrifying America*. Cambridge: MIT Press, 1990.

Patterson, Walt. *Transforming Electricity*. London: Earthscan Publications, 1999.

Pomerantz, David. "Getting Politics Out of Utility Bills." Energy and Policy Institute, 2023, https://energyandpolicy.org/utility-political-machines.

Ramsey, M. L. *Pyramids of Power: The Story of Roosevelt, Insull, and the Utility Wars*. New York: Bobbs-Merrill, 1937.

Rhodes, Richard. *Energy: A Human History*. New York: Simon & Schuster, 2018.

Stokes, Leah Cardamore. *Short Circuiting Policy*. Oxford: Oxford University Press, 2020.

Vaitheeswaran, Vijay. *Power to the People*. New York: Farrar, Straus and Giroux, 2003.

Wasserman, Harvey. *Energy Wear: Reports from the Front*. Westport, CT: Lawrence Hill & Co., 1979.

Index

Abbott, Greg, 66
accountability, transparency of utilities industry and, 59, 79
AEP. *See* American Electric Power
Akin (public affairs firm), 17, 18
Akins, Nick, 27, 64
Akron, Ohio, 7, 67. *See also* FirstEnergy
Alabama Political Reporter (newspaper), 90
Alabama Power, 89–90
Allegheny Energy, 8
Alliance Resource Partners, 18
America First Policies, 17
American Electric Power (AEP) Ohio, 13, 23, 25, 27, 59
American Petroleum Institute (API), 39
Anderson, Dave, 60
anti-corruption, 45, 102, 104, 107
anti-referendum, 41, 63
API. *See* American Petroleum Institute
APS. *See* Arizona Public Service Company
Arizona Free Enterprise Club, 97
Arizona Public Service Company (APS), 95–96, 97
Artiles, Frank, 83, 84
Athletic Club, lobbyists meeting at, 22, 23, 33, 67, 68–69

attorney, US on FirstEnergy corruption, 46, 48
attorney general. *See* Yost, David

bailouts: DeWine, M., support of, 67–68; FirstEnergy and, 1, 7, 12, 13, 16, 37–38; HB 6, 32; Kiani support of, 64; legislation for, 26; "Nuclear Bailout Bill Discussion," 64; Ohioans Against Corporate Bailouts, 40–41; for reactors, 26
ballot threat of HB 6, 39, 40
bankruptcy: FirstEnergy Solutions, 19, 20, 63; Westinghouse, 93
Base Load Review Act, 90, 91, 92
Bechtel, Virgil C. Summer project audited by, 91
Black, Timothy, 48, 49, 51
"blockers," 40, 63, 86, 97
"Bob and Betty Buckeye," 15, 26, 27
Bonneville Power Authority, 6
Borges, Matt, 33; federal trial of, 47–48, 51; Fehrman and, 42; punishments of, 50–51; racketeering and bribery, 49; spying by, 41; Yost and, 43
Brandt, Don, 2, 96–97
bribery, 99; ComEd, 2, 73, 80; Exelon guilty of, 80, 109; FirstEnergy using, 11–12, 22–23, 47; Insull using,

153

3–4; for legislation, 2; McDonnell accepted, 103–4; of political campaign, 1; racketeering and, 2, 45, 49, 55; of Randazzo, 22–23, 55, 57, 61; referendum organizer, 40; scandals related to, 20, 63, 81; schemes, 69, 81; state legislators, 108; of Yost, 56
Buckeye State. *See* Ohio
bully, FirstEnergy as, 52–53
Byrne, Stephen, 92–93

campaigns, 17, 46, 50, 87; Householder, L., 71; Husted, 70; scheme, 84. *See also* political campaigns
Capitolist (website), 87–88
CARE. *See* Clean Affordable Renewable Energy
CEJA. *See* Climate and Equitable Jobs Act
Centerior Energy, 8. *See also* FirstEnergy
CEO, scandals of, 2
Cespedes, Juan, 21, 30; on Clark, 33; sentencing for, 50
Chack, Dennis, 57, 63
Chicago alderman, 4, 75, 78
Chicago Arc Light and Power, 4
Chicago Edison Company (1892), 3
Chicago's Thirteenth Ward, 74, 75
Citizens for Energizing Michigan's Economy (dark money group), 93
Citizens Policy Institute, 65
Citizens United v. FEC, 6, 32, 70, 86, 100, 102, 103
civil lawsuit, against FirstEnergy, 55–56, 69
Clark, Neil, 32, 33, 43, 65, 102; FBI and, 52; as "hitman," 53; Longstreth and, 41; suicide of, 51
Clean Affordable Renewable Energy (CARE) for Michigan, 94
clean-air regulations, 8
clean energy, 26, 34, 77, 96, 97, 101; Climate and Equitable Jobs Act, 78–79; Ohio initiatives for, 12–13

Clean Energy Future, 38
Cleveland Plain Dealer (newspaper), 34, 42–43, 52; on DeWine, M., 66; on Householder, L., 30
Cleveland Public Power, 38
Climate and Equitable Jobs Act (CEJA), 78–79, 104
coal plants, 10, 16, 28, 35; AEP and, 59; APS purchasing, 95–96; environmentalists and, 31; FirstEnergy and, 8–9, 11
Cold War, 27, 28
Commonwealth Edison (ComEd), 104–5; bribery in, 2, 73, 80; "ComEd Four," 78, 80–81; legalese-laced settlement, 78; lobbyists, 76, 81, 82; Madigan, M., involvement with, 73, 74
compensation committee, of FirstEnergy board, 57
competitors, of utilities, 3, 4, 83, 100, 108–9; FirstEnergy, 12, 13, 16, 35, 39; monopolies protecting, 7, 11
conservation groups, hindering referendum, 41
construction work in progress (CWIP) bill, 90, 91
Consumers Energy, 93, 94
Corporation Commission, Arizona, 96, 97
corruption, 3, 6, 11, 43, 46, 99, 109. *See also specific topics*
Cove Key Management, 20
Craft, Joseph, 18
Crowds on Demand, Entergy hiring, 94–95
Cuomo, Andrew, 104
Curry, Lenny, 88–89
CWIP. *See* construction work in progress

Daley, Richard J., 74
Darin, Jack, 79
dark money, 2, 46, 61, 63, 102; Borges and, 51; DeWine, M., election

supported by, 69; elections paid for by, 27, 32, 65, 69; FP&L funneling, 85, 86; groups for, 32, 45, 46, 48, 65, 67, 90; Householder, L., management of, 27; refunded illegal revenue, 106–7; Silagy and, 84–85. *See also* Citizens for Energizing Michigan's Economy; Empowering Ohio's Economy; Freedom Frontier; Generation Now; Grow United; Partners for Progress; Save Our Future

Davis-Besse nuclear facility, 8, 26, 27, 62

Dawson, Laurel Pressler, 34, 66–67

Dawson, Michael, 34, 37, 66

"decoupling" policy, 25, 35, 66

Defense Production Act (1950), 19

Department of Energy, US (DOE), 17

Department of Justice, US, 28, 60

deregulation of utilities, 9

DeSantis, Ron, 88

Deters, Joe, 50

DeWine, Alice, 67

DeWine, Mike, 21, 35, 64; bailouts supported by, 67–68; dark money groups supported by, 65; FirstEnergy support of, 66, 69; HB 6 signing, 36–37; Husted and, 66; Jones relationship with, 23; McCarthy and, 67; Randazzo and, 23

DOE. *See* Department of Energy, US

Doherty, Jay D., 76–77, 78

Dominguez, Joe, 78

Dowling, Michael, 21, 34; FirstEnergy firing, 57; Husted and, 70; indictments of, 57–58; Jones and, 22, 24; SEC and, 58; as Speaker of House of Representatives, 20, 24

DTE Energy, 94

Dunn, Terry, 89–90

Dynegy, 10; NRG Energy and, 13, 27

Edison, Thomas, 3

Edison Electric Institute, 46

Edison Illuminating Company, 3

EIMA. *See* Energy Infrastructure Modernization Act

elections, 28, 47; dark money payments for, 27, 32, 65, 69; Election Day, 39, 66, 69; utilities "buying," 5

Electric City (magazine), 4

electricity. *See specific topics*

electricity generators, 5; manufacturers of, 3; for nuclear power plants, 15–16

electricity grid, 12; emergency for, 18–19; foreign investments and, 41; manager of, 13; modernization of, 14; PJM Interconnection and, 16; smart meters for, 3, 74, 110

Elisar, Scott, 60

Empowering Ohio's Economy (dark money group), 64

Energy and Policy Institute, 60, 98, 105

Energy Harbor, 20, 34, 62; API comparison to, 39; Generation Now and, 40; HB 6 effecting, 38. *See also* FirstEnergy Solutions

Energy Infrastructure Modernization Act (EIMA), 73

Energy News Network, 15

Entergy, 94, 95

environmentalists: coal plants and, 31; FirstEnergy and, 41

Environmental Law & Policy Center, 13

Environmental Protection Agency (EPA), US, 18

ethics committee, 107; CEJA, 104

Exelon, 73; bribery, 80, 109; FERC auditing, 81; labor-union allies, 79; Pramaggiore overseeing, 77–78. *See also* Commonwealth Edison

FBI, 101; APS investigated, 97; Clark and, 52; on FirstEnergy lobbyists, 21–22, 37; FirstyEnergy lobbyists arrested by, 45–46; investigations, 29, 31; McClain raided by, 78; Randazzo and, 53, 66; wiretaps by, 42, 48, 75

federal agents. *See* FBI
Federal Energy Regulatory Commission (FERC), 13–14, 18, 58, 102, 105; Exelon audited by, 81; Generation Now charges from, 62
Federal Power Act, 18
federal prosecutors: misconduct of, 6; schemes exposed by, 1–2; Zahn and Wannemacher charged by, 89
Federal Trade Commission (FTC), 5–6, 15
federal trials: Borges, 47–48, 51; broadcasted, 108; Householder, L., 47–48, 101
Fehrman, Tyler, 41–42
FERC. *See* Federal Energy Regulatory Commission
Finnigan, John, 12
FirstEnergy: advertising, 34; Athletic Club and, 22, 23, 33, 67, 68–69; audit of, 15, 19, 62; bailouts and, 1, 7, 12, 13, 16, 37–38; board of, 57; bribery, 11–12, 22–23, 47; bullying of, 52–53; civil lawsuit against, 55–56, 69; coal and, 8–9, 11; competitors, 12, 13, 16, 35, 39; DeWine, M., supported by, 66, 69; "DOE Team," 17; environmentalists and, 41; exploitation of political systems by, 11; FBI arrests, 45–46; FBI on, 21–22, 37; HB 6 bailouts and, 32; House of Representatives and, 1; indictment avoided by, 2; internal investigations of, 61–62; Jones and, 1, 9–10, 56–57; lobbyists, 2, 21–22, 51–52; NRC citations, 8; Partners for Progress, 21, 29, 46–47, 67, 71; political campaigns backed by, 20–21, 33; prosecution of, 60; PUCO illegal charges to, 14–15; Randazzo payout from, 54; regulators pushed by, 62; reregulation of, 10; scandals, 61, 71; secret money payments of, 38, 54, 65, 70; shareholders, 9, 10, 47; Statehouse-based lobbying, 32–33; subsidies, 13–14. *See also specific topics*
FirstEnergy Solutions, 9; bankruptcy of, 19, 20, 63
Floodlight (investigative newsroom), 85
Florida Power & Light (FP&L): dark money funneled, 85, 86; Florida Public Service Commission against, 85–86; JEA and, 89; leveraged funds, 86; scandals, 87–88; Supreme Court ruling avoided by, 83
Florida Supreme Court, US, 87; FP&L diverted, 84; on solar energy, 86
Floridians for Affordable Reliable Energy, 86
FP&L. *See* Florida Power & Light
fracking, 7, 8, 9, 11, 39, 84
fraud, 99, 102; political, 73; rise of, 99; SEC charging, 81–82; utility, 71, 79; wire, 46, 54, 61, 89, 92
Freedom Frontier (dark money group), 65, 70
FTC. *See* Federal Trade Commission
Future Energy Jobs Act, 77

General Motors factory, 25
Generation Now (dark money group), 20; Energy Harbor and, 40; FERC auditing, 62; Longstreth and, 21, 30
George, Tony, 20, 21, 65
gerrymandering, 61, 107
Goldwater, Barry Jr., 96
Great Depression, 5
Greenspan, Dave, 31
Grow United (dark money group), 84–85, 86, 89
Gulf Power, 88

Hadden, J. B., 23
Hagan, Christina, 32
Hague, Asim, 15
HB 6. *See* House Bill 6
Hill, Ned, 38
Hooker, John, 74

House Bill 6 (HB 6), 15, 17, 20, 26, 34; bailout, 32; ballot threat of, 39, 40; DeWine, M., signing on, 36–37; Energy Harbor effected by, 38; legislation, 30, 70; referendum, 71; scandal, 10–11, 12, 69; subsidies associated with, 60, 64; Tully and, 35–36
Householder, Larry "Big Larry," 20–21; barred from public office, 50; campaign committee, 71; FBI arrest of, 45–46; federal trial of, 47–48, 101; Jones and, 22; Ohio House of Representatives, 29–30; as Perry County auditor, 28; protection of HB 6, 39; racketeering and bribery, 49; schemes involving, 58
Householder, Taundra, 45, 49
House of Representatives, Illinois, McClain serving, 76
House of Representatives, Ohio, 1, 28; Dowling and, 20, 24; Householder, L., 29–30; Jones pressuring, 32
Huffman, Matt, 34
Husted, Jon, 65, 69; campaign, 70; DeWine, M., and, 66

Illinois Commerce Commission, 5, 75
Illinois House of Representatives, 76
independent power producers, 9, 10
Indiana-based Fort Wayne Electric Company, 4
indictments: FirstEnergy avoidance of, 2; Insull, 6; Jones and Dowling, 57–58; Madigan, M., 79; Randazzo, 68
Industrial Energy Users of Ohio, Randazzo controlling, 55
insider trades, Jones engagement in, 58
Insull, Samuel, 3–4, 9, 99–100; indictment of, 6; Roosevelt on, 5
internal investigations, of FirstEnergy, 61–62
Internal Revenue Service (IRS), 67, 93
International Brotherhood of Electrical Workers, 37
IRS. *See* Internal Revenue Service

Jacksonville Electric Authority (JEA), 88–89
JobsOhio, 27, 67
Joint Legislative Ethics Committee, 55
Jones, Charles "Chuck": "decoupling" policy and, 25–26; Defense Production Act (1950) and, 19; DeWine, M., and, 23; Dowling and, 22, 24; firing of, 57; FirstEnergy and, 1, 9–10, 56–57; HB 6 legislation and, 30; indictments of, 57–58; insider trades of, 58; Ohio House of Representatives pressured by, 32; subsidies and, 7, 10, 15, 16; swaying votes for Householder, L., 30; xenophobic assertions by, 42–43
Jones Day law firm, 18, 61
journalists, reporting on corruption, 108; *Alabama Political Reporter*, 90; *Capitolist*, 87–88; *Cleveland Plain Dealer*, 34, 42–43, 52; *Miami Herald*, 84, 86; *Ohio Capital Journal*, 28; *Orlando Sentinel*, 85, 86, 89; *Post and Courier*, 93; *Toledo Blade*, 67, 68
Justice, Jim, 109

Kagan, Elena, 103
Kasich, John, 12–13
Kelter, Rob, 13
Kennedy, Anthony, 102, 103
Kiani, John, 20, 52, 63–64, 71
kickbacks, 28, 107
Klaffky, Robert, 21, 30

LaFollette, Robert, 4
LaRose, Frank, 41, 71
legislation: bailout, 26; Base Load Review Act, 90, 91, 92; bribery for, 2; Climate and Equitable Jobs Act, 78–79, 104; ComEd agenda for, 80; CWIP bill, 90, 91; Defense Production Act (1950), 19; Energy Infrastructure Modernization Act, 73; Federal Power Act, 18; Future Energy Jobs Act, 77; HB 6, 30,

70; power corporation prohibited by, 106; Public Utility Holding Company Act, 6, 107; Racketeer Influenced and Corrupt Organization Act, 45; Senate Bill 221, 70; for States with privately owned utilities, 4–5; Trump tax-cut, 17
Leppla, Miranda, 35
Lewandowski, Corey, 17, 18
lobbyists: ComEd, 76, 81, 82; Commonwealth Edison, 73; FirstEnergy, 2, 21–22, 51–52; frustration toward, 100–101
Longstreth, Jeff: Clark and, 41; Generation Now, 21, 30; Householder, L., and, 48; sentencing for, 50
Louisiana, Entergy, 94–95
LS Power, 38

Madigan, Lisa, 74
Madigan, Michael: Chicago alderman and, 75, 78; ComEd involvement with, 73, 74; FBI wiretapping of, 75; indictments against, 79; racketeering trial, 80
Marcellus Shale, 9
market prices, 16
Marquez, Fidel, 76–77
Marsh, Kevin, 90, 92
Matrix (political consultant firm), 85, 86, 87
McCarthy, Dan, 21, 67, 70–71
McClain, Michael, 74, 75, 76, 78
McConnell v. FEC, 6
McDonnell, Bob, bribery of, 103–4
McKinley, William, 5
McNees Wallace & Nurick (law firm), 60
Miami Herald (newspaper), 84, 86, 87
Michigan, 93–94
Middle West Utilities, 4, 5
misconduct: ComEd, 78, 109–10; Exelon, 109–10; FP&L, 88; utilities, 73

modernization: of electricity grid, 14; state infrastructures, 26; transparency and, 111
monopolies: competitors of utilities protected by, 7, 11; corporate, 2; corruption as result of, 83; electricity, 110; gross investments and, 107; Silagy supporting, 86; state-sanctioned, 26–27; technology and, 100, 110–11; utility executives and, 5
Moody, 11
Morgan Stanley, 35
Morningstar Research Services LLC, on fraud, 99
Murray, Robert, 18, 31
Murray Energy, 18

natural gas: competitive markets in, 9; fracking, 7, 8, 9, 11, 39, 84; prices, 16, 28
Natural Resources Defense Council (NRDC), 52
"net metering," 96
NextEra Energy: FP&L, 85; Gulf Power, 88
NRC. *See* Nuclear Regulatory Commission
NRDC. *See* Natural Resources Defense Council
NRG Energy, 10; Dynegy and, 13, 27
"Nuclear Bailout Bill Discussion," 64
nuclear power plants, 8, 12, 18, 19, 35; generators for, 15–16
Nuclear Regulatory Commission (NRC), 8
"Nukegate scandal," SCANA Corporation and, 90

OCC. *See* Ohio Consumers' Counsel
Ochoa, Juan, 75–76
Ohio, 7; American Electric Power, 13, 23, 25; chief regulator of, 22, 64, 97; clean energy initiatives, 12–13; consumer charges in, 12, 14; corruption in, 71; Empowering

Ohio's Economy, 64; Environmental Law & Policy Center, 13; Industrial Energy Users of Ohio, 55; JobsOhio, 27; Perry County, 28; referendum overturned, 39; Securing Ohio's Future, 65; Supreme Court, 15; Sustainability Funding Alliance, 23. *See also* House of Representatives, Ohio; Public Utilities Commission of Ohio; regulators of Ohio; Yost, David

Ohioans Against Corporate Bailouts, 40–41

Ohioans for Energy Security, 40

Ohio Association of Foodbanks, 69

Ohio Capital Journal (newspaper), 28

Ohio Consumers' Counsel (OCC), 11–12, 13, 26, 59; PUCO subpoenaed, 28

Ohio Edison, 7, 8

Ohio Environmental Council, 36

Ohio Manufacturers' Association, 13, 59, 62

Ohio Power Siting Board, 35

Ohio Valley Electric Corporation (OVEC), 27, 59

Oliver, John, 7

Orlando Sentinel (newspaper), 85, 86, 89

outmoded generators, 1, 3, 9, 99, 110, 111

OVEC. *See* Ohio Valley Electric Corporation

Paduchik, Bob, 17

Partners for Progress (dark money group), 21, 29, 46–47, 67, 70–71

pay-to-play: demonstration of, 30; Kagan on, 103; scandals, 21, 38–39, 50

penalties for corruption, 106

Perry, Rick, 17–18

Perry County, Ohio, 28, 45, 48

Pierce, Gary, 97–98

Pinnacle West Capital Group, 96

PJM Interconnection, 16, 26

plants. *See* coal plants; nuclear power plants

political campaigns: bribery of, 1; FirstEnergy backing, 20–21, 33; racketeering of, 1, 100–101; subsidies through, 1

political expenditure, of utilities, 104, 105

political fraud, 73

Pomerantz, David, 98

Post and Courier (newspaper), 93

power corporation prohibited by legislation, 106

power plants: Insull and, 4; nuclear, 8, 12, 15–16, 18, 19, 35; Southern Company, 88

Pramaggiore, Anne, 2, 73–74, 75; Exelon overseen by, 77–78; resignation of, 78

prices: market, 16; natural-gas, 16, 28; shareholder, 9

Pritzker, J. B., 79

privately owned utilities, 38, 46, 108–9; legislation for, 4–5

prosecution, of FirstEnergy, 60

Public Utilities Commission of Ohio (PUCO), 12, 13, 28; FirstEnergy illegal charges from, 14–15; Randazzo and, 22, 23–24, 35, 46, 53

Public Utility Holding Company Act (PUHCA), 6, 107

PUCO. *See* Public Utilities Commission of Ohio

PUHCA. *See* Public Utility Holding Company Act

Racketeer Influenced and Corrupt Organization Act (RICO), 45

racketeering, 3, 71, 81, 111; bribery and, 2, 45, 49, 55; Madigan, M., trial for, 80; measures to reduce, 106–9; of political campaign, 1, 100–101; transparency of utilities industry and, 2, 99

Randazzo, Samuel: bribery and, 22–23, 55, 57, 61; "decoupling" policy of, 25; DeWine, M., and, 23; FBI and,

53, 66; FirstEnergy payout to, 54; HB 6 and, 36; indictment of, 68; Industrial Energy Users of Ohio and, 55; PUCO and, 22, 23–24, 35, 46, 53; racketeering, 55; secret money payments from, 54; suicide of, 55
recusal standards, for utilities, 106
reduction measures for racketeering, 106–9
referendum: anti-, 41, 63; conservation groups hindering, 41; Debtors assisting, 20; Florida, 86; HB 6, 71; Ohioans Against Corporate Bailouts, 40–41; Ohio overturning, 39
referendum organizer, 40, 41, 43
regulators of Ohio, 12, 13, 16, 59; chief regulator, 22, 53, 64, 97; FirstEnergy pushing, 62
renewable energy, 12; APS against, 96; CARE, 94; DeWine, M., ignoring advocates for, 35; Future Energy Jobs Act, 77; Illinois transitioned to, 79; Randazzo against, 23
Republican Governors Association (RGA), 65
reregulation of FirstEnergy, 10
Reyes, Victor, 74, 75
RGA. *See* Republican Governors Association
RICO. *See* Racketeer Influenced and Corrupt Organization Act
Rockford, Illinois, power-and-light business in, 4
Roosevelt, Franklin, on Insull, 5
Rubin, Josh, 33, 67

Sammis Plant, 33–34
Santee Cooper, 91
Save Our Future (dark money group), 96
Scalia, Anthony, 102
SCANA Corporation, 90, 91, 92
scandals, 62, 110; bribery, 20, 63, 81; CEO, 2; chief regulator of Ohio, 53; ComEd and Exelon, 81–82; Consumers Energy, 94; electric utilities facing, 2–3; Entergy, 95; exposed, 101; FirstEnergy, 61, 71; FP&L, 87–88; HB 6, 10–11, 69; Insull, 6; "Nukegate scandal," 90; pay-to-play, 21, 38–39, 50; SCANA Corporation, 92; Silagy, 88; state commissions, 5; subsidies, 7; utilities, 100, 101, 109
SCE&G. *See* South Carolina Electric & Gas Company
schemes: bribery, 69, 81; campaign, 84; consequences of, 1–2; corruption, 57, 82; HB 6 and, 58
SEC. *See* Securities and Exchange Commission
secret money payments, of FirstEnergy, 38, 54, 65, 70
Securing Ohio's Future, 65
Securities and Exchange Commission (SEC), US, 5, 19, 47, 102; Dowling and, 58; fraud charges from, 81–82; Marsh charged by, 92
Senate, US, investigations of, 5
Senate Bill 221, legislation for, 70
shareholders: FirstEnergy, 9, 10, 47; prices, 9
Shaw, Kate, 104
Silagy, Eric, 2, 83; dark money organizations and, 84–85; monopolies supported by, 86; scandals, 88
smart meters, 3, 74, 110
Smith, Frank, 5
Smith, Ryan, 29
Snyder v. United States, 81, 103, 104, 141n53, 149n24, 149n29
solar energy, 86, 96; APS and, 96; fees imposed on, 87
South Carolina: corruption, 93; CWIP bill in, 90, 91; SCANA Corporation, 90
South Carolina Electric & Gas Company (SCE&G), 91
South Carolina Public Service Authority. *See* Santee Cooper
Southern Company: Alabama Power, 89–90; power plants, 88

state legislators, 2, 12, 59; bribery and, 108
state regulations: clean-air, 8; utilities influencing, 2, 4
Stephens, Jason, 59
Stevens, John Paul, 103
Stigler, George, 110
Strah, Steven, 57
subsidies, 107, 108; FirstEnergy, 13–14; HB 6, 60, 64; Jones and, 7, 10, 15, 16; from political campaigns, 1; scandals related to, 7; utilities seeking, 11, 101
Supreme Court, US, 45; *Citizens United v. FEC*, 6, 32, 70, 86, 100, 102, 103; deregulation of political money and lobbying, 104; Florida, 84, 86, 87; Ohio, 15
Sustainability Funding Alliance, Ohio, 23

technology, 1, 2–3, 11, 19, 26–27, 108; modernization of electricity grid, 14; monopolies and, 100, 110–11
Tennessee Valley Authority, 6
Three Mile Island accident, 8
Tierney, Brian, 47, 61
Time (magazine), Insull in, 4
Toledo Blade (newspaper), 67, 68
transparency, modernization and, 111
transparency, of utilities industry, 3, 11, 61, 106, 107, 111; accountability and, 59, 79; corruption curbed by, 102; Kennedy on, 103; racketeering and, 2, 99; short-lived, 109
Trump, Donald, 1, 18, 32, 49, 50, 104; America First Policies, 17; Borges supporting, 33; inauguration celebrations of, 21
Tully, Pat, 35–36

United States (US): attorney, 46, 48; Department of Justice, 28, 60; DOE, 17; Environmental Protection Agency, 18; Securities and Exchange Commission, 5, 19, 47; Senate, 5. *See also* Supreme Court
University of Akron, 7, 67
US. *See* United States
utilities. *See specific topics*
utility executives: Jones as, 1, 15; monopolies and, 5

Virgil C. Summer project, 90, 91; abandonment of, 93; Byrne and Marsh on, 92
Vistra Vision, 64

Wall Street, 37, 38, 56; Byrne and, 92; corruption influenced by, 100; Jones and, 19
Wannemacher, Ryan, 89
watchdogs, 62, 68, 98, 108
Westinghouse, 91; bankruptcy, 93
whistleblowers, 93, 108
Willis, Maureen, 59
wind farms, 13, 17, 35
wire fraud, 46, 54, 61, 89, 92

xenophobic assertions, 1, 42–43, 63
Xi Jinping, 42

Yost, David, (Ohio Attorney General), 40, 43; bribery, 56; lawsuit against FirstEnergy by, 46–47

Zahn, Aaron, 89
zero emission nuclear (ZEN), 15

Acknowledgments

Many of the revelations reported in this book come from dogged journalists, analysts, and prosecutors. With apologies to those I failed to mention, I thank and commend:

JOURNALISTS

Mario Alejandro Ariza, Kristi Swartz, and Miranda Green with Floodlight
Tony Arnold and Dave McKinney with WBEZ Chicago
Jessie Balmert and Laura Bischoff with the *USA TODAY* Ohio Bureau
Tony Bartelme with the *Post and Courier* (South Carolina)
Jackie Borchardt with the *Cincinnati Enquirer*
Ana Ceballos, Samantha Gross, Mary Ellen Klas, and Sarah Blaskey with the *Miami Herald*
Steve Daniels with *Crain's Chicago Business* until October 2023 and as of this writing with the *Chicago Tribune*
Renee Fox with WOSU, part of the NPR network, and David Folkenflik with NPR
John Funk, formerly with the *Cleveland Plain Dealer* and as of this writing with *RTO Insider*
Dan Gearino, formerly with the *Columbus Dispatch* and as of this writing with *Inside Climate News*
Jo Ingles with the Ohio Public Radio and Television Statehouse News Bureau in Columbus
Kathiann Kowalski with *Eye on Ohio* and the Energy News Network
Randy Ludlow with the *Columbus Dispatch*
Annie Martin and Jason Garcia for the *Orlando Sentinel*

Hannah Meisel with *Capitol News Illinois*
Jason Meisner and Ray Long with the *Chicago Tribune*
Nate Monroe, Christopher Hong, David Bauerlein, and Mark Woods with the *Florida Times-Union*
Jim Provance with the *Blade* (Toledo)
Ryan Randazzo and Laurie Roberts with the *Republic* (Arizona)
Marty Schladen and David DeWitt with the *Ohio Capital Journal*
Josh Sweigart with the *Dayton Daily News*
Andrew Tobias, Jeremy Pelzer, and John Caniglia with cleveland.com/the *Plain Dealer*
Morgan Trau with News 5 Cleveland WEWS
Jake Zuckerman, formerly with *Ohio Capital Journal*, and now with cleveland.com/the *Plain Dealer*

Analysts

Dave Anderson and David Pomerantz with the Energy and Policy Institute
Ryan Augsburger, Eric Burkland, and John Seryak with the Ohio Manufacturers' Association
Andrew Barbeau with the Accelerate Group
Rachael Belz with Ohio Citizen Action
Sandy Buchanan, Cathy Kunkel (now an independent consultant), and David Schlissel at the Institute for Energy Economics and Financial Analysis
Tom Bullock of the Citizens Utility Board of Ohio
Trent Dougherty, formerly with the Ohio Environmental Council and now a lawyer with Hubay Dougherty
John Finnigan, my former colleague at the Environmental Defense Fund who's now with the Ohio Consumers' Counsel
Rob Gramlich with Grid Strategies
Hannah Halbert with Policy Matters Ohio
Christie Hicks, another former colleague at the Environmental Defense Fund who's now with Earthjustice
Ned Hill at Ohio State University
Rob Kelter and Howard Learner at the Environmental Law & Policy Center
David Kolata, formerly with Citizens Utility Board, Illinois, and now with Sealed
Randi Leppla, formerly with the Ohio Environmental Council and now with the Case Western Reserve University School of Law
Sarah Moskowitz with the Citizens Utility Board, Illinois
Tracy Sabetta with Initiative Consulting
Daniel Sawmiller with the Natural Resources Defense Council, based in Ohio
Heather Taylor-Miesle, formerly with the Ohio Environmental Council and now with American Rivers

Catherine Turcer with Common Cause Ohio
Sierra Club's Neil Waggoner, in Ohio, and Jack Darin, in Illinois
Jen Walling with the Illinois Environmental Council
Bruce Weston, who was executive director for many years of the Ohio Consumers' Counsel

Prosecutors

In Ohio, leading the federal charge were Vipal Patel, Kenneth Parker, Emily Glatfelter, Matthew Singer, and Alexis Zouhary with the US Attorney's Office for the Southern District of Ohio; as well as Blane Wetzel, J. William Rivers, and Chris Hoffman with the Federal Bureau of Investigation. Also active has been Ohio's attorney general Dave Yost, and his staff, including Jonathan Blanton, Martin Cordero, Margaret O'Shea, and Bradford Tammaro.

In Illinois, the prosecutorial team was coordinated by Morris Pasqual, acting US attorney for the Northern District of Illinois; Robert W. "Wes" Wheeler Jr., special agent-in-charge of the FBI's Chicago field office; and Justin Campbell, special agent-in-charge of Internal Revenue Service criminal investigation in Chicago.

Thanks also to John Finnigan, Catherine Ittner, Erica Fick, Colin Rowan, Ellen Bell, John Hall, and Jim Marston—former colleagues at the Environmental Defense Fund who helped craft and promote a series of blogs on FirstEnergy's machinations. I want to particularly thank John Finnigan, Randi Leppla, and David Pomerantz for reading—and improving—sections of the book; mistakes, of course, remain mine.

I appreciate Deni Remsberg and Ashleigh Cooke at Rowman & Littlefield Publishers (now part of Bloomsbury Publishing), for their encouragement and guidance. Mary Kay Zuravleff, as she's done with several of my book projects, offered good cheer and improved writing. Kathryn Munson continues to inspire.

About the Author

Richard Munson wrote *From Edison to Enron*, a history of the electric power industry, and he participated in clean-energy debates while with the Environmental Defense Fund and Recycled Energy Development. He's also crafted biographies of Benjamin Franklin, Nikola Tesla, and Jacques Cousteau, as well as wrote *From Tech to Table*, offering profiles of food and farm innovators.